KOMPROMAT

JEFF PEGUES

KOMPROMAT

HOW RUSSIA UNDERMINED AMERICAN DEMOCRACY

Prometheus Books

59 John Glenn Drive
Amherst, New York 14228

Published 2018 by Prometheus Books

Cover design by Jacqueline Nasso Cooke
Cover design © Prometheus Books

Inquiries should be addressed to
Prometheus Books
59 John Glenn Drive
Amherst, New York 14228
VOICE: 716–691–0133
FAX: 716–691–0137
WWW.PROMETHEUSBOOKS.COM

22 21 20 19 18   5 4 3 2 1

Library of Congress Cataloging-in-Publication Data

Identifiers: LCCN 2018010834 (print) |
ISBN 9781633884304 (ebook) | 9781633884298 (hardback)

Printed in the United States of America

CONTENTS

Let us never forget that government is ourselves and not an alien power over us. The ultimate rulers of our democracy are not a President and senators and congressmen and government officials, but the voters of this country.

—Franklin Delano Roosevelt

PREFACE

In late December 2017, I began to watch old Watergate movies. I was enjoying the holiday break with my family and finally had a modicum of free time to settle into my favorite blue chair in my basement, looking straight at my seventy-inch television. My back pressed against the small pillow that my oldest daughter, Jordyn, had made for me, in 2012, when she was eleven years old.

I picked up the remote and scanned the movies I could stream to my television and settled on *All the President's Men*.[1] I'd seen the film before, but watching it in December was different, since I'd spent a year and a half witnessing remarkable things while working on the Russian espionage story for CBS News. By the end of 2017, there were eerie parallels between Watergate and the Russia investigation.

All the President's Men tells the story of *Washington Post* investigative reporters Bob Woodward (played by Robert Redford) and Carl Bernstein (played by Dustin Hoffman) who were instrumental in exposing the Watergate scandal that eventually led to the resignation of President Richard M. Nixon on August 9, 1974. It is a film that might be viewed as a journalism cult classic.

I watched, mesmerized, as the team sat in the gritty newsroom bullpen, sweating in their suits as they pecked away at onion skin and carbon paper on antiquated typewriters. They ran around DC discovering colorful forms of "ratf—ing," a slang term for political sabotage that began when five men who were CREEPs (working for the Committee to Re-elect the President) broke into the Watergate Hotel, the headquarters of the Democratic Party, and were found trying to bug the place and rifling through files. Gradually, Woodward and Bernstein uncovered the Nixon reelection committee's "dirty tricks" campaign against Democrats, which included wiretapping phones of people who had been critical of Nixon (like journalists), enlisting spies, stuffing ballot boxes, and creating propaganda-like fake campaign literature. The *Post* reporters were digging deeper into the scandal when Nixon turned over tapes of phone calls he recorded that alluded to his involvement in these tactics.[2]

It was interesting to view the team's mysterious source "Deep Throat" and the way they protected both him and his identity.

The film was anchored in the reporters' collective integrity in uncovering and sharing the truth—that there were members of the Nixon administration who were dirty, including Nixon himself. Woodward and Bernstein had an unflinching belief that the administration committed a moral wrong by deceiving the American people for its own selfish reasons and essentially seeking to undermine democracy.

The world would later learn in 2005 that Deep Throat was Mark Felt, the FBI's number two in the early 1970s.[3] In 2017, Felt would be the subject of another eponymously named Watergate movie, which I also watched that late December. Part of the movie's plot covered Felt's effort to push back against an administration that he believed was breaking laws and trying to short-circuit the FBI investigation. I had an appetite for the issue. Watergate was a domestic crisis. The Russia investigation is a domestic crisis involving a foreign adversary—a Russia controlled by former KGB agent Vladimir Putin.

Many Americans (including government officials) were distracted when Russian-backed hackers weaseled into federal and state databases. Cyberattacks are a new kind of warfare—the type average Americans don't notice until it's too late. After the attack is over you're still left wondering what happened, who invaded the local voter database, or who planted propaganda on Facebook or Twitter for you to follow and to sway you toward a candidate or political camp. In that way, it was personal. The information manipulated you through your personal computer or phone. Perhaps worse, you may sense that foreign entities could have contributed toward stirring up dormant feelings in you to become prejudiced toward blacks, Hispanics, Muslims, or to have hatred for Democrats or Republicans.

The power of the Russian intelligence operation was its covert nature. More than three years after it began, we—as Americans—still don't know the extent of what really hit us. It was a multipronged attack, the most potent aspect of which was its influence campaign. The Russian propaganda machine seeped into the fabric of our democracy by poisoning our free speech. Over and over, US investigators and government officials insisted that the Russian intelligence operation did not alter votes. But the Russian plan may not have been to change actual votes, which would have been harder to do because the election system is dispersed and—to borrow a word from former FBI director James Comey—"clunky."[4] Their bar was likely lower and an easier target to hit. What if you pervert the information American voters hear and read? Doesn't that ultimately change how they vote? Furthermore, what would happen if it was determined that votes were changed? Then what? How would the country solve that?

Chapter 1

THIS IS WARFARE

I was sharing a meal of filet mignon and Maker's Mark with an intelligence source. As a journalist I have come to rely on certain sources for details of investigations and frankly potential scandals circulating around government. It is the kind of information that is not readily available to the public. It is often highly classified and not intended for public consumption. At least not until government officials decide to declassify it. The source I was meeting with on that day was a man who had once recounted, with disquieting calm, what it was like to watch the enemy get bombed in war zones by a predator drone. There are live feeds from the armed drones over the battlefield, and you can go to a specially designed enclosed area in a building or Sensitive Compartmented Information Facility or SCIF to see the strike. The "Pred feeds," as they've been dubbed by insiders, show the dust settling after the strike while the "viewer" waits to see how it turned out or the "reflections"—whether you have hit the target or not.

That day, as he described the "Pred feed" to me, my source's voice remained even-keeled. The muscles in his face barely moved. During my career covering the Justice and Homeland Security beat for CBS News, many of the law enforcement and intelligence operatives I've come into contact with spoke of horrible things with this same kind of composure. It's not that they didn't care. They cared. But they were professionals trained to maneuver through emergencies regularly, unnerved. I learned to see their humanity beneath their stoic demeanors. I was getting better at deciphering their cryptic language. So, when these individuals started to panic, I knew something serious was going on.

My source looked me in the eye and casually alluded to problems that he believed were undermining our democracy. He couldn't state any specifics. I knew if I pressed him, he would stop talking to me altogether. He switched the subject to our country's more pressing long-term problem. This was the topic I had become almost exclusively obsessed with since the summer of 2016. I couldn't let it go—the Putin-led cyber-espionage attacks.

"So, you are saying this is just the modern-day version of tradecraft for the Russians?" I asked.

I had been piecing together the evolution of how Russian operatives functioned throughout history. I appreciated the John le Carré–like glamour of the old KGB days in which spies used invisible ink, performed dead letter drops, and buried mounds of cash in the woods.

Then there were the more recent incarnations of Russian-government-led attempts to use our vulnerabilities against us, which spoke to the questions of how any of this stuff affects us directly or why we should care.[1] In the 1960s, Russian-led operative units tried to exploit the country's Achilles' heel—racism—and Jim Crow laws.[2] For example, they tried to portray Dr. Martin Luther King Jr. as an Uncle Tom who had been bribed by President Lyndon Johnson to quell the fire of the movement and keep black people in subordinate roles.[3]

In 2016, the internet allowed Russian-government-led cyber-espionage hackers to embed themselves in our institutions, gathering and releasing intelligence to the public to undermine our politicians in a more succinct and effective manner.[4] They used social media platforms like Twitter and Facebook and exploited these platforms' capacity to incite hate.[5] They attempted to compromise our voting booths and influenced us, without our knowledge, thereby waging an invisible war.

This is warfare. It's not typically discussed in these terms, but the United States and its allies are already engaged in a war with Russia. The hackers messed with our minds by exploiting our divisions with information warfare.

"Is it complicated then, because they play by a different set of rules?" I asked.

My source nodded. He was silent a long time. He seemed grave. He took a sip of water as I wondered to myself if anybody even knew what those rules were. Several sources had spoken to me about the intricate web of alleged collusion between Russian officials and the Trump administration, which was just one in a series of White House–based problems they couldn't talk about but had shaken. There was such intensity to them in how they described what had happened.

I kept feeling as if I had been living in a movie or a dream for months. This simultaneously thrilled and frightened me.

It also made me feel an urgent responsibility to uncover more and to relay what I had learned to other people.

"Do you think the cyberattacks destabilized our democracy, that we are verging on a constitutional crisis then?" I asked.

My source nodded so slightly that it was barely discernable. This is the way many of my sources operate. They never feed you all the information you want. They seem to dole it out in small nuggets. It's like an intricate puzzle you have to put together by gathering the pieces from different people, different agencies, and at different times. One must be tenacious in doing this job. You get a taste of something good and you want more. The Russia investigation for me started just as other stories I report. However, the pieces I gathered with my Justice unit at CBS News kept leading to bigger stories and ever more troubling revelations.

Chapter 2

MINING FOR CLUES AT THE DNC

JULY 24, 2016

The Democratic National Convention in Philadelphia in 2016 was like the halfway point of a brutal marathon, one that only allowed the briefest cooldown in between interviews, and during which I prayed my college-football-weakened knees didn't give way to jelly legs. There was a heat wave, with temperatures climbing well past ninety degrees, and humidity that made my clothes feel like a straitjacket.

It was Sunday, and I was sitting on the edge of my bed at the Westin Hotel, waiting to go to a press conference at Philadelphia's Emergency Operations Center. The police would field questions about security measures they had taken for the convention, which was expected to draw an average of forty thousand protestors a day. I was ready, with my shined shoes at the door and my navy summer blazer steamed and pressed. I didn't really want to move too quickly.

I was, quite frankly, exhausted. I had just driven a rental car from the Republican National Convention in Cleveland to Pittsburgh and had arrived in Philly the day before. It was a nice extended relaxing trip. I had blasted the AC and coasted along I-76 past hills and farms, eventually careening into Heinz Field to eat a burger and watch all the Pirates fans. The next morning, I took my golf clubs to a driving range.

That drive back was euphoric, largely because I was relieved. Covering security for Republican National Convention protests had at first felt like stepping onto streets wired with land mines. We were living through a strange time. Colleagues had shared stories about covering rallies where candidate Donald Trump incited stadium-sized crowds to boo the media. Others had been present when he overtly advocated for violence against protestors.[1] Worst-case scenario, some had been expecting something like the anti–Vietnam War protests that occurred at the Democratic National Convention in 1968 in Chicago, at which thirty thousand protestors and police clashed, and even reporters were beaten to the ground. We were bracing for the worst.

Protests had always been a part of my personal history. As a kid, I had often sat at my parents' dinner table and listened to them share stories with their friends about civil rights activities during the 1960s. They were both raised in Alabama—my mother in Montgomery, my father in Birmingham—and fought hard for equal treatment and for their success. Whether they were talking about marching with Dr. King or getting hauled away by police, they spoke with great pride because they knew they had done what was necessary. That wasn't lost on me. Growing up, I wondered what my contribution would be. I often wondered if I would have the courage to do the same if faced with similar circumstances.

Protests had become a part of my professional life, too. I spent several years interviewing police and protestors around the United States in the aftermath of uprisings such as the one that followed the death of Freddie Gray in Baltimore. Yet the 2016 election had been the closest I had come to covering convention protests on the ground as they occurred.

It turned out that Cleveland was nothing like Chicago in '68; it was nothing like Birmingham or Selma. The police deliberately underplayed their hand so that the protestors didn't feel defensive. A maze of barricades and checkpoints was set up at the Quicken Loans Arena, where the convention was being held. Across the street at the Public Square near the Renaissance Cleveland Hotel, ordinary police on bicycles circled the protestors like herders, separating the two factions. I had also seen the officers in full gear—with riot shields and pepper ball guns—who had been instructed to stay out of the protestors' line of sight.

The police strategy worked. There were a few flare-ups, but the streets in Cleveland remained relatively peaceful. We'd dodged a bullet.

It wasn't clear whether we would be so lucky at the Democratic National Convention. The heat alone, which was also breaking historic records, was enough to set people off. I had already interviewed law enforcement officials and learned about the hostage negotiators, SWAT teams, and sharpshooters. They had been running through drills all week long, practicing things like how to respond to a lone-wolf attack on a motorcade. I was always hungry for breaking news, but it had already been a long year for reporters. I could have done without getting caught in the crossfire of another uprising.

It was certainly one of the most surreal and volatile periods for the country that my generation had seen. People were caught in a hotbed of collective emotions: anxiety, anger, terror and outrage. We were all heavily distracted. Few of us saw the real culprit or threat to our freedom.

In my hotel room, I stood up and looked in the mirror. There were slight bags under my eyes from exhaustion, and I was happy it was just a press conference. It had been an easy Sunday so far.

I sat on the bed and ran down the news I had heard from a friend in the lobby of the convention hall. I had been on I-76 on July 22, the day WikiLeaks placed an announcement on Twitter inviting readers to visit its page to "Search the DNC email database."[2] When readers clicked they gained access to over nineteen thousand emails plucked by hackers from Democratic National Committee (DNC) servers.

These included details of perks for party donors attending the convention, and emails from DNC chair Debbie Wasserman Schultz, which included notes about her appearing to favor Hillary Clinton over Vermont senator Bernie Sanders as candidate for president.

Later, the number of leaked emails from the DNC grew to sixty thousand. Someone named Guccifer 2.0 claimed ownership over the hacks, which were distributed through WikiLeaks, DCLeaks, and a conference event. This persona denied any ties to Russia.[3]

Having had enough noise for one day, I embraced the peace and quiet of a room without a television on or the radio blaring in the background. I pulled the hospital corners off the bed and lay down on my back with my feet crossed.

My iPhone was vibrating, indicating that a producer was trying to reach me with breaking news. I picked it up and saw an email from a CBSN producer, our streaming network. He wanted to know if I had enough information to go on the air to talk about the FBI investigation into the DNC hack.

"We'll take you as soon as possible," he said.

He wanted me to come on Josh Elliott's TV show and discuss whether Russia was behind a hack to the DNC servers. They would broadcast from a skybox overlooking the convention floor. I deliberated. The show was in a couple of hours, and I had mixed feelings about doing it.

On the one hand, I was always grateful to be brought in as an expert on subjects related to my Homeland Security and Justice beat. It would be an easy in-studio gig that wouldn't require me to swelter outside in my suit. But I just didn't have a lot of information on the hacks at that time. Most people, including those at the FBI, didn't have a lot of information. The *Washington Post* had released a report the previous month suggesting that Russian government hackers had penetrated the computer network of the DNC and obtained access to their database.[4] The hacking was obviously embarrassing the Democrats and undermining the convention.

I was so consumed with trying to stay on top of the protestors at the convention that I didn't at that point stop to consider what we were witnessing with the hacks. The weight of it all had not yet hit me.

Distortion had become the norm since the campaign had started. All our platforms had devolved. The internet was buzzing with provocative tweets from candidate Trump and counter tweets from candidate Clinton. Then there was the almost minute-by-minute smackdown on cable television. The candidates' campaign chairpersons, managers, and supporters argued. Cable news anchors stoked the discussion with the latest accusations. The volume of the discourse had reached an unprecedented decibel level that drowned out just about everything else going on.

No wonder we didn't see it coming.

I thought about what I already knew. It wasn't much.

The month before, the DNC disclosed that Russian hackers had accessed their servers and leaked information to WikiLeaks.[5] The cyber security firm CrowdStrike had nicknamed the hackers Fancy Bear and Cozy Bear. Hackers leave a kind of digital fingerprint behind—some biometrics pattern that experts can discern.[6]

In May, James Clapper, director of national intelligence, informed both the Trump campaign and the Clinton campaign that they were being targeted for cyberattacks.[7] It was amazing that the Democrats didn't do something sooner to prevent this from happening.

A few days later I'd be in Baltimore, covering the hearings of the police officers who shot Freddie Gray. I was mildly disappointed that I wouldn't be able to rest before hitting the road again. I had gone live on television with much less information. I decided to do it.

When I agreed to race over to the Wells Fargo Center that afternoon, I turned a corner on terrain I never knew existed. The next month an intelligence source whom I knew well and trusted became my cartographer—drawing a metaphorical map and guiding me toward a beat based almost exclusively on stories about Russia.

Chapter 3

MEANWHILE, BACK AT THE WHITE HOUSE . . .

The first White House meetings following the Democratic National Convention leaks took place in a secure, classified conference room in the Eisenhower Executive Office Building, an architectural anomaly that Mark Twain called the ugliest building in America. The building's late-1800s French Second Empire style is simultaneously monolithic and gaudy with a double-pitched mansard roof, cast-iron columns, and granite façade dominated by cookie-cutter windows. A tunnel connects the White House to the building and the beehive of government employees who wind through its tiled corridors and who are cloistered in 550 offices spread out over two miles, some with cast-insignia doorknobs indicating whether they once belonged to the War, Navy, or State Department. The "Old Executive Office Building" now houses representatives of the Office of the Vice President, the Office of Management and Budget, and the National Security Council who may occasionally play a game of tenpin in the Truman bowling alley in the basement—but don't always share information.[1]

It isn't surprising, then, that among the dozens of people in the conference room, including members from the FBI, CIA, NSA, DOD, State, ordinary policy wonks, and anyone else you'd find at a national security meeting, nobody knew what others knew or when they had found out about it. Information wasn't restricted as much by security clearance as by party affiliation. Those involved with the Democratic National Committee (DNC) were more likely to have been tipped off. Polarization between White House policy and political campaigns is intended to protect the integrity of US elections.

This is one of several staples of our democracy that now makes us vulnerable to attack.

It was surprising to find out that nobody in that room seemed to know much about the hacks. The Russian influence campaign didn't start with the cyberattack on the DNC's computer networks, though that seemed to be the point at which White House officials first took notice. The breach of the computer systems had been in the works for years. The Russian hackers gained access to DNC computers in the summer of 2015. They maintained access to the DNC networks until at least June 2016.[2] Russian military intelligence then compromised the personal email accounts of Democratic Party officials and political figures. By May 2016, US intelligence officials assessed that the hackers had stolen "large volumes of data from the DNC." The hackers' dormant code had activated and "come to life." The Russians' cyber fingerprints were all over the DNC computer systems.[3]

Michael Daniel, who was then special assistant to President Barack Obama and was White House cybersecurity coordinator, admits that he first found out about the hacks from an article in the *Washington Post* on July 23. He then penciled the investigation onto the agenda of the regular Cyber Response Group.[4]

Daniel explained that the White House had been expecting election-related cyber-espionage, nation-state hackers mining for intelligence, which is what happened during the 2008 and 2012 election cycles.[5] The way WikiLeaks was circulating this information publicly, however, was unprecedented. Accordingly, we knew neither who was behind it nor what the hacker's endgame was. The intelligence groups sloughed through scenarios. They first tried to determine if the hacker left a kind of cyber fingerprint, a pattern that could lead them to him/her.

"We start raising the question of, okay, what's the actual threat here? What's actually happening? And can we understand? The first couple of questions are going to be like, so who the heck do we actually think Guccifer 2.0 is? You know, do we really think he's a Romanian hacker?" Daniel said, and laughed.

It was information warfare that heaped another level of absurdity on an already absurd year. Guccifer 2.0 associated his name with "Guccifer," a Romanian hacker named Marcel Lazar, and claimed to be a Romanian himself who had no ties to Russia. This is a comparison akin to a teenage tagger in Nebraska claiming to be associated with legendary New York graffiti artist Banksy.[6]

The investigating firm CrowdStrike gave the hackers the code names of children's stuffed toys. Guccifer 2.0 and his counterpart DCLeaks are believed to be linked to a Russian cyber unit security experts have come to call Fancy Bear or APT28 (Advanced Persistent Threat—a high-level, generally state-sponsored hacker). Simultaneously, another Russian cyber unit nicknamed Cozy Bear or APT29 is believed to have quietly embedded itself in the DNC and other government and political networks.[7]

"Was this an inside job?" Daniel said this question was brought up.[8]

They tried to determine how vulnerable we were.

"If the goals were to disrupt our elections in some way, how would you do that? And what do we need to do to protect ourselves against that?" Those were just a few questions White House officials at the time were trying to answer.

"What would a misinformation campaign look like?"

More experts were invited into the room. Edward Felten is a Princeton professor, a computer wunderkind who trades in his tweed sports coat for a navy-blue suit when called into the White House to assume his post as deputy chief technology officer. He has a physicist's brain that somersaults over cyber terrain, and his work tends to anger company head honchos by proving their systems aren't impenetrable. As witness for the US government in the antitrust lawsuit against Microsoft, he demonstrated nineteen ways it was possible to remove the Internet Explorer function from Windows without damaging the operating system.[9] He broke a digital watermark created by Secure Digital Music Initiative, a forum of companies and IP professionals developed in 1998, to quash music piracy over the internet. The group, in September 2000, had put out a letter to IT professionals challenging them to break the watermark, and Felten's team claimed to have done so.[10] Felten also identified critical problems with the accuracy of Sequoia voting machines in New Jersey and demonstrated how they could be easily hacked and compromised.[11]

Felten helped the group to conclude that although voting machines could be hacked, they weren't likely a target. The hacker would have to know the specific location he/she wanted to target ahead of time and would have to predict how close the election will be in that locality. You'd have to rig the system to flip enough votes to change the outcome but not set off warning alarms.

In later meetings, the Cyber Response Group queried the Russia director at the National Security Council (NSC) and Russia experts at various agencies. They wanted to figure out what the Kremlin's strategic goals might be.

"They were talking about this idea of sort of disrupting and undermining confidence in the electoral process being one of the top goals. There was the discussion pretty early on that Vladimir Putin particularly hates Hillary Clinton—like, at a very personal level," Daniel said. "That was certainly acknowledged as a factor."[12]

Chapter 4

THE DOSSIER

There is a thirty-five-page document entitled *U.S. Presidential Election: Republican Candidate Donald Trump's Activities in Russia and Compromising Relationship with the Kremlin.*[1] It alleged that Trump had been in cahoots with the Kremlin and President Vladimir Putin for at least five years and that he "accepted a regular flow of intelligence on Hillary Clinton." It also contains what it purports to be evidence that proved Trump had been compromised. Information, if true, could be used to blackmail him, including substantial financial connections to Russian oligarchs and by extension the Kremlin. A former MI6 Moscow field agent, Christopher Steele, had been commissioned by Fusion GPS, a commercial research and intelligence agency cofounded by former journalist Glenn Simpson, on behalf of the firm's anonymous client at the Democratic National Committee to investigate Trump's business dealings in Russia.[2] Steele sent a series of sixteen memos to Fusion beginning in June 2016, revealing most of the materials that would be compiled into the dossier.[3] He also noted that Russian-government-based intelligence sources, at the request of Putin, had spent years collecting material about Hillary Clinton during her frequent visits to Russia, but that these were mainly bugged phone calls and conversations that contained no incriminating information. The FBI would eventually see the dossier but not until after it had launched its counterintelligence investigation in late July 2016.

At the Halifax International Security forum in Canada held on September 2, 2017, Senator John McCain (R-AZ) learned about the dossier from Sir Andrew Wood, the United Kingdom's former ambassador to Russia. Wood stressed that the document contained information that concerned a mortal threat to the US democratic system. According to my sources, McCain had requested someone to meet with Steele, find out what he knew, and pick up the document.[4]

My producers and I had done some research and figured out who McCain had sent to London to pick up the dossier. Our research showed that the envoy for this secret mission was David Kramer, a former assistant secretary of state, whom McCain seemed to trust. Here was a man who traveled to London and walked around Heathrow Airport with a former operative for MI6 who had collected information that could contribute toward a scandal as big as Watergate with our new president-elect, information that could shift the playing field of our country and possibly the free world as we know it. I had read all about Steele. I knew he had been an MI6 operative during the Cold War. He'd operated in Paris, Russia, and the Foreign Commonwealth Office in London. As a Russia specialist, he is believed to have been integral to the investigation into Alexander Litvinenko's murder.[5] Litvinenko was a Russian spy who died after drinking green tea laced with radioactive polonium-210. I wondered what that work entailed. I imagined high-speed car chases, covert meetings in train tunnels and caves inside parks, stamp-sized cameras, and bugs in hollowed-out coins so conversations could be monitored.

A spokesperson for Putin dismissed the dossier as *kompromat*, which means "compromising material." President Trump has called it "fake."[6] According to my sources, by sending Kramer on that secret mission, McCain obviously believed the dossier was worth obtaining.[7]

If anyone appreciated freedom and democracy, it was the senator from Arizona. His story is well known by now. While he was a naval aviator in 1967, he was shot down during a bombing mission over Hanoi. After being captured by the North Vietnamese he was held as a prisoner of war until 1973. He was tortured but refused to betray his country after being offered unconditional release. McCain decided that he would adhere to the POW code of honor, and that meant remaining in a North Vietnamese prison. He didn't want to be repatriated ahead of the other American prisoners who had been there longer.[8]

McCain wasn't a Trump fan, having been a frequent target of then candidate Trump's barbs about preferring people who hadn't been captured in battle. Trump said, "He's a war hero because he was captured. I like people who weren't captured."[9] McCain has been in the House and Senate for nearly forty years, and he ran for president twice, so he seems to have thick skin by now. But he is sensitive about protecting the nation from Russia, and he has not minced words about his distaste for Vladimir Putin. He often calls him a dictator or "the most important threat, more so than ISIS."[10]

After Kramer came back to the United States with the dossier, McCain hand-delivered it to the FBI.[11] That, in itself, was extremely unusual, and it shows the urgency with which McCain viewed the matter. Is it possible McCain knew more than just what was in the dossier?

In late 2016 and throughout 2017 I would monitor McCain's interviews because I knew about his connection to the dossier and his well-known reputation for being a maverick. He's the type of politician who can't be controlled or muzzled to uphold the party line. Remember the campaign rally in 2008 when a woman stood up and called then candidate Barack Obama an Arab?[12] It would have been so easy for McCain to ignore the comment—there are too many people (sadly) who would have done just that. But McCain corrected the woman, and for good measure said, "No, ma'am, he's a decent family man [and] citizen that I just happen to have disagreements with on fundamental issues."

On the issue of Russia and collusion McCain has been persistent in trying to get the public to pay attention and to appreciate the gravity of the Russia investigation. In the dozens of interviews I've seen when he's asked, he always answers the same way: "I told you months ago that this was a centipede and shoes would drop, and I guarantee you more shoes will drop."[13]

Chapter 5

THEY ARE HACKING
THE HELL OUT OF US

AUGUST 2016

Linda Power, a US intelligence operative, first tipped me off to the extent of the Russian operation. I was upstairs in my office after I finished delivering a report close to the top of the 7:00 a.m. hour on *CBS This Morning*.[1] It was about the time of day I try to reach sources I depend on. Linda was always at the top of the list, mostly because she and I had developed an easy rapport. I enjoyed talking with her. I always learned something new, and it wasn't always the kind of information that would end up in one of my reports on the *Evening News*. I would often keep the substance of our discussions to myself.

I dialed her number, and after we had exchanged some quick small talk, I asked her what was going on.

"Jeff. They are hacking the hell out of us," she said.

"What do you mean they are hacking the hell out of us?" I asked.

"The Russians. They are hacking the hell out of us, and we're not doing anything."

There was a bite of anger in her tone. Normally, Linda was plain-spoken. She didn't connect her emotions to her work. If she didn't want to answer a question, she'd flat out tell you.

"Did something new happen since the convention?" I asked. "Did a new attack occur?"

She sighed and then drew in a deep breath. She was putting

not only her job on the line by talking to me, but potentially her freedom, since she could be imprisoned for divulging classified information.

"Did you hear Trump on the campaign trail? Did you hear what he said about Putin?"

"Yeah. You mean where he says Putin was nice because he called Trump a genius?" I said and then laughed.

She didn't respond.

"Oh, and he called him a strong leader, too, right?" I coaxed. Trump's statements on the campaign trail had US intelligence officials scratching their heads.[2]

"Why is he saying that? How could he say that? Putin is KGB," she said.

At this point I didn't know a whole lot about Russia. But I did know Linda wasn't alone in this sentiment about Trump's relationship to President Vladimir Putin. The prevailing feeling in Washington about Putin was that he was a manipulator and couldn't be trusted. When Trump praised Putin during his campaign, it was inordinately offensive to people in intelligence circles.

It was dangerous, too. While in the United States there are limits on a president's powers—checks and balances—in Russia there really is no cap on how far Putin can extend his influence. So the consensus in US intelligence circles is that anything big related to Russia has Putin's fingerprints on it. He is the one who gives the go-ahead.

Linda was a real pro, and a patriot. If she sensed something was off-kilter, there was a reason she was telling me.

I asked her what she thought about Trump telling the Russians to find Hillary's thirty-three thousand illegally deleted emails. The whole campaign had seemed so surreal.

I was referring to a press conference that occurred on July 27 when Trump, after calling on Russia to find the emails, said the media would thank them. Trump believed that the media was like pigs to mud when it came to any new revelation about Hillary Clinton.[3] He was speaking of Hillary Clinton's use of a private email server (rather than secure federal servers) for work communications while she was secretary of state. Her use of these servers was exposed publicly in March 2015, one month before she announced she was running for president, and an FBI investigation began. Clinton maintained the legality of using her personal email for these communications. On July 2, 2016, Clinton underwent an intensive interview by the FBI, and on July 5, 2016, FBI director James Comey cleared Clinton of any wrongdoing but scolded her when he said the way she dealt with classified information was "extremely careless."[4]

Linda sighed. I waited. Other sources had clammed up when they were asked about Clinton's emails. I presumed it was because the FBI was already under scrutiny for being too lenient with Clinton.

"Did anything new happen? With the hacks, I mean? Did they find anything new?"

She said no.

I tried a different tack. I asked Linda if there was a human component to all of this.

"*Kompromat*," she said.

"What?"

"Russian operatives are renowned for compromising people. They use Russian operatives to contact people; they get them to trust them. You may not know you are being compromised, but they are using you. That's what Russian operatives do."

Of course, it was obvious to anyone who had ever read John le Carré's *The Spy Who Came in from the Cold*, but at that point I still needed those things spelled out.

I took a sip of coffee and put it down, reminding myself to stay cool. And, truth be told, at that point I wasn't that hungry for the story. It would be a few weeks before I recognized it for what it was, before I ran down the stairs into the newsroom essentially stomping and ranting that we had to shift our focus from terrorism to the Russia story.

Still, I could tell there was something more Linda wanted to divulge.

"What else?" I asked quietly.

She drew in her breath again. "Nothing new happened. Nothing new." She sounded agitated.

"Something old then? They've known about this longer than we thought?" I asked.

Linda was referring to some US officials who had been aware of the Russian cyber intrusions for some time. But at that moment there were only a handful of people who knew before word began to spread to a larger group.

"It's been going on longer than we thought," she said.

"What has? The hacking? Breaches? Computer breaches? Like cyberattacks or what? Espionage from Russia specifically? What are we talking, like years here?"

"I don't understand how nobody knew," she said.

It is true many government officials didn't know about the hacking. Surely, this was the case with many of the men and women in that situation room with Michael Daniel, who was special assistant to President Barack Obama and White House cybersecurity coordinator. Daniel himself admits his team only found out about the hacking after WikiLeaks started dumping the DNC emails and they read about it in the *Washington Post.* Over the years, many of my sources admit to learning about major threats to our country due to information from inquiring reporters. Of course, it is possible that some of these sources may have "known" about the hacks through official channels but chose not to reveal the information to me in order to protect their jobs and the classified information. However, I am certain the siloed nature of the information kept many from finding out about the cyberattacks until the media broke the story, which also parallels how Watergate was exposed.

In the 1970s as details of Watergate were emerging, Nixon's attacks on the media grew more intense. This is noteworthy because the Trump administration seems to have taken the same adversarial approach toward the media (except for Fox News). President Trump overtly attacks and tries to discredit the media, advising the public that news outlets don't tell the truth. There are bad apples in every profession. In journalism, I like to think that 99 percent of us work to uncover the facts. That is certainly the case at CBS News, where everything we put on the air is checked and vetted through numerous filters. We take pride in what we do because we have a tradition that is deeply engrained in the culture of the organization. A culture born through legendary journalists like Walter Cronkite, Edward R. Murrow, Ed Bradley, Bob Schieffer, Leslie Stahl, Scott Pelley, David Martin, and many others.

Even as a target for a White House that seeks to discredit the media, reporters must persevere. We cannot be deterred. But we must also continue to get the story right.

As for the Russian cyberattacks, top US officials knew about them prior to any kind of media report, at least as early as June 2016 when the Democratic Party hired the cybersecurity firm CrowdStrike to investigate. Adam Meyers, vice president of CrowdStrike, posted a blog about their findings, called "Bears in the Midst. Intrusion into the Democratic National Committee," in early June.[5]

> CrowdStrike Services Inc., our Incident Response group, was called by the Democratic National Committee (DNC), the formal governing body for the US Democratic Party, to respond to a suspected breach. We deployed our IR team and technology and immediately identified two sophisticated adversaries on the network—COZY BEAR and FANCY BEAR. We've had lots of experience with both of these actors attempting to target our customers in the past and know them well. In fact, our team considers them some of the best adversaries out of all the numerous nation-state, criminal and hacktivist/terrorist groups we encounter on a daily basis. Their tradecraft is superb, operational security second to none and the extensive usage of "living-off-the-land" techniques enable them to easily bypass many security solutions they encounter.[6]

Meyers, who wears black wire-rimmed glasses, three earrings in his left ear, and has spiky gelled hair, may not fit preconceived ideas about how a cybersecurity expert should look. He has over fifteen years' experience in security, and his territory includes more than seventy "criminal, state sponsored and nationalist cyber advisory groups around the world."[7]

The team flew out from CrowdStrike's offices in Sunnyvale, California, which looks like a place that might fit the mold for brilliant and young security experts: replete with a break room filled with video games and a large-screen television. CrowdStrike was the firm that investigated the Sony Pictures hack, and uncovered (within forty-eight hours) that the attack came from the North Korean government.[8]

I wanted to interview Meyers to learn more about the DNC hacks and how these cyber investigators knew that it was indeed the Russians. Meyers spoke in the crypto-language of computer code and explained how CrowdStrike deployed their technology at both the DNC and the Democratic Congressional Campaign Committee (DCCC), which "provided visibility and saw the Russian intrusion activity against the DNC." He explained how the "surreptitious monitoring tools" associated with Fancy Bear and Cozy Bear went by different names, including a remote access Trojan, an implant, or a remote access tool kit. Meyers and his team used their own tools to poke around and see what was happening. "Imagine somebody breaks in to a bank, and they use a special saw to cut through the safe. We found that saw as they were using it and were able to then analyze it and track it back to the actor."[9]

That actor (computer security professional speak for the hackers) was most likely Russian, Meyers said. The tools that were used were known to be "uniquely associated with this Russian threat actor." He explained how the infrastructure (for example, the domain names) the actor used to put in the implant and poke around had the Russian hackers' style and cyber fingerprints all over them. He spoke specifically about the implants. "These things, somebody has to control them; it's not like a drone, where you just fire it off and it comes back with the stolen data: there are people operating that malware, that implant, and using it to move within that environment."[10]

The malware used was in line with Russian objectives, and had been used in other Russian attacks, he explained.

> The malware that we've identified that's not widely available is something specially built by this actor. We've seen this actor use this malware across multiple platforms, so they've targeted Windows and Mac and Linux and mobile devices like Apple and Android. Having that same tool, being developed across platforms is pretty unique in the malware world. You don't see a lot of that, so that kind of leads us to the assessment that this is something that they've built and they control and they've continued to develop over the last ten years.[11]

Meyers said this attack was likely orchestrated by hundreds of people. Those who broke in with the malware probably belonged to a different team that was connected to the people who disseminated the information. He noted it was hard to ping their location.

> We don't know exactly where they are. I think it's reasonable to assume that there's probably an element in Moscow and they may also have other elements across the rest of Russia. We have some belief that this is tied to the Russian Main Intelligence Directorate, the GRU, which can have locations elsewhere within Russia.[12]

Hackers' fingerprints are essentially clues. "We have to make some assertions or . . . intelligence assessments around what we believe to be true based on having a piece of the story," Meyers said. He notes that story is hard to decipher because of the nature of computers. "These things are deliberately obfuscated. They're not trying to make it very obvious where it ties back to," he said. Just as the intelligence folks are cautious about their language, so are the cybersecurity firms. In this case they speak in confidence levels. They had a "high degree of confidence" Russian hackers were behind the attacks.[13]

They were, however, clear on the timeline.[14]

"We went through the timeline pretty well," Meyers said, "which was that the attacks began over a year before with Cozy Bear around September 2015, probably this past spring [2016] with Fancy Bear, and that they released the data from that intrusion back in June concerning the DNC and the DCCC later, and that we stand by the initial analysis and assessment that we made that this ties back to Russian intrusion operations that were deliberately targeting political entities within the United States."[15]

Meyers explained how the hackers didn't even try to hide their tracks, because it is part of their culture in the cyber-espionage realm; they don't "necessarily pull back after something like that happens; you know they're doing their thing."[16]

The Russians have done their thing in their own unique manner for generations. Cyber espionage is just the most recent way they have employed tactics they have been using for years to target their enemies for information, or to undermine their institutions. It has a long and fascinating history.

Chapter 6

DEAD DROPS, INVISIBLE INK, PROPAGANDA, AND DEEP COVER

Pre-internet espionage seemed like a lot more fun. Spies used pens that fired bullets, jack-in-the-box dummies that popped out of suitcases and stood in for you while you rolled out of a car during surveillance, and combustible letters that ignited after you read them.

The television series *The Americans* dramatized two KGB sleeper spies posing as a married couple living in the suburbs near Washington, DC, during the Reagan administration.[1] The show started in 2013 and is entering its sixth and final season at the time of this writing. *The Americans* details the couple's efforts to gather intelligence. It explores the psychological splitting that occurs when living a double life, as the couple navigates between loyalty to the KGB and attraction/revulsion toward their handpicked ordinary lives.

The series was created by former CIA officer Joe Weisberg, who also published the novel *An Ordinary Spy.* Weisberg mined his memory of tradecraft to insert features into the program such as dead drops—one person dropping an item off in a secret location for another person to come pick up. His conversations with colleagues may have inspired other tricked-out Cold War spy gear like a secret panel leading to a clandestine intelligence storage room in the couple's house, honey traps, a bugged copy machine, breathy code words whispered in pay phone booths, and a trove of disguises.[2]

OPERATION GHOST STORIES

The Americans is also partially based on the real-life tradecraft of ten Russian deep cover spies targeted by the FBI's Operation Ghost Stories. They were deported to Russia and traded for four American intelligence agents in a remote corner of a Vienna airport in 2010 in one of the largest spy swaps in history.[3]

The FBI complied with the Freedom of Information Act in 2011 and released nearly one hundred photos, videos, and documents of the Russian operatives who had embedded themselves in locations throughout the country and passed themselves off as ordinary Americans. Their mission was to connect with pundits in business, education, energy, and the government to gather intelligence. Ultimately, they sought to gain influence over US policy.

Although the FBI maintains that the group was apprehended without gaining any major intelligence, the Associated Press reported that the group was "getting very close to penetrating U.S. policy-making circles." One of the members developed a close relationship with a cabinet member during the Obama administration.[4]

This operative was Lydia Guryeva, who posed as Cynthia Murphy, a vice president of an exclusive accounting company in Manhattan. She homed in on Alan Patricof, a venture capitalist who was finance chairman for Hillary Clinton's 2008 campaign. Guryeva was probably targeting Clinton and at least five other people who were closely related to her. The FBI's unclassified reports note only that Guryeva was targeting a member of the Obama administration who took care of foreign policy work, following the person running for a high-level public office. The *Daily Mail* concluded this person was Clinton, since she was "the only person fitting that description."[5]

INTERGENERATIONAL SPYING

Although the investigation concluded in 2010, many of the older spies used classic Cold War–era spy techniques. Five used a technique called "Dead Doubles" or "Legends," in which they snatched their identities from people who died. The project code name,

Operation Ghost Stories, came from this practice. Other classic techniques reportedly utilized included James Bond–like moves, such as using invisible ink, hiding bugs in hollowed-out nickels, and hiding cameras in pipes.[6]

The FBI's website contains fascinating video of some of these classic cloak-and-dagger moves. In one video, a spy, Chris Metsos, participates in a brush pass with a Russian mission official. This essentially means he walked by the man and brushed against him, and in the process Metsos passed him something without anyone in the vicinity knowing they had made contact.[7] Metsos was believed to be the man who handled the cash. He was also the intermediary between the operatives and Russia's foreign intelligence service, the SVR.

Another video shows Richard Murphy, who posed as Cynthia Murphy's husband in suburban New Jersey, receiving a money-filled paper shopping bag from another Russian official at a train station.[8] A spy from the group was videotaped in the woods digging up a package delivered during a dead drop.[9]

The younger generation of spies in the ring brought modern techniques to the group. Anna Chapman, the daughter of a Russian diplomat, assumed the identity of a New York real estate agent using her real name. She was fluent in several languages and spent years perfecting her American accent before arriving in the States for her assignment.[10]

Chapman was depicted in several videos working on her laptop at Barnes and Noble, and meeting at a downtown coffee shop with an FBI agent posing as a Russian consulate official. In one video she pretended to be shopping at a department store while transmitting wireless information to her handler on a high-end burst transmitter, sending encrypted information via radio waves in a split second. Another twenty-first-century technique some of the younger spies used included cryptographic programs that embed messages within online photos.[11]

Chapman became the tabloid superstar of the lot after her capture. Fame followed her back to Russia. Rather than maintain a low profile, as is the MO for most former spies after they are caught, she capitalized on her notoriety. Chapman worked as a model, was a spokesperson for a famous Russian bank, and became a popular television host.[12]

Deep cover spies still exist all over the world, but the practice is becoming less common. This ring showed us techniques that were easily adapted to the cyber realm, which included garden-variety compromising of intelligence targets in the United States. The practice of "spotting and assessing" was integral to their work. This is an operative's method of determining whether neighbors or friends would be good spy targets, and identifying future leaders or influencers.

AKTIVNIYE MEROPRIYATIYA

Weisberg set *The Americans* in the 1980s because in 2013, prior to Donald Trump running for president, the American public was no longer focused on Russia. In the years following the Cold War, we were on seemingly friendly terms with the country's leadership.[13] The Russian government had attempted to undermine elections with misinformation campaigns in the 1980s, again using techniques that have now been upgraded for today's digital world. According to the *New Yorker*, in 1982, then director of the KGB Yuri Andropov ordered foreign-intelligence operatives to carry out "active measures" (in Russian it was *aktivniye meropriyatiya*) against the reelection campaign of President Ronald Reagan. The Russian spies tried to use forgeries and other Cold War methods to spread false information to influence events. This included perpetuating the idea that Reagan was a figurehead for the military-industrial complex, and associating the slogan "Reagan Means War!" with him. The efforts didn't seem to work. Reagan won the election.[14]

Chapter 7

MODERN-DAY SPIES

Cyber espionage is a new version of an old game, one that will probably never disappear from the "virtual streets" of any city in the world. Spies are not an anomaly. Anywhere you go in the world there are probably spies. Just as US officials have authorized cyber espionage in other countries (albeit they play with what we believe is a more honorable rule book), there are also US spies who still disguise themselves and participate in clandestine activities abroad.

Of course, in-the-flesh Russian operatives likely still exist here.[1] The expulsion of thirty-five diplomats, including those who may have also functioned as intelligence operatives, is a big deal. But that doesn't mean the United States will not continue to find operatives on our soil. Again, let's be careful and not jump on the bandwagon of suspicion. There are millions of Russian immigrants and Russian American citizens who are truly ordinary folks, many of them who are exceptionally accomplished, but they are not spies. They are in no way connected to the Russian government or to the Russian operatives who may spearhead cyber-espionage operations against the United States.

There certainly are spies here. No doubt we would be surprised if there weren't. We seem to find them fascinating, partly because they live the kind of colorful double lives we watch on television shows like *The Americans* or in movies like *Salt.* Learning how they operate and how they are caught can also teach us about techniques of modern-day spy tradecraft that often play out in a new form in the cyber arena.

One of the most intriguing modern-day Russian operatives (in my humble opinion) is Evgeny Buryakov (aka Zhenya), who functioned like many of the Ghost Story spies.[2] Zhenya spent the years between 2010 and 2017 pretending to work at a Russian bank called Vnesheconombank (VEB) in New York City while covertly serving as an operative for the Russian External Intelligence Service, known as the SVR.[3]

The SVR is really just the most recent incarnation of the KGB, which handled the Soviet Union's domestic and worldwide intelligence and counterintelligence operations. The KGB was officially abolished with the dissolution of the USSR. SVR took over its foreign operations division, while the Federal Security Service took over its domestic and counterintelligence work. These are all distinct organizations from the Glavnoye razvedyvatel'noye upravleniye, or GRU, which takes care of military intelligence and is part of the Russian armed forces.[4] The SVR is meant to be a more "modern special service employing talented ambitious people devoted to the Motherland and their military duty" than the KGB.[5]

Zhenya was caught and prosecuted on March 11, 2016, by Preet Bharara, the US attorney for the Southern District of New York (who was fired by President Trump approximately a year later), and John Carlin, assistant attorney general for national security.[6] Zhenya was sentenced to thirty months in prison for "conspiring to act as an agent of the Russian Federation without providing prior notice to the Attorney General." He was also ordered to pay a ten-thousand-dollar fine and a one-hundred-dollar special assessment, given an additional three years of supervised release, and ordered to be deported to Russia after his prison sentence was completed.

Essentially, he was convicted not because he was a spy, but for not telling the US attorney general he was a spy. It's an odd catch-22. Buryakov was working under nonofficial cover. If he'd reported himself as an official with the Russian intelligence agency, he would not have been officially convicted. This is how the law reads, although it is an odd espionage loophole.[7]

Bharara's statement included in a Department of Justice press release suggests that he, too, may also be interested in the idea of tradecraft.

"Evgeny Buryakov, in the guise of being a legitimate banker, gathered intelligence as an agent of the Russian Federation in New York.

He traded coded messages with one of his Russian spy codefendants, who sent the clandestinely collected information back to Moscow. So long as this type of Cold War–style spy intrigue continues to go on in present-day New York City, the FBI and the prosecutors in my office will continue to investigate and prosecute it."[8]

Buryakov was part of a group whose members were gathering intelligence on subjects including US future alternative energy sources and future US sanctions against Russian banks. The second member of the group was Igor Sporyshev, who was under deep cover as a trade representative for the Russian Federation of New York.[9] They used classical techniques such as coded messages to share intelligence-related information while disguising their connection to each other.

The group also included Victor Podobnyy, a Russian whose official cover was an attaché to the Permanent Mission of the Russian Federation to the United Nations. In 2013, Podobnyy met with Carter Page, who later became a Trump campaign foreign policy advisor in 2016. Page shared information about the US energy industry. He maintains that he had no idea Podobnyy was a spy. "I shared basic immaterial information and publicly available research documents with Podobny[y]," Page said in an emailed statement to CBS News. "In doing so, I provided him nothing more than a few samples from the far more detailed lectures I was preparing at the time for the students in my Spring 2013 semester 'Energy and the World: Politics, Markets and Technology' course, which I taught on Saturdays at New York University."[10] Therein lies part of the problem when investigating the possibility of collusion between President Trump's campaign and people highly trained in the art of deception. In the United States this level of deception is an anomaly. The list of players involved in the scandal keeps growing, reading like the cast of flawed characters in a blockbuster movie, one that gives you a headache as you try to piece together the various plot elements. It is difficult to discern who is a willing participant and who has been compromised.

Sporyshev, forty-one, and Podobnyy, twenty-eight, were "charged," which was later tempered down to "accused," with the same charges Buryakov faced in court. They were also "accused" with second-count charges for aiding and abetting Buryakov.[11] Both Sporyshev (a trade representative) and Podobnyy (an attaché to the UN) had diplomatic immunity, and have left the country. They were "charged in absentia."[12]

SECRET SPY GEAR

The FBI used creative and old-school methods to find the spies. They sent in an undercover agent (aka Undercover Employee One—UCE-1) who pretended to be a professional analyst working for an energy company based in Manhattan. UCE-1 allowed Sporyshev to try and recruit and compromise him. In the process, he brought to Sporyshev tons of paperwork inside three-hole-punch binders that contained fake documents about the energy industry. Miniature superspy cameras were hidden in the hard binder covers and other secret cubbyholes in the binders. Sporyshev carried the binders everywhere, including to the "Residentura," the SVR's home base in New York.[13]

It was a simple method that yielded fantastic results. Sporyshev and Podobnyy were recorded discussing the federal agent's official cover, the nuts and bolts of their roles as SVR officers, and the FBI's arrest of the "illegals" (in other words, secret spies found in the United States, much like those depicted on *The Americans* TV series). The two operatives spoke about Buryakov's other undercover work posing as a representative of VEB for five years in South Africa, and in doing so essentially outed him during a dinner with another member of the SVR.

The spy team revealed methods in which they directed Buryakov to gather intelligence and transmitted his reports back to SVR headquarters in Moscow.[14] The dynamic duo also discussed attempting to recruit Manhattanites to be covert operatives for Russia.[15]

During their operations, the three men regularly communicated using "clandestine methods and coded messages,"[16] in order to exchange intelligence without being recognized as associating with each other or disclosing their secret lives as members of the Russian intelligence service. The FBI found this out by using top secret interception methods of calls between the two ringleaders, in which they noted they needed to meet for some seemingly mundane purpose, like giving them a "ticket," "book," or "list," or for some phony social occasion. This was part of the code they used to alert one or more of the others that they needed to meet to exchange what they found.

During these meetings, they often exchanged paperwork or small items. The FBI broke their secret code through ordinary and logical methods. For example, although the team said twelve times that they needed to exchange tickets, they never were seen attending events like a concert or football game that would require tickets. Once, they spoke about going to a film at a cinema.[17]

The Department of Justice press release about the capture of the operatives revealed a few close calls and near attempts at gaining important intelligence.

ATTEMPT TO GAIN SENSITIVE INFORMATION ABOUT THE NEW YORK STOCK EXCHANGE

On May 21, 2013, Sporyshev called Buryakov and tasked him to connect with his sources and find out what questions ITAR-TASS, a Russian news service, could pose to the New York Stock Exchange. When he called Buryakov again, he had the answers. He said the news service could ask questions about (i) exchange-traded funds (ETFs), including the "mechanisms of their use to destabilize the market"; (ii) "curbing of trading robot activities"; and (iii) "technical parameters" and "other regulations directly related to the exchange." On July 8, a man posing as the ITAR-TASS bureau chief emailed these questions to an employee of the New York Stock Exchange.[18]

SANCTIONS

An investigation that may have served the Russian government intelligence well in 2017 occurred on March 28, 2014, when Buryakov was instructed to research "the effects of economic sanctions on our country."[19]

The FBI listened to an intercepted conversation on April 2,

2014—where Sporyshev noted he hadn't heard from Buryakov in a while and asked to meet outside the VEB office. The FBI later conducted a court-authorized search of Buryakov's computer and found at the time of the call that Buryakov had been conducting internet searches for "sanctions Russia consiquences [sic]" and "sanctions Russia impact." Was Buryakov a slacker who wasn't doing his homework right away?[20]

Another intercepted conversation, on April 4, 2014, revealed that Buryakov called Sporyshev and said that he "wrote you an order list," and suggested that they meet. Twenty minutes later, Sporyshev was in the driveway at Buryakov's home. Video surveillance cameras revealed that the two met for less than two minutes and appeared to exchange a small object.

Later, Buryakov was given documents he believed were obtained from a US government agency about US sanctions against Russia, and other classified material, which could be useful to the SVR and its Moscow-based officials.

As some of these stories unfold, one might wonder if there is any uniform way to deal with an operative once he/she has been captured and why some sentences are stiffer than others. For example, Buryakov has to do prison time while the people whom he was working for, and as we have seen "the illegals" and the thirty-five spies President Obama sent home as a form of sanctions intended as punishment for covert actions, were simply notified that they were being expelled and required to leave the country within a specific period of time. In this high-stakes game of tradecraft, the operatives themselves are bargaining chips.[21] Some, like Buryakov, become sacrificial lambs, while others, like Anna Chapman, become heroines. As a newshound who has spent years interacting with intelligence operatives, I suspect there is more to these stories than what we've been told. I wonder about who is conducting these operations. Are they high-level employees or largely grunts who spend nights sitting in their cars nursing coffee and hoagies, watching for lights in windows or people walking through doors, who spend days monitoring fuzzy surveillance cameras. I wonder who purchases the tiny cameras or discovers the trapdoor space in a binder.

Mostly, it fascinates me to wonder what information is out there, what secrets Russian operatives may have about the United States. How many more spies are out there, and what are the things we have not been told about them? Were any of the people responsible for the hacking of the DNC databases former old-school spies who used classical techniques, yet dropped them into the cybersphere of the modern age? Do they work in tandem with people like Buryakov or Chapman, utilizing the information that the ground operatives have gathered? How does the spy game really work?

To find this out I spoke with Eric O'Neill, whose former career as a "spy catcher" was the subject of a major feature film.

Chapter 8

CONVERSATION WITH A GHOST

Eric O'Neill's appearance kind of resembles what one might imagine a former FBI surveillance operative would look like: somebody chameleonlike who can easily blend in with the crowd. He is simultaneously nondescript and ruggedly handsome, about average height with olive skin, deep-brown eyes, and a runner's build.

His expression was somewhat guarded, but amiable. He was also extremely easy to talk to. O'Neill's career surveilling Robert Hanssen, a "spy catcher" higher-level counterintelligence officer, is the subject of the film *Breach*.[1] O'Neill poses as Hanssen's assistant. Over the course of several years he gathered intelligence showing that Hanssen had been in bed with the Russians since 1984, had disclosed information to the Russians that had killed US agents, and he leaked a plethora of classified secrets.[2]

Hanssen was ultimately apprehended in 2001, after making a dead drop under a bridge in Virginia for his Russian handlers to pick up. He copped a plea and was spared the death penalty, but remains in solitary confinement for life in a prison in Colorado.[3] O'Neill was only twenty-seven years old at the time, and decided to leave the FBI to become an attorney.

When I met him in the CBS third-floor interview room, he was a national security expert and public speaker with the firm Carbon Black. We sat in two chairs in front of a simple black background to chat. Two cameras were set up around us. I was excited to interview O'Neill because his journey following Hanssen was interesting to me.

First, I was intrigued by how young he was when he'd been pulled from his regular work and unexpectedly was asked to play a role in bringing one of the country's biggest traitors to justice. I wondered what it felt like to be part of taking down a guy like Hanssen.

I could certainly guess why he may have decided to leave the FBI after that experience, but I was curious to know more. He had seen how Russian spies operate and was willing to talk about it. I wanted to know how he viewed the current Russian cyber-espionage threats in the context of spying in a pre-internet world.

My interest gained traction as soon as we started to talk.[4]

Pegues: Let's talk about the unit you were in, in the FBI.

O'Neill: Right, so one of the misconceptions was that when I was in the FBI I was an agent.

Pegues: You weren't an agent?

O'Neill: I was not a special agent; I was an investigative specialist, otherwise known as [a] ghost. It's little known although no longer classified. You can go on the federal government jobsite and apply for it. It is a group of individuals who are specially trained in undercover operations, counterterrorism, and counterintelligence, who are the primary assets in the FBI who do the surveillance for the FBI and the undercover operations.

Pegues: All right, so it wasn't an agent. It was a . . .

O'Neill: An investigator.

Pegues: And they called you ghosts?

O'Neill: The idea was [that] you never saw us, and if you saw us we didn't look like a threat. Your eyes would slide right off us, and you might see us three or four times during the course of a day, but we'd look different every time.

I imagined O'Neill wearing the kind of secret disguises I had read about: fake scars, mustaches, reversible clothing, etc. I told him that his old position sounded like something out of a movie. He agreed.

O'Neill: For quite some time it was not a publicized role. It's still quasi-secret, not classified secret, but not a lot of people know about it. The ghosts do most of the field work in counter terror and counterintelligence for the FBI.

We spoke for a while about Russian cyber-espionage techniques, and how good the Russians were at what they do. O'Neill explained the Russian spies' best skill sets. He explained something called HUMINT.

O'Neill: So, human intelligence, or HUMINT, is recruiting sources, taking people who work in areas where they want access and through either bribery or blackmail or ideology—you think more like me, your politics are more like me, help me out—they recruit people to give them information. We call those trusted insiders; you trust them, but they've sold out to the Russians in this example. That human intelligence is something they've been excellent at collecting.

Pegues: Better than the Americans?

O'Neill: Well, about the same. We're very good at it, too. But there's been this change in the last number of years.

Pegues: In what way?

O'Neill: We stopped putting information in file cabinets; we started putting all our information in computer systems.

Pegues: And that's a problem?

O'Neill: It is a problem if you're trying to protect information. It's great if you're a spy.

Pegues: Storing all of your valuable information in computers is a problem because it opens you up to hackers?

O'Neill: That's right, but I don't like the word "hackers."

Pegues: Why not?

O'Neill: I don't like the word "hackers" because what's happened. What I like to say is [that] there are no hackers . . . there are only spies. Hacking is nothing more than the natural evolution of espionage.

Pegues: You think so?

O'Neill: Those people, [for whom] we coined the term "hackers" some time ago, were mostly people who were interested in breaking into systems either for mischief or the challenge, and sometimes because they were criminals. That's not the level of what a spy does. A spy is someone stealing information to further a cause or to gain information that helps the policies of the government, or, as we've seen in recent years, disrupt another government. That's something more than [a] hacker. The hackers—those people have all gone—they work for security companies now. Those who are penetrating systems are spies, and the spies are well funded, and they have a lot of time to manage their attacks.

O'Neill explained how spies fit every piece of information they gather into a puzzle board, and how they work as a unit.

O'Neill: One thing that makes the Russians so good at HUMINT is everyone who works in the embassy works for the master spy there.

Pegues: Everyone?

O'Neill: Everyone. Everybody is part of it; even families can be used. Everybody's working toward a common goal; it's a little less [like] the way we operate. It's one of the distinctions between the Russians and how we operate. So, everybody who's collecting information: it all gets sifted, it all goes through the machine, and there can be facts that can help, even from conversations that might seem to be something different than anything that would help espionage.

Pegues: So, any conversation that you might think is totally innocent, the Russian spy could be looking at that in a different way.

O'Neill: Sure. Remember, spies get their information from everywhere; there are old stories from the old days when I was in the FBI, before the proliferation of information on the internet, where the first thing that the top spies in the Russian embassy would do every morning was read through all of the US papers, cover to cover, to find . . . information, [and] reporters were some of the best sources because they can uncover things that a spy might not have access to. [I]t's a start, it's all information that helps create this whole, and the whole is information about what we here in the US are going to do or plan to do that informs the policies and the directives and the decisions back in Moscow.

When O'Neill said that, it reminded me of the Russia investigation and the contacts between the Russian ambassador Sergey Kislyak and several members of the Trump campaign. Throughout 2016 and 2017 those contacts had raised concerns for US law enforcement officials.[5]

> **Pegues**: Do you think as a former . . . ghost . . . that's why US law enforcement/intelligence pays such close attention to contacts with Russian contacts, Russian operatives here in the US?
>
> **O'Neill**: It's important. Everyone in the government who is working with the Russians has to understand that what you say to them is going to go to Russian intelligence, and they do.
>
> We are trained for that, but there has to be that understanding that you're not just talking to a politician or a diplomat; you are talking to someone who will feed intelligence. We do the same thing overseas. We are hiding our spies within [embassies] as well because that's how you get diplomatic immunity.

I asked him how to combat state-sponsored spying that transcended simply gathering intelligence, but instead deliberately leaked information to cause disruption to a society, an election, a candidate. He spoke about the goals of cyber espionage.

> **O'Neill**: A phishing attack is attacking a person, not a computer. You attack the person. You fool the person; you trick the person into doing the work for you, so you're turning the person who mistakenly clicks on something that they trust into a virtual trusted insider. You have just recruited that person as your spy, and they have no idea that it's happened, so it's that old spy tradecraft in a modern system.

We spoke about what distinguished the DNC hacks from others—namely, in the dissemination of information. O'Neill said he believed (in 2016) most people assumed Hillary Clinton would be president, including the Russians. US officials believe that the intelligence the Russians gained was then weaponized through its delivery to WikiLeaks, a company headed by Julian Assange, who made maximum use of it by leaking it slowly.

> **O'Neill**: I think that there is no argument that both Putin and Julian Assange were pretty contrary to Hillary. None of them liked her very much. And I don't think either of them wanted her to win, or if she did, they wanted that new presidency to begin in disgrace.
>
> Both have their problems with her in the past. I think that if Putin was going to give [the stolen DNC data] to some[one] where he was going to provide the maximum damage or really weaponize it, handing it over to Assange was a good way to assure that was going to happen.
>
> So many people believed that there was journalistic integrity to WikiLeaks. I never did. I saw WikiLeaks as just another spy agency. The day it was founded I think I called them the fast food of spying. You can drive by and spy and go through the drive-by window. I was never fond of them, and I think what happened here is Assange has proven that there is no integrity there. If he wanted to claim anything of that sort he would have posted all of those emails at once, but the way that he dribbled them out bit by bit curated them almost.
>
> And remember that he was almost gleefully tweeting and giving [press] conferences and saying a big revelation is coming out, almost like he was doing publicity for his company. I truly think that there was a lot of information there that these things [emails] were coming.

Perhaps the warning signs were there prior to 2016, but too many people missed them. I know I didn't see it coming. Prior to the summer of 2016, my producers and I were focused on police shootings and the threat that ISIS posed to Americans. At that time, I was digging into the backgrounds of people who could be inspired or directed to carry out terrorist attacks on US soil. There had been the Paris attacks in 2015, in which more than 130 people were killed and hundreds injured.[6] Then the San Bernardino terrorist attack, during which the attackers killed fourteen people and injured over twenty others.[7]

There is no doubt that we had plenty to be distracted by in late 2015 and early 2016. This cyber realm we have entered where we are connected to the world wholly and instantaneously is relatively new. Yet, in hindsight, knowing that I was so underinformed about the topic of the Russian attack embarrassed me a bit.

Listening to Linda Power, Adam Meyers, and O'Neill made me wonder, though, how it was possible in the twenty-first century for a superpower to fall behind the curve in recognizing that Putin had perhaps employed an army of hackers who had embedded themselves into our systems. We had been dealing with Russian operatives' propaganda for years.

Linda's voice ran through my head. *"I don't understand why nobody knew."* Did more people know more than they had let on? That prospect made me, quite frankly, angry; the response time in alerting the American public, even after Putin's army was going after the throat of our election, was alarmingly slow.

Chapter 9

VLADIMIR PUTIN: WHO IS THIS GUY?

About a year ago, I saw a Reuters photo of a bare-chested Vladimir Putin holding a gigantic rifle. He was wearing a silver cross and fingerless leather gloves and trudging through dry, junglelike terrain in the Tuva region of Siberia. There was sweat on the bald spot pushing back tufts of parted blond hair. His forehead was cinched, as if he was in deep concentration.[1]

The photo was taken in 2007, one of a rock-star-like portfolio bearing testament to President Putin's physical prowess. He is a hunter who often goes on research expeditions with scientists who track and tag animals. He has black belts in Kaikan karate and judo (he wrote an entire book about judo and his signature harai goshi moves). He was given the nickname "Abaddon" ("the destroyer" in Hebrew) by the high council of Russian bikers, and often brags about his prowess swimming for fun in frigid Siberian lakes.[2]

I had known Putin was a hotshot who often boasted of his athleticism, but something about that Reuters photo struck me as curious. It was an image that stuck in my mind and wouldn't go away. I couldn't figure out why. Perhaps the work was getting to me.

As an observer trying to gather information from well-placed law enforcement and intelligence sources, I realized things were becoming increasingly surreal. The movie I was watching unfold was definitely a thriller, a certain Hollywood blockbuster that involved espionage, cyberattacks, a presidential campaign, a reality TV star, and a woman being painted as unscrupulous, all entrenched with a Russian president who liked being photographed shirtless and armed.

I looked at the photo of the odd man who was at the helm of the US cyberattack, a man who led an invisible strike force of hackers, who swooped in, gathered intelligence, and slipped away undetected until it was too late.

It is truly impossible to understand the character of high-ranking political leaders. Their public and private personas become enmeshed. Their political actions are not their own but determined and undermined by a multitude of other people, motives, and storylines. In a perfect world, their political actions would speak for themselves. But this is not quite a perfect world.

The lineup for the 2016 presidential election could not have been more bizarre. Trump and Putin's rough public personas could at times seem (or be made out to be) driven largely by ego and machismo. While these qualities may make for fine actors or quarterbacks, when they come from political leaders, boundaries can be and often are crossed. There is no harm when that ego is sequestered from the political arena. For example, Putin was playing at a recent hockey game and the players let him score eight goals.[3] I could understand that because all men know people like that. He's just a guy who has to win, who other people have to let win, because if he doesn't win, then everyone knows there is going to be a problem. And I have heard that Trump can also be like that, especially when he is playing golf.

Putin had been known to cross lines to intimidate political adversaries. For example, he brought out his giant black Lab, Koni, during a meeting with German chancellor Angela Merkel in 2007 about energy supplies.[4] He knew she was terrified of dogs and had once been bitten. Putin remarked how big Koni was. Merkel joked in Russian that at least the pooch "doesn't eat journalists."[5] Former president George W. Bush has embraced his artistic side and painted a brooding portrait of Putin that he describes as "hollow." Bush explained the inspiration for his painting was his bone of contention with Putin, who trotted Koni out at a meeting with Bush while mocking the size of Bush's late, prized Scottish terrier Barney. Bush explained that line of attack revealed Putin's character.[6]

The script has sure changed.

THE CONTEXT

It is hard to avoid creating caricatures out of leaders these days. A game is being played with our country and our lives, and the rules were never explained to us. Perhaps to understand Putin better we might examine the context. Russia's political system is counterintuitive to ours. Since 1999, Putin has been either Russia's president or prime minister. In 2018, he won his fourth term as president in typical fashion.[7] Many believe he has maintained his status mainly by pushing limitations (regulated by the Kremlin) on election laws, intimidating potential rivals, and quelling independent news outlets.

Some of the chess moves he has made during his most recent term in office that were controversial and detrimental to the US government include granting asylum to Edward Snowden, a former CIA employee and government contractor who leaked classified National Security Agency (NSA) information. The classified information included details Snowden believed the American public should know about, such as global and domestic surveillance programs. One of the most controversial things he leaked was an NSA program that required US phone companies to give them every single customer's phone records.[8]

Snowden was charged with violating the Espionage Act. But he has been recognized as a hero by some and a traitor by many of those I've spoken with who work in the area of national security. Accordingly, some folks in the government believed Putin's harboring of Snowden was an aggressive act.[9]

Putin has been widely criticized for international human rights violations in the physical (non-cyber) world. The United Nations and organizations like Human Rights Watch have condemned Putin's practices, which include torture, the killing of at least ten thousand people, and the illegal transport of thousands of residents of Crimea to Russian prisons. Crimea is a peninsula in the Black Sea that was snatched from Russia by Ukraine in 1954, and later occupied by Russia and annexed in 2014.[10]

Global protest has followed Putin's stringent anti-gay laws, which include making it illegal for gay couples in Russia to get married or have children. Russia's crackdown on terrorists has also led to violations against Muslims in Russia. For example, in the North Caucasus region of Russia, reports surfaced that Putin was ordering saliva samples to be collected from Muslim women purportedly to locate "black widows," or female suicide bombers.[11]

Vladimir Vladimirovich Putin was born in Leningrad to a working-class family. His father was a factory foreman, and he grew up in a communal apartment shared with three other families.[12] He was born in 1952, five years after the Cold War between the Soviet Union and the West began.

To place Putin's formative years in context, the Cold War is a phrase that essentially describes the tricky relationship between the United States and its NATO allies, "the West," and the Soviet Union or what was officially termed the Union of Soviet Socialist Republics (USSR) from 1945 to 1989 (or 1991, depending upon your perspective). The USSR included fifteen republics comprising a gargantuan swath of land that made it the biggest country in the world in territory. Its capital was in Moscow from 1945 to1989. The conflict was essentially an ideological one—communism versus capitalism, democracy versus dictatorship—with both sides zealously promoting their way as correct. Although each side had substantial power (nuclear and otherwise), no actual fighting occurred between them. Rather, they used the world as their chessboard, each having spheres of influence with client states duking it out on their behalf. Most notably North Vietnam was pro-Communist, and its arms were supplied from Russia or China. South Vietnam was anti-Communist and received its weapons from the United States and its allies.

Putin graduated from Leningrad State University with a degree in law in 1975. He served in the KGB for sixteen years, rising through the ranks to become a lieutenant colonel. In 1991, he retired from the KGB and returned to his hometown, which had been renamed Saint Petersburg, and entered politics.[13]

The revolutions of 1989 included millions of people protesting on the streets in countries across Eastern Europe (what had come to be called the Soviet Bloc). Major events included the collapse of the Berlin Wall, which marked the division of Europe; cutting down barbed wire fences marking borders in Hungary; and the end of Communist rule punctuated by candlelight vigils all over Europe. Many note the end of the Cold War as occurring in 1989 at the time of the widespread revolutions against Communist rule, while others note it as having taken place in 1991 when each republic succeeded and the Soviet Union formally dissolved. During that year Mikhail Gorbachev, the eighth president of the Soviet Union, resigned and handed the reins of power over to Russian president Boris Yeltsin. Yeltsin appointed Putin as prime minister in 1999. He was then made president, when Yeltsin retired in 2000.[14]

Putin's cyber strategies have been described by many of my sources as "very Russian." This means that the Russians have their own elaborate strategic system, developed over years, of provoking conflict in a country by using stealthy former spies, mathematicians, and current spies. Russia's citizens know they live in a country where it is a given that people are often under government suspicion, particularly outsiders. Although many of my intelligence sources have studied Russian operatives, nobody seems to have suspected they would gain such unfettered recent access to our cyberspace. Many admit that the United States is ill prepared because we don't really understand the context in which Putin is operating.

Laura Rosenberger of the Alliance for Securing Democracy explains how foreign Russia's strategy was viewed by the US intelligence community at the time its military occupied Ukraine, beginning in 2014 (and including the annexation of Crimea). She describes how difficult Russian political culture is to understand, even for the experts.

> I was at the National Security Council at the White House when we were dealing with Russia's intervention in Ukraine. We were really looking at other things that Russia might do along its periphery and elsewhere with this asymmetric tool kit. One of the things that was clear to me was that theirs was a playbook that we in the national security community in the United States, at least at the time, were not really equipped to fully wrap our heads around, nor to respond to in a comprehensive way.

Its asymmetric and cross-cutting nature doesn't sit well with how our bureaucracy is organized. That sounds like a very bureaucratic answer. But the reality is that if we aren't able to analyze, understand, and respond to the tool kit in a way that is just as comprehensive as what we're getting on the incoming side, we're just going to keep playing whack-a-mole.

That's a very long way of saying that, "No, I don't think that we have a responsive playbook, because I don't think we really yet fully understand the threat that we're facing."[15]

Chapter 10

THE PLAYBOOK

In general, spying is integral to politics and warfare, but it has been a separate entity. Much of today's espionage, politics, and warfare are becoming intertwined in the cyber realm. In 2016, NATO officially recognized cyberspace as an operational domain—a place where conflict can be carried out. The term "cyberwar" has been coined to indicate how nation-states can disable one another to gain advantage in conflict.[1]

When incidents are related to Russia, the phrase "Cyber Cold War" is now in vogue. There are different levels at which these attacks are believed to be occurring worldwide. A cyberattack may occur online but have repercussions in the physical world. The most infamous of these occurred in 2015 when the Ukrainian power grid was disabled, leaving 230,000 customers without power. The cyber criminals, who utilized sophisticated techniques in their attack, thoughtfully planned it over a period of months and used reconnaissance methods to study the facilities. Many believed the Russian government was behind it.[2]

Likewise, two hacking groups called Dragonfly and the Energetic Bear that have been linked to Russia have breached security systems at approximately one hundred electrical and nuclear plants in 2017 with about half of them occurring in the United States, according to Symantec, a computer-security company.[3]

"Fake news" or misinformation campaigns may spur a conflict, as we saw in the case of Estonia. In 2007, when the country's leaders decided to move a statue of a soldier in a World War II Red Army uniform, it sparked a cyberattack. When it was unveiled by the Soviets in 1947, it symbolized the USSR's victory over Nazism. But for Estonians the bronze soldier was a symbol of Soviet oppression.

When the statue was moved, it sparked outrage in Russian-language media. False stories generated by Russian-language media stirred up protests. There were two nights of riots, with 156 injured, one fatality, and one thousand people were detained. But Estonia was also smacked with weeks of cyberattacks that many believed were ordered by the Kremlin.[4]

It is also believed that Russian hackers have intruded on electoral systems throughout the world. Data was seized following a hack by Russian-backed APT28 on the Bundesstadt, the Federal City of Bonn, Germany.[5]

Subsequently, Hans-Georg Maassen, the top spy chief in Germany, told the German public that Russia had threatened to publish embarrassing documents about members of the German legislature, which they believed to be a tactic to destabilize their September 2017 elections.[6] At the time Maassen said, "We have the impression that this is part of a hybrid threat that seeks to influence public opinion and decision-making processes." He also cautioned that it was important to call it out for what it was. "When people realize that the information that they are getting is not true . . . then the toxic lies lose their effectiveness."[7]

Although the Russian hackers may have wrought confusion by sidling into cyberspace and attempting to compromise trust in various electoral systems, there was a clear and well-defined methodology behind their madness. Officials believe Russian hacking in Estonia, Ukraine, the Netherlands, the United States, as well as in half a dozen other locations around the world were part of a new approach to warfare. It has been called the Gerasimov Doctrine, which is outlined in an article General Valery Gerasimov, the chief of general staff of the Russian armed forces, wrote and published in 2013 in a military journal.[8] The article, titled "The Value of Science Is in the Foresight: New Challenges Demand Rethinking the Forms and Methods of Carrying out Combat Operations," essentially articulates Russia's modern form of warfare, which is rooted in the Cold War strategies the country's intelligence agents have always used.[9]

The doctrine calls for a bombastic multilevel attack that places politics and war on the same nonmilitary playing field—cyberspace. It intends to sow chaos and undermine societies, often in a way that is so covert that nobody knows what is happening. Spies slip into computers rather than hotel rooms, targeting everyone from media to businesspeople, using traditional Soviet strategies including conventional and asymmetrical methods.

Conventional warfare is war between two evenly matched military powers abiding by international laws of war. Asymmetrical warfare is just what it sounds like. It is a lopsided, wonky form of warfare in which one side has a markedly different strategy or power than the other side. It is unconventional warfare. The term "asymmetric" is often used to refer to guerilla warfare, and has also been used to describe insurgency or terrorism. In the case of cyberwar, asymmetrical methods could include elements like phishing, spear attacks, or distributed denial of service attacks—commonly called DDoS. The covert, invisible nature of cyberwar also fits into the definition of asymmetrical. The nation under attack often doesn't know their enemy is there. Thus, they are mismatched.

This approach is intended to destabilize. People who subscribe to the strategy believe it is more effective than traditional war. In his article, Gerasimov lays out a perspective that is thought to be the prevalent view in Russian intelligence of warfare, having evolved from a physical war playing out on the battlefield: it costs a lot of money and sinks resources into a war that occurs behind the scenes and largely in the technological realm. The war he describes is sophisticated trickery, an often invisible and covert psychological global chess match that causes government processes and policies to devolve and destabilize.[10] In the article, Gerasimov writes of using covert and propaganda tactics to turn a "perfectly thriving state" into a victim of "foreign intervention," causing it to "sink into a web of chaos."[11] Does that sound familiar? Just look at 2017 in the United States. Political chaos—the likes of which we have not seen in this country in decades. No need to ascribe blame just yet, except to say that it is clear that Russian internet trolls are playing a role in our country's domestic politics. They latch onto certain issues in the news and then hype them up. For example, in February 2017 when Republican members of the House Intelligence Committee voted to release a controversial memo alleging that the Russia investigation was tainted because of bias within the FBI against the Trump campaign, Russian bots helped the hashtag "#Release the memo" go viral. It was just the type of issue the Russian bots and their allies had been embracing to deepen divisions between Americans. The German Marshall Fund's Hamilton 68 dashboard flagged the Russian campaign.[12] Hamilton 68 had been founded to spot Russian bots' activities online in the United States.

The Gerasimov Doctrine essentially pits us against ourselves. Think back to what happened after the Democratic National Committee emails were leaked and more than twenty state election databases were scanned and probed.

Adam Meyers of the internet security firm CrowdStrike is among those who believe the Gerasimov Doctrine inspired these incidents. Meyers explains how information warfare was used as "a way of influencing the events that occur without [the involvement of] troops." He stresses that using the term "cyber warfare" to qualify the playbook strategy is limiting, that cyber is only a component. "Broadly, it's information warfare in that they're not constrained to use only cyber mechanisms; they're going to use media and social media and things that they can use to sway or put out the things that they want people thinking about," he said.[13]

The way they used the information to influence the public's choice of one candidate over another by employing irregular/asymmetric actions is a playbook strategy. When the special counsel investigating whether there was collusion between the Trump campaign and Russia announced an indictment in February 2018 against thirteen Russian nationals, some of those actions were outlined.[14] The court documents alleged that, dating back to 2014, a Russian internet troll factory sought to "sow discord in the U.S. political system." Internet "specialists" scanning social media planted online posts attacking Hillary Clinton, and promoted Bernie Sanders and then candidate Donald Trump. The court documents also said that the Russian internet trolls wanted to suppress the vote leading up through Election Day 2016. For example, an Instagram message from a fake group called "Woke Blacks" advised against voting for either party's nominee: "We cannot resort to the lesser of two devils," it said. "Then we'd surely be better off without voting at all."

Separately, Kremlin-backed hackers phished information from private databases, dumped it into the public realm through WikiLeaks, and launched a misinformation campaign around hyping and distorting this information—while at the same time creating alliances with polarized groups in the United States.

The leaks caused dialogue points used by television, radio, social media, and print outlets. Their success was measured by the fact that they changed the narrative around the election, first by demonizing Clinton and her campaign officials. Russian-backed hacking units scanned and probed state databases and caused us to question the security and sanctity of our electoral process. When citizens in states like North Carolina found that they were unable to vote, they questioned how the voting booths had been compromised.[15] Had they been manipulated by Americans siding with certain candidates, or by a foreign entity? If they had been manipulated by a foreign entity, what does that say about our security system? In tapping into several coordinated tactics, Russian hackers pitted us against ourselves, and caused us to question the legitimacy of our electoral system.

Meyers explains more in his blog. "The mark of success of an irregular/asymmetric action against the US election may not necessarily manifest as one candidate winning over another. Simply causing the American people to question the validity of the results would likely cause widespread disruption across the US media, legal and political systems."[16]

It did cause disruption. The misinformation campaign drew on and applied a century of knowledge gleaned during the Cold War to manipulate public opinion and alter our democratic system.

THE PLAYBOOK IN UKRAINE

Meyers also details how the playbook was utilized to compromise electoral systems in Ukraine. For example, in a mayoral election in Odessa, embarrassing video was leaked depicting twenty-one-year-old mayoral candidate Valeria Prokopenko performing a strip tease, public exposure of which caused her to drop out of the election.[17]

Simultaneously, the other mayoral hopeful, Gennadiy Trukhanov, who was pro-Russian, was exposed through the Panama Papers as having potentially dirty business dealings in Russia. The Panama Papers revealed that Mossack Fonseca, an offshore law firm, had dealings with politicians who used offshore tax havens. These involved 143 politicians, including twelve national leaders. Among these is Putin, who was affiliated with $2 billion in a tax haven. Sergei Roldugin, a cellist and Putin's best friend, was connected with a scheme in which money from Russian state banks was hidden offshore. A ski resort where Putin's daughter was married in 2013 also received some of the flow of this money. The firm's dealings were leaked to *Süddeutsche Zeitung*, a German newspaper. They were then given to the International Consortium of Investigative Journalists and spread to top-notch reporters at major outlets throughout the world.[18]

CyberBerkut, a hacking group, deleted files, stalling the vote-tallying mechanism, and even briefly changed the results during Ukraine's 2014 presidential election.[19] During this election, outdoor digital screens in Kiev were compromised and displayed violent photos accusing nationalist politicians of war crimes. These activities, including the massive power grid blackout, while seemingly haphazard and unrelated, may have been part of a coordinated strategy to undermine the Ukrainian population's faith in their government and its ability to protect them.[20]

The playbook strategy is most debilitating because most of it occurs under cyberspace deep cover, where spies are simply bringing smoke-and-mirror tricks they have perfected for years to a new arena. In the United States, the course of the past few years would have been destabilizing enough with the carnival sideshow acts performed along the primary and campaign trail, even before we became aware of the potential that we were being compromised.

Let's face it, even before the 2016 presidential election, the United States was doing a decent job of undermining its own political system. We made ourselves vulnerable. At least that's what the Obama administration's cyber czar Michael Daniel told me: "I'm a student of history, too. And we should not ascribe superpowers to the Russians. They're very good at what they do. But some of that was luck on their part, right? I mean, there's no way that they could've predicted that we would have somebody like now president Trump, who would fuel that kind of atmosphere. There's no way they could've predicted that the Democrats would choose as polarizing a figure as Hillary Clinton in some ways, right? And so, some of that was them capitalizing on the situation."[21]

Chapter 11

PUTIN'S GRUDGE AGAINST CLINTON

Hillary Clinton was a polarizing figure—although it is possible the rifts between her supporters and her opponents wouldn't have been so pronounced if Trump and/or Putin weren't sowing the seeds of hatred against her.

Clinton will always be remembered as the person who had been tenacious and devoted enough to become the first woman to win the presidential nomination for a major political party in the United States. She will also be remembered for her dogged determination in standing up to a candidate who held her responsible for her husband's sexual transgressions.[1] Because of the impact of social media and an unyielding twenty-four-hour news cycle, she was heckled and jeered at while campaigning in a manner that has never occurred in our country in the past. Then Trump riled up his crowds to chant phrases like "Lock her up" and "Crooked Hillary."[2] Clinton also stood up to a candidate whose multiple attempts at verbal and physical intimidation during debates were so remarkable they were prominently featured in domestic comedy skits like *Saturday Night Live*.[3]

As the campaigning became more brutal and rifts between party members in the United States deepened, Clinton came to represent one of several ideals. Some people vehemently opposed to the election of Trump felt that voting for Clinton wasn't a choice, but more of an obligation because that would ensure he didn't get into office. Others passionately supported her because she was a woman and they wanted to see the first female president of the United States get into office—just as they had seen Barack Obama as the first African

American president. Her position would ensure women fought for and maintained equal economic, social, and political rights. Her presidency would stand for our collective evolution, proof that our society had changed. Many people in this camp believed Clinton was a good choice because she had stood her ground for decades in a political environment that was largely dominated by men, and had made tough choices.

There are educated, informed people who didn't like Clinton due to some of the choices that she'd made throughout her career, for example being largely responsible for coining the phrase "super predator"—a myth referring to gangs of bloodthirsty, remorseless (black) kids roaming the streets—and for supporting policies that led to mandatory sentences of life without parole for thousands of teenagers, the majority of whom are still in prison.[4] Some held her responsible for what happened at Benghazi, on September 11, 2012, where four Americans were killed in Libya.[5] Even the Clinton Foundation had become a liability for her. Some Republicans had succeeded in branding it as a corrupt vehicle for donors to curry favor with Secretary of State Clinton. The Clinton Foundation began in 1997 as a way for the Clinton family to raise money for humanitarian work across the globe, and there was no hard evidence presented that it had done otherwise. There were people who had strong political opinions about why they didn't want Hillary Clinton as president.

If you ask the majority of people vehemently opposed to the election of Hillary Clinton, however, they generally parrot the rhetoric Trump spouted during the campaigns, calling her "crooked," or a "criminal," and citing the investigations into her email server as evidence.

PUTIN WAS BEHIND HILLARY BASHING

It is becoming well known that the Putin-led Russian influence campaign helped sway public opinion against Clinton, and that some of its primary objectives "were to undermine public faith in the US democratic process, denigrate Secretary Clinton, and harm her electability and potential presidency."[6] This information was made public in a declassified report called *Assessing Russian Activities and Intentions in Recent US Elections*, a compilation of assessments from the CIA, FBI, and NSA, released in January 2017. US officials said that what was revealed to the public was a declassified version of another "highly classified assessment" that only a small group of people had been briefed on.[7]

The source of this condemnation was Putin's hatred of Clinton. This hatred stemmed back to 2009, when Clinton had just been appointed secretary of state, and Obama charged her with overseeing his "Russian reset" program, which was established to try and sow some semblance of goodwill between the two countries. Putin didn't trust Clinton from the get-go. He believed she was harder on policies relating to Moscow than other US officials and that she advocated for Russian "regime change" measures that could have ousted him from power.[8]

Russian reset followed on the heels of a threat to Putin's power in 2009, when Putin's elongated term was limited and he became prime minister and relinquished the presidency to Dimitri Medvedev. Putin was hurt when Medvedev veered from the trade Putin schooled him in and when Medvedev expressed himself as a liberal with a penchant for the West and their fun technological gadgets.[9]

In 2011, Putin ran for president again (it would be his third term). He won the election by a landslide, but was accused of rigging the vote.[10] Shortly afterward, Clinton spoke out, saying citizens' votes should count and that she supported free, fair elections. Subsequently, the most substantial anti-government protests since the fall of the Cold War occurred in Moscow and other cities across Russia.[11] Kremlin officials feared they could lead to a revolution. Putin largely blamed the protests on Clinton's remarks. The idea that she had made these statements mainly to serve US agendas had been a belief held by factions in the Kremlin since Russian reset began.[12]

And Putin certainly had it in for Clinton. "He was very upset [with Clinton] and continued to be for the rest of the time that I was in government," said Michael McFaul, who served as the top Russia official in President Obama's national security council from 2009 to December 2011 and then was US ambassador to Moscow until early 2014. "One could speculate that this is his moment for payback."[13]

That payback began with Putin's army of hackers, including two units nicknamed after children's stuffed toys, Fancy Bear and Cozy Bear, who hacked into the email servers at the DNC and passed off the data to a team of drive-through cyber spies to leak them over the internet. That was only phase one. One of my sources explained that after the hack was publicly attributed to Russia, the actors didn't retreat or go into a shell, as many other operatives would have. Instead they doubled down. This was also what Meyers meant when he said the "Russians didn't hide their tracks and were doing their thing."[14]

Phase two was more aggressive. Putin went for the jugular of our electoral system—our electoral databases.

Chapter 12

THE SEPARATION BETWEEN FEDERAL AND STATE GOVERNMENT

Michael Daniel sat at another meeting of the Cyber Response Group. The people who gathered in the room had gradually become more alarmed, as their hypotheses were beginning to come true. Daniel held a printout of a report made through the Cyber Threat Intelligence Integration Center, a kind of a fusion center for intragovernmental reporting—including everyone from White House staff to senior policy makers. Information about viruses, hacks, espionage, etc. are cherry-picked from the FBI, the National Counterterrorism Center, intelligence analysts, and other officials to create a consolidated picture.[1] The system was established in 2014 by the National Security Council.

The critical report detailed hacks into Illinois voter registration databases. The hackers had essentially absconded with names, social security numbers, and addresses of registered voters.

Forensic investigation tried to determine if a specific hacker's fingerprint could be traced to the Illinois hack. Daniel couldn't say if they confirmed the Russian hacker's involvement at that point. They created a tracking matrix to see whether other states were affected, and eventually discovered at least twenty-two states had been potentially compromised. They couldn't decipher a pattern or verify if any information plucked from the databases had been manipulated. Again, they didn't know much at all.[2]

There was a more significant barrier to weeding out the hack than identifying its roots or even how many states had been invaded.

For many, the atmosphere of the campaign had the disconcerting quality of being lost in the space-time continuum, with people on the Far Right seeming to revisit perspectives related to race and gender, predating events like the Voting Rights Act of 1965, *Roe v. Wade*, even the Nineteenth Amendment, and people leaning toward the Left reacting vehemently. This deepened the division not just between parties, not just between red and blue states, but between the states and federal government.

It wasn't a great time to be compromised. When Daniel and other members of the National Security Council reached out to states to see if they could do anything to help protect their voter registration databases—in places where elections had been viewed as local matters that states were most protective of—they were reproached.[3] Federal employees responding to the cyber-espionage attacks were caught in a bureaucratic quagmire. Again, freedom became a liability.

In late 2017, I met Daniel at Sequoia, a Georgetown restaurant, for lunch to discuss what was happening during the late summer of 2016. The sun beat down on the restaurant plaza, set along the wide banks of the Potomac.

I sat by myself for a few minutes and looked outside at the stunning iconic view. It was so close I could make out slight waves on the muddy river, and see across it all the way to Arlington, Virginia, and down the street to the Kennedy Center and the Watergate Hotel.

I recognized Daniel as he arrived, and we shook hands and exchanged formalities before Daniel sat down. I set up my recorder and started the interview.[4]

Daniel spoke of the Russian hackers' goal in 2016.

> **Daniel:** I think that their goal was, first and foremost, to undermine Americans' confidence in the . . . electoral process. The Russians very much wanted to put themselves on the same moral playing field as the United States. And they want to do everything they can to basically [be] able to argue, "See, the United States is no better than anybody else. So, when they tell you that you should follow their examples, don't believe them. Look how crappy they are at running their own elections."

And you know, I think that they were also strategically hoping to weaken the United States. The Russians don't view that as an isolated thing. They view it as part of a larger continuum of efforts to push back against the West. They're not going to just view that as just an isolated thing.

Next, we started talking about the difficulty Daniel and other members of the National Security Council had in trying to offer reconnaissance to the states.[5]

Daniel: I'm a career civil servant. I've been in the national security field for over twenty years now. My first instinct is not to think politically in the sense of party dynamics, even though I live in Washington, DC, you know . . . and have for my entire professional career. And so . . . I was completely taken aback at the reaction that we got from the states when we did . . . some of those outreach calls, at the amount of pushback that we got.

Pegues: How would you describe it?

Daniel: Some of them were the secretaries of state, on that initial call that Jeh Johnson did, were outright hostile.

Pegues: Georgia?

Daniel: Among them.

Pegues: Florida?

Daniel: Yeah. I don't remember the exact breakdown. But certainly, Georgia was among them. And they saw it completely as an Obama, political, Democratic Party attempt to horn in on their election space. And I'm completely flabbergasted. Because I'm like, "There's a foreign power trying to screw with us. And you know, you're being willfully blind to this." And it was a real wakeup call for me that this was going to be way harder than we were anticipating, because of that political overlay.

Pegues: What month was that in?

Daniel: That was August. And so what we also realized as we were going along is that there's a couple of things here, which is that, frankly, what we can actually offer the states in terms of real hardcore capability is pretty limited.

You know, we can offer the scanning services. We have

some ability, if the states request it, to send assessment teams to help them shore up their systems. We can make some recommendations on best practices.

But we don't have a whole lot else that we can really offer the states or local governments, especially on the time frame that we're in, which is, for many of them they had already, long since, locked down their voting machines. They had already locked things down. [Princeton professor] Ed Felten refers to it as "the Election Valley of Death." What he means by that is there's a misalignment between when people tend to focus on election cybersecurity and when anybody could actually do anything about it, which is, when anybody could do anything about it, nobody's paying any attention. And by the time people are paying attention, you can't do anything about it.

Pegues: It's too late.

Daniel: In many ways, we were already too late. And at the same time, we're . . . trying to think of all the different ways that we can assist with election security.

At the same time, we're also thinking through, how do we push back on the Russians diplomatically? How do we ready some options? How do we work on a communications plan, in case things go sour? At the same time we're trying to maintain the public messaging about confidence in the underlying electoral system.

Pegues: That was going all the way up to the president. He was on that message, as well? Were you part of that advisory process to brief him on how to respond to these questions, to emphasize this over that?

Daniel: I mean, sure. You know, we were certainly providing that. I can't say that I briefed the president personally on that. But we were feeding the folks who were.

Pegues: What was important at that point in terms of messaging?

Daniel: Well, you know, one of the things we were trying to do was not do the Russians' work for them. We didn't want to be causing people to panic by what we were doing, either. We didn't want to feed the narrative that "Oh, the electoral infrastructure is unreliable."

Pegues: But it was already out there. Because you had a candidate who was saying that the system was rigged.

Daniel: Right. But then that just added the extra political overlay on it, right? And you know, it was very clear, from the president on down, the chief of staff, that they did not want us to do anything that looked like we were putting our thumb on the scale one way or the other, for one candidate over the other, that we, from a national security perspective, needed to treat this as a national security issue that was not partisan in that sense. And that was very clear guidance from the president on down.

Pegues: I understand what the White House was trying to do. But in hindsight, did that lead to an atmosphere where the administration was too cautious?

Daniel: You know, it's hard to say. It's also hard to say what would've happened if we had been more aggressive. You know, I think that, for me, the larger lesson is that this issue is not going to go away. These information operations are going to continue.

Other people, other nations are probably going to start. Other groups are going to start playing in that space, because of the perceived success that the Russians had. We need to invest in the cybersecurity of our electoral infrastructure. Because that's been shown to not be where it needs to be.

And I think we should think of it like we think about the power grid or our telecommunications grid or our healthcare system or the financial services industry. It's critical. It's a process and a thing that is critical to the functioning of our democracy.

After the interview, I was headed back to CBS and processing what Daniel had said. I looked out the window while passing through Georgetown and stopped near the Watergate Hotel. It suddenly struck me as ironic that Daniel and I had interviewed across from that building as historical parallels to the Watergate scandal started to be revealed in 2016.

My mind drifted. I was happy. I felt like the interview went well and provided me with a new perspective on the story.

I learned more about how we behaved collectively at this point in history. It was interesting to note how genuinely confused, even heartbroken Daniel was when the states accused his office of pandering to a particular party or interfering with their elections. I was puzzled by the fact that by the time anyone in the federal government discovered the state hacks, the machines were essentially in lockdown mode—Felten's Election Valley of Death. Even if the machines weren't locked down, the federal government wouldn't have been able to offer much help. Were we amazingly underequipped to deal with this type of emergency? Again, how could one of the most modern, Western, purportedly technologically advanced nations in the world be unprepared for an attack on our voter databases, one of the crown jewels of our democracy? It just didn't make any sense.

It was still unclear whether the separation between the states and federal government made voter databases more or less secure. Sources had told me the lack of a cohesive collective election system across all the states and counties in the country made them more difficult for hackers to penetrate as a whole. James Comey, who was the FBI director at the time, called the system old and clunky.[6] The hackers may be able to reach twenty-three states, for instance, but they couldn't get every state's database. On the flip side, the federal government's reluctance to inform the public until it was too late (or in many cases state representatives found out long after the elections, or not at all) was shameful and dangerous; it was as if the federal government didn't trust us enough to tell us and, hence, protect us. The states' distrust of the federal government also made us vulnerable. But was it warranted?

I headed along K Street and then passed the World Bank, where my father worked as a senior banking sector specialist.

I frequently ruminated over this issue during the course of this investigation. Millions of people, including women and African Americans, had fought for the right to vote, to be part of a society that addressed everyone's needs. United we stand. Divided we fall. I could also understand where the states were coming from in distrusting and resisting the federal government. There is a historical precedent for that, most notably in the South. I reflected on that concept while traveling back to Birmingham, Alabama, with then CIA director John Brennan.

Chapter 13

FROM CIVIL RIGHTS TO RUSSIAN INTELLIGENCE

SEPTEMBER 14, 2016

I stood squinting at the motorcade slinking up the tarmac of Andrews Air Force Base in Prince George's County, Maryland. It was a hot, dusty day. My luggage had already been screened and was on board the jet.

I had met the director of the CIA, John Brennan, before, but I had never had this kind of access. When he emerged from his black SUV and walked up to me to shake my hand, I wasn't nervous, just eager to get the interview underway. Brennan was a barrel-chested, immaculately dressed six-foot-three-inch-tall guy. Although I had been a wide receiver in college and could hold my own, I was only five feet seven, and he towered over me.

Brennan was imposing for reasons beyond his size, though. As I shook his hand, I immediately began to consider the breadth of experience he has had. Here was a man who had been with the CIA for thirty years and who had served under every president from Jimmy Carter to Barack Obama. I had read that his office was in the West Wing directly below the Oval Office during his role as assistant to President Obama for Homeland Security and counterterrorism. In 2013, he was nominated to be the director of the CIA, the person responsible for protecting the country from everything from nuclear holocaust to terrorist attacks.

I was granted an exclusive twenty-four-hour interview with him to talk about anything at all, which included highlighting the fact that the purpose of his trip to Birmingham (my family's hometown) and to Miles College, a predominantly African American college where my grandmother went to school, was to recruit new CIA agents and encourage diversity within the ranks of the agency.

It was an exciting opportunity. No television crew had been allowed to spend that kind of uncensored time with a CIA director, although Brennan had assumed a more public persona than any of his predecessors.

We boarded the plane, an unmarked jet that just about seated the nine or so people in the cabin. I was surprised that it was so small and unadorned.

I sat at the window, Brennan settled into a seat across from me, and we pulled our seat belts on. Brennan's top press aide sat across from us.

Unlike the commercial flights I usually take, I noticed that the one flight attendant on board did not tell us to fasten our seat belts, nor did she speak over the intercom about what to do in the event of an emergency. Probably not necessary, I thought, given that the plane was carrying the man assigned to deal with every emergency imaginable.

There was so much about the trip that was unprecedented and unique to our time. Brennan was on a mission to recruit more diversity to the ranks of the CIA because he had ordered a study that concluded that the agency was staffed mainly by older Caucasian men, a fact already obvious to anyone who was paying attention, including Brennan.[1]

Brennan, as director, was not only encouraging more diversity, but he was also repositioning the agency to counter the most pressing cyber threats.[2] In his view, the two goals weren't mutually exclusive. The CIA needed people from all cultures and ethnicities to form a collective front in defending the United States against all kinds of attacks.

These two factors made the trip personal to me. My family's history was deeply engrained in the civil rights movement, and touching down in Birmingham with a CIA director willing to take a good look at that history and amend it was a great, albeit surreal, privilege.

Brennan's new position also brought him to the cyber realm,

where he believed the United States was most vulnerable to attack. I believed that, too. It was the issue I had become nearly obsessed with over the previous few months. Race was still our country's weakness, but now that was just one factor making every American vulnerable. Russian-led cyber-espionage attacks were quietly undermining our free election system. That it had been so easy for the Kremlin to meddle in our democracy was, in my view, the single biggest threat to our freedom—more than terrorism. The Russians had been waging a war against the United States, and the Obama administration had been caught flat-footed. It infuriated me that in the latter stages of the 2016 election the Russian threat had not yet become widespread public knowledge. What the public knew had been coaxed out of intelligence or law enforcement officials by journalists.

The CIA's response to the Russian threat (in conjunction with other intelligence and law enforcement efforts) would consume the remainder of Brennan's career, but he wasn't able to acknowledge that at the time I interviewed him.

I wanted to hear what the CIA knew about Russian interference and how the agency planned to stop it. But these are topics I had to work my way up to, particularly with the director of the CIA.

For much of the flight we discussed the depravity of the radical jihadist group ISIS. Brennan said that the terror group "knows no bounds" and that it had "fewer limitations than al-Qaeda." He was referring to its use of chemical weapons, which by then had become available on the battlefield. I was intrigued by the fact that whatever topic we discussed always had a component in the cyber realm. For example, we were speaking about how ISIS had suffered some setbacks in recent years.[3]

> **Brennan:** So, I think it has reached its peak from the standpoint of the numbers that [it] has been able to attract to the organization and its global reach. But that doesn't mean by any stretch of the imagination that they do not have lethal capability. There's an even greater lethal capability than what we've seen so far because they had invested in this over the past several years. And right now, I think they're trying to reap the harvest of those investments.

Pegues: With operatives they were sending out?

Brennan: Sure. I mean, it's not just sending. It's what they've been able to do across the digital domain and the cyber environments in terms of trying to get people in different countries who never have traveled to Syria or Iraq, who've never touched the organization, to pick up arms to carry out strikes. And that's what they've done. They have preyed on individuals who may be disaffected, may be on the fringes of society. They believe that they have no other purpose in life.

An hour into the interview I asked him how serious the cyber threat from Russia was and if his agency saw signs of Russia's intent to influence and disrupt the election in the United States.

Brennan: Well, I think there have been some reports about that. . . . But it has happened in other parts of the world, where Russia uses different type[s] . . . of things. Sometimes it's through cyber, sometimes it's through influence, and sometimes it's through individuals who have been working on behalf of Russia. But it is not something that is strange and unusual for Russia to try to take advantage of the opportunities that are out there. . . .

And there was a threat assessment in February [2016]. And it had a pretty interesting paragraph on Russia's cyber. When you look back at that today it was very impressive. . . . It didn't say, "Russia will do this." It said, "Russia has growing capabilities and has done x, y, z in the past."

I nodded. Some of this was already revealed at a May press conference by Director of National Intelligence James Clapper. I pushed Brennan a little.

Pegues: The scope is bigger?

Brennan: The scope. And also, what we've been able to see over the past couple of years as far as disclosures and things that have gone out of there. I think it wasn't a bit unusual that it's not just [the Russians] going in and collecting information; it's collecting it, and then all of a sudden [that information] gets pushed out there by WikiLeaks and others. So it's exposing it. Traditionally foreign adversaries collected [intelligence] for their own use.

That was the first time I had heard it put that way. But it made sense especially when you consider and compare it to the data breach of the Office of Personnel Management (OPM) that was revealed to the public in 2015.[4] OPM houses some of the most sensitive information, including the records of people who have undergone background checks. Both current and former government employees. In the wrong hands, the information can be used to blackmail someone in law enforcement, intelligence, or any type of government service with access to classified information. At least that was what US officials were concerned about when news of the breach leaked out. At the end of the day, more than twenty-one million people were affected, their social security numbers, names, dates and places of birth, and addresses likely in the hands of Chinese intelligence. But unlike Russian intelligence, the Chinese government wasn't leaking what their hackers had swept up.

I tried to process what Brennan had said: essentially the CIA had not known anything specifically about Russia either. I thought about what Linda Power had mentioned, what we'd all been thinking. If the CIA, the FBI, and the White House did in fact miss something this big, how could they have missed it?

Pegues: In the media world, when you miss a story and your competition has it, your boss says, "Why don't you have this?" When something like Russia happened—you know, trying to influence the election—or the OPM data breach, does the president say, "Why didn't you have this? Why didn't we know this was coming?" And do you worry and say, "Oh, gosh. I should have had that. We should've seen that coming"?

Brennan: Well, I am under no illusions that, as good as the CIA is, we're going to be able to have insight into all the future that may take place. Clearly, whenever there is some type of important development around the globe that affects US national interests, I would like to have the CIA know about it in advance. And sometimes we do. Sometimes we don't. Certainly, we feel disappointment if the president is surprised over something. . . .

At the same time, the president [Barack Obama] has a very, very astute and deep understanding of how big and complicated this world is and how, even with our tremendous intelligence capabilities—and there is no country that comes close in terms of our breadth and depth of capability on the intelligence front—that stuff will happen. We're not going to see it all. But he relies on us also in the aftermath of something like that happening [to try] to understand the consequences, the implications, how can we disrupt—maybe—a path that is going to be problematic for us? . . .

So, it's not just forewarning, although forewarning is great. We do it a lot. We are able to disrupt activities and events and cut them off. But the president also wants to know, "So what are our options now in light of this knowledge, this understanding?" And particularly in the cyber world and the digital world, we know that our systems are so accessible in various ways to individuals who want to do us harm or people who just want to see what they can do and accomplish.

We shifted to talking about all kinds of technological topics from how the government would clear the air space when miniaturized drones have the capability of delivering flowers to our doorsteps, to how to prevent an army of drones flying chemical weapons into the country. He spoke about the incredible things cyber technology has done for us over this generation. The conversation always veered back to defending the nation against all sorts of adversaries.

Brennan: We have to recognize that along with the great convenience of the internet, there is tremendous dependence on it. I can't imagine where we're going to be thirty years from now in the technical arena. . . . This is the thing that really makes my head hurt. When I was at the White House and I was the president's assistant for counterterrorism and Homeland Security, it was the Homeland Security element of it that really made my head hurt in terms of cyber. How are we going to protect this country? How are we going to be resilient and respond to that type of major cyberattack?

Pegues: You think about that?

Brennan: Yeah. I do. So, you look to the next fifty years and you say, "My goodness gracious. What does science technology hold for us?" Can it begin to cure cancer? But defense always lags behind offense.

It would soon become clear to the world that US defense had lagged behind Russia's offensive cyberattacks on the US election in 2016. But that wasn't the only vulnerability at the time. Russia's multipronged espionage operation included massive cyberattacks and likely traditional spies.

The plane started its descent to Birmingham. My mind was spinning, partially from the altitude but also from the breadth of topics we'd spoken about. Of course, I'd heard people speak about futuristic things before; some of them were plausible while others seemed completely ridiculous. It took on a whole different tone when the director of the CIA was talking about these scenarios as if they were not only plausible but likely.

The campaign trail was surreal enough. When I'd started covering the Russia investigation earnestly, it became clear that collectively we were losing equilibrium. On the plane, talking with Brennan about Russia, that sensation intensified. We were clearly entering a new phase in the world. This knowledge actually made me feel a little bit nauseous.

Chapter 14

LIVING THE DREAM: BIRMINGHAM

SEPTEMBER 2016

John Brennan's broad face remained stoic whether he talked about his 4:00 a.m. weight lifting or how to stop an army of drones from flying chemical weapons into our country, and I wondered how he slept at night.

Outside the tinted windows of the SUV we rode in, cottonwood trees drooped in the still-humid September air. Moss hung from water oaks. The SUV seemed displaced careening down the narrow, one-lane roads.

Brennan wasn't particularly jovial, but I was beginning to see why the people who worked for the man really liked him.

The director of the CIA isn't exactly the poster child for entitlement one might expect from someone in his position. His was a classic Horatio Alger story. Brennan was a first-generation Irish American. His father had been a blacksmith in Kilkenny who slept above his employer's horse stables and immigrated to New York City. Brennan had been a self-proclaimed mediocre liberal arts undergraduate student who toiled for his grades, and eventually answered a *New York Times* ad recruiting for the CIA. Over a period of thirty years he'd worked his way up the ranks.[1]

Even though he was sixty-one and nearing the end of his career, his ethics still guided his life. He wasn't just paying lip service to his call for diversity; he was out here pounding the pavement. He seemed earnest about it.

It was the tail end of our journey. Earlier that morning Brennan and I went to the Sixteenth Street Baptist Church, where four young girls had been murdered during a 1963 bombing. We'd walked the streets of Birmingham together, the same streets on which the city's commissioner of public safety Eugene "Bull" Connor had ordered officers to turn fire hoses on African Americans during protests in the 1960s, and where my own grandparents had drunk from Colored-only water fountains. Returning to those haunted Southern streets reminded us of how close we were to our past. We are only a few generations removed.

It wasn't that long ago that we also gained real entrance into a democracy that was now being threatened. Some of our most influential citizens had also been raised in Birmingham, such as federal judge Cecil D. Poole and US Secretary of State Condoleezza "Condi" Rice. My father, Joseph Pegues, had also been raised in Birmingham. This was the South where he and my mother had joined thousands of civil rights workers to march with Dr. King and were encouraged to help register other blacks to vote.

I sat in the SUV with Brennan and thought about how that right was again being threatened, how the not-so-long-ago raw struggle for self-determination now made us vulnerable to a foreign invader. It was difficult to explain this transition to citizens who were still walking streets that were haunted with our own history.

We had just left for our final destination, Miles College, a predominantly black school where Brennan had gone to recruit new members. Incidentally, my grandmother Louise Pegues graduated from Miles with a teaching degree. This was of course no small feat for an African American woman raised under Jim Crow laws in the Deep South. At Miles, Brennan spoke about Omego Ware, the first African American CIA operative, who happened to gain entrance in 1955 because he neglected to fill in the race question on his application, spoke fluent Russian, and was well schooled in espionage.[2] Brennan also spoke of how we need diverse talent to counter our biggest threats in the cyber realm.

He'd said, "I believe that this change at CIA can continue to draw inspiration from the larger aspirations of the civil rights movement. Now, this is not to diminish the unique significance of the historic struggle that played out here in Birmingham. But as I see it, at the core of CIA's modernization effort is the belief that our own internal integration makes us better. By creating our new Mission Centers, we are breaking down the barriers that kept our people isolated inside their own professional communities. We are allowing our officers to work together as one team."[3]

In the car ride, we discussed topics touching on everything from the internet to whether North Korea posed a credible nuclear threat. I circled back to Russia, as I had wanted to do for half the day.

Pegues: Going forward do you expect that there will be more cyber intrusions from Russia or Russians leading up to the November 8 election?

Brennan: I believe that as we come to the election there will be additional attempts to exploit, to collect, and possibly to disclose information that is related somehow to the presidential campaign.

Pegues: Is it already happening?

Brennan: I do think that it will prove to be fertile ground for individuals to try to exploit those electoral systems. At the same time, I think Russia will continue to carry out intelligence activities in the cyber domain. And they may or may not be directed against the US electoral system. But Russia has formidable capabilities in the cybersphere, and [Russian intelligence has] very sophisticated cyber actors. This is one of the things that we as a country need to be on guard to make sure that whatever adversary might be out there—countries, hackers, or hacktivist groups—we protect the systems as best we can.

As the SUV slowed down, Brennan looked out his window, and I did the same. The whole experience had been surreal. In part, the feeling came from traveling with the CIA director to my family's hometown—the place where they had fought for the most basic equalities and my grandfather, a tough disciplinarian who owned a television repair shop, inadvertently forced the integration of a small town. I knew that he would be proud of me.

This was the place where my father had grown up. He'd gone from getting arrested during civil rights protests to becoming fluent in French and working for the World Bank, the International Monetary Fund, and Citibank. Both my father's and mother's struggles and accomplishments were responsible for my charmed childhood.

Now, on the one side, we had a CIA director who was revisiting the battle scars of our history and advocating for diversity. On the other, we spent the day talking about alien intelligence, drones, and an impending war carried out through cyberattacks and for which we weren't prepared. If there was something to stand up for in this age, this was it.

We were less than two months away from the election. Brennan had said he was expecting more disclosures of stolen emails and hacked Democratic Party data the closer we got to November 8. He was anticipating a more pronounced effort by Russian intelligence to get further involved in the US election. I also suspected that if he was willing to acknowledge that in this interview with me, there was a lot more he wasn't sharing about the seriousness of the Russian cyber operation. Within months of our interview, Brennan would testify on Capitol Hill about the Russian influence campaign and what he knew.[4] He testified that he had been aware of contacts between Russian operatives and people working in the Trump campaign as early as July 2016. He also testified that he was the first to warn the Russians to back off.

In September 2016 while I was in Birmingham with the director, all of that was classified information.

When we arrived at Miles College, I stepped out of the SUV and Brennan jumped out behind me on the same side. It soon became clear he was exhausted, too. I almost said goodbye, but something in his eyes stopped me.

"Do you ever stop asking questions? My God you are just a reservoir of questions," he said.

He wasn't smiling. Instead, he looked almost as if he wanted to punch me. I didn't regret asking any of those questions, though admittedly we'd been talking for a long time about his worst nightmares. I stood there. Brennan straightened his jacket and turned on the dusty road.

Chapter 15

MOSCOW ON THE HUDSON

OCTOBER 6, 2016

J ust over a month before the November election, some of my intelligence sources were in full-on alarm mode. They were being briefed on what were then the early stages of the FBI counterintelligence investigation into Russian interference in the election. By then word had not spread far and wide that there was suspicion about whether the Trump campaign was colluding with the Russians to influence the election. But there were suspicions among a relatively small group of US officials in the White House, the intelligence agencies, and federal law enforcement. They were seeing troubling signs in real time.

It was the perfect storm for America's adversaries to invade.

And that is exactly what US intelligence officials believe Vladimir Putin and Russia had done.[1] Thousands of hackers and an elaborate misinformation army helped Putin invade the United States through disruption and division. By October 2016, American voters were primed for "influencing."

Many Americans were worn down by the campaigning. Polls showed that both candidates were among the most unpopular presidential picks in US history.[2] FiveThirtyEight, a website that uses statistical analysis to make predictions, projected that Clinton had a 75 percent to 80 percent chance of winning.[3] No one had yet accurately gauged the impact of Russian interference in the election, or how Putin had been covertly tipping the scale to get Trump elected.[4]

At 1:45 p.m. on October 6, perplexed office workers in DUMBO

(Down Under the Manhattan Bridge Overpass), a rapidly gentrifying neighborhood in Brooklyn, looked out their windows and saw two men struggling to unfurl a gargantuan twenty-by-thirty-foot banner over the side of the Manhattan Bridge. The men left and the banner remained. It featured a photograph of a larger-than-life, dark-suit-and-tie-clad Putin in front of the Russian flag, which is three equal horizontal swaths of white, blue, and red. The word "peacemaker" was printed in block letters underneath Putin. It was a windy October day, and the banner billowed over the East River.[5] What do you do when you see a random banner with the giant face of the Russian president flapping in the breeze in New York City? You call 911. An hour later, police took down the banner.

People promptly tweeted their accounts of what happened.

"2 dudes just hung a giant Vladimir Putin 'Peacemaker' flag off the manhattan bridge."[6]

"The Manhattan bridge, right now. (Vladimir Putin, peacemaker???)"[7]

"This just dropped on the Manhattan Bridge. Living in some weird and scary times."[8]

It was a confusing symbol. At that moment in history, many Americans had little context for assessing the strange Russian leader, or what the word "peacemaker" under his face could possibly mean. Putin-led interference in the election had been usurped by the highly contentious and uncharacteristically emotional battle for the presidency, and wouldn't become front-page news for several more months. In New York City, the Russian hackers were more the domain of computer geeks and conspiracy theorists. It is possible Russian investors had figured into some of the urban legend–like stories circulating about what was really going on with those glass tower condominiums that had been built by wealthy foreign investors (or investors who bought them on spec) and had remained largely empty. People wondered whether the buildings remained empty because they had just been a pipe dream for overly enthusiastic investors and had lost market value, or whether they had been bought up for more covert, even ominous purposes. The hackers may have become part of that storyline. But Russian hackers weren't mainstream watercooler or cocktail party conversations.

Still, the banner made people pay attention, both those who were following the cyber-espionage angle and those who weren't. It was a wonky image that stuck in people's minds, largely due to the fact that it didn't make any sense. It wasn't your ordinary poster wheat-pasted onto the side of a tunnel by a guerilla artist. It was a political message promoting the leader of another country. This occurred during a year when a sector of the population feared that Trump had a fascist agenda and that we'd be doomed if he was elected to the White House. All kinds of doomsday scenarios were seeping into people's minds.

Nobody knows who made that banner. Yet whoever created it likely added to the overall paranoia surrounding that month. The banner stands for me as a physical example of the kind of propaganda Russian operatives have engineered over time. This propaganda didn't really make sense to most people who hadn't lived in Russia long enough to understand the cultural and political consciousness. The propaganda always made people pause and look. It often achieved its goals. People didn't recognize it as propaganda and believed it to be truth.

US intelligence analysts closely examine images like this. They weigh the timing of events, study human reactions, and ascertain whether there is a connection to something bigger. The banner on the Manhattan Bridge was hanging above New York City for a matter of minutes, so it didn't have a major impact on the election or the people who saw it. But moments like that stand out, especially if you're a US intelligence operative or a White House official tracking Russian meddling in the election. It may not have been a coincidence that the banner was hoisted in such a way that you could see New York City's iconic Freedom Tower—our newest symbol of resilience—behind it.

Chapter 16

THEY'RE TALKING

I met Linda Power, my trusted source on the Russia investigation, in early November 2016 for lunch at a restaurant inside a Georgetown hotel. It was a quiet weekday afternoon, and the spacious restaurant seating with its tall, ionic stone columns and private tables with windows overlooking the outdoor garden offered the right blend of propriety and comfort that made for successful interviews. I was surprised to hear that she wanted to meet in person since she was likely as slammed with assignments as I was with Election Day nearing.

It had been a busy month. Both Clinton's and Trump's dirty laundry was brought out, and both were being publicly harangued. On October 7, WikiLeaks started dumping twenty thousand pages of emails it plucked from Clinton's campaign chair John Podesta. These had been attributed to a spear-phishing attack by Russian hackers.[1] Phishing is when hackers pose as trustworthy individuals to obtain passcodes, usernames, and other information from users. Spear phishing is a more targeted attack on a corporation or individual, although the emails didn't reveal anything we didn't already know, such as some of the Clinton Foundation's in-house conflicts and excerpts from paid speeches she made to Wall Street corporations that one of her staff members noted may make her vulnerable politically, for example, supporting a no-fly zone in Syria.[2]

Also on October 7, Homeland Security secretary Jeh Johnson and Director of National Intelligence James Clapper made a public statement noting that Russian cyber-espionage experts were trying to influence our election.[3]

That significant revelation was overshadowed later that day when the *Washington Post* released what was later dubbed "Pussygate" in

Mother Jones and other magazines. This was a video recording of Donald Trump and *Access Hollywood* TV host Billy Bush on their way to a set during which Trump described inappropriately touching women: "I don't even wait. And when you are a star, they let you do it, you can do anything, even grab them by the pussy."[4]

Trump later made a public apology for his remarks, which some lawyers and psychologists equated to promoting sexual assault. In the ensuing months, I spoke with federal law enforcement sources who were still angered by how the *Access Hollywood* tape had overshadowed their announcement about Russian interference in the election. It was a revelation that they considered monumental. But then again, the WikiLeaks disclosures of Podesta's emails had also overshadowed the announcement of Russian meddling in the election. Was the timing of the WikiLeaks disclosures made by the Russians to overshadow that moment?

On October 28, 2016, a few days before I met with Linda, FBI director James Comey announced that the FBI started looking into newly found emails on a Clinton aide's husband's laptop that could be relevant to the email investigation.[5]

I knew Linda had arrived in the restaurant before I saw her, since I heard her laughing with a waiter and heard her heels clicking on the floor. I often wondered if she, as a member of the intelligence community, knew how to walk through a room unnoticed.[6]

"Hey, stranger," she said as I stood up. "How are you?" Then she looked at my tired face and laughed.

"About as good as me, I see. And the fun is just beginning," she added.

After a few minutes, we ordered. I knew better than to inundate Linda with questions before she'd had some food.

We made small talk about the campaign for a while and replayed our own version of the *Saturday Night Live* reel of Trump stalking Clinton onstage during the presidential debate.[7] We did that quietly, laughing and allowing ourselves the relief. Election Day was around the corner, and we were both on overload.

Linda and I had an unwritten code between us. Our humor had boundaries. We didn't voice our opinions on any of the even more disconcerting features of the campaign race—the way Trump riled the crowds to chant "Lock her up" or booed the media at the rallies, or whether Clinton's email investigation would yield anything about Benghazi, the Islamic militant group Ansar al-Sharia's attack against two US government buildings in Libya, during which four Americans (including the US ambassador Chris Stevens) were killed on September 11, 2012, when she was secretary of state.[8]

"So, what do you think about the Comey investigation? Are they going to find anything?" I asked.

"Who knows?" she replied.

"But you have to admit. That was a gutsy move for Comey to make, practically on the eve of the election. He could have let it slide. But he thought he was doing the right thing," I said.[9]

"The email investigation, that's not the real question."

I nodded. The trail Linda and other sources had been leading me down over the past several months led straight back to Putin, WikiLeaks, and Clapper's statement.

"There's more to this than I'm seeing, isn't there?" I asked.

Linda didn't respond.

I waited awhile and drank some water. The waiter brought our food and set it down.

"My theory, the way Obama is dealing with this is because he doesn't want to come off as influencing the campaign and favoring Hillary. I mean, if stuff's going down," I said.

And then there were several other instances of Comey trying to do what he thought was right. Because he considered himself an honest man who believed in the truth, and it ended up getting him in hot water along the way. But he may have been doing the right thing. It's just that in this politically charged environment it doesn't look that way.

What I liked about dealing with Linda was her ability to measure everything she was willing to tell me against her sense of right and wrong. That sense didn't come only from her internal barometer, but from a stick-to-your-ribs patriotic code she'd subscribed to in service to her country. She had that no-nonsense moral fortitude that made me trust her.

This was one thing I felt I had in common with not just Linda but many of the intelligence officials I had interviewed. Intelligence folks, like journalists, are supposed to remain even-keeled and neutral. I like to believe that I have that kind of personality. People are supposed to stick to certain moral guidelines. I believe deeply in our free election system, the vote my parents and grandparents had fought for the right to cast.

People like Linda were the courageous ones. They risked their jobs and jail time in order to communicate the truth. I was sitting with her because she had something important to say. I gave her space to say it.

"They're talking," she said.

"Who is talking?" I asked. "Trump?"

"His campaign, people connected to him," she said.

"Talking to whom?"

"Who do they think is responsible for the spear phishing on Podesta's emails? Who do they think is responsible for Assange's dumping all those emails out there?" she questioned. "They're traitors."

I looked up.

"They have committed treason," she said. She had used that word in the past. Subsequently, I did some research. Legally, treason is something that only exists in times of war as I understood it.

"Yes, but even if it's true, does anyone think it's going to matter?" I asked. "I mean, do people believe Trump will win the election?"

"The election is close."

One of the most frustrating things about both the Russian cyber-espionage attacks and possible collusion between the Trump campaign and Russian operatives was that we could all sense something unnerving and extremely serious was going on. There were people in intelligence circles who undoubtedly knew details about both things they weren't revealing.

Yes, it was frustrating to be fed nuggets rather than the full meal of the Russian influence campaign and how much coordination there may have been between some Trump campaign officials and the Russians. But that's just the way this level of reporting usually works. You end up having to piece together different sources of information. It's like a puzzle. You're putting together as many of the pieces as possible and trying to make sense of the bigger picture.

I kept peppering Linda with questions. I kept pushing for more of the details. How do you know this information? Was it coming from human intelligence gathering? Or was it from wiretaps? I would ask those questions, but I knew getting specific answers would put Linda in danger. This is all highly sensitive information that the US government keeps under wraps for a reason. Mainly because they want to protect their sources and methods for information gathering around Putin and in the Kremlin. A great deal of US espionage originates in the cyber realm these days.

Most people weren't aware of our cyber-offensive or cyber-defensive strategies. Cyber operations was an exclusive field with a history that only stemmed back to the late 1990s, when people were switching up their Commodore 64s for faster desktop computers, and when the internet had just started to become mainstream. It's conceivable nobody back then could predict a time when terrorists recruited suicide bombers through the internet, or operatives could attempt and possibly succeed in undermining an election and a democracy in this realm. In the beginning, cyber espionage was lawless, like the Wild West, and there were unwritten codes of honor.

To find out more about these unwritten codes, I spoke to Michael Hayden, former director of the National Security Agency and the CIA. Hayden was one of the first Americans to function as a cyber operative himself.

Chapter 17

THE CYBER REF: A CONVERSATION WITH MICHAEL HAYDEN

NOVEMBER 1, 2016

O n the north side of Pittsburgh there is a street called General Michael V. Hayden Boulevard, named in honor of the former director of the NSA and CIA. Hayden, who is one of the foremost authorities on intelligence on earth, is a Pittsburgh native and has as much pride for his hometown as he does for his country.[1] The street is just a few blocks from Heinz Field, where the young Hayden served as an equipment manager for the Pittsburgh Steelers, the football team he protects ferociously.

So when Trump trash-talked the Steelers for joining two other NFL teams in a protest by locking arms and refusing to stand on the field during the national anthem before a game, Hayden defended them.[2] He wrote an op-ed in the *Hill*, a top US political website that has a wide readership among DC politicians, noting that his hometown was patriotic, because they opted out of the emotional poker game being played between Trump and their team.

"As a 39-year military veteran, I think I know something about the flag, the anthem, patriotism, and I think I know why we fight," he wrote. "It's not to allow the president to divide us by wrapping himself in the national banner. I never imagined myself saying this before Friday, but if now forced to choose in this dispute, put me down with [Colin] Kaepernick."[3]

Hayden is still a football-minded, no-nonsense guy who tends to explain his actions or those of the government as if he were a ref explaining tackles, touchdowns, interceptions, a game in play, or the overall rules. He is one of the few leaders who knows the rules of cyber espionage that have evolved since he became NSA director in 1999, at the dawn of the new information age.[4] While in the past the NSA focused mainly on collecting information over the airwaves, the playing field has changed. He was in a sense among our country's first hackers, the first cyber juggernauts, who broke into other countries' computer realms and poked around. He noted that this was exciting, although the NSA was limited in what it could do once in that area. For example, NSA operatives were unable to do anything that may constitute an act of war, such as compromising other countries' military computers.

In an interview with CBS News national security correspondent David Martin, Hayden described how he graduated to becoming the first head of cyber command. In that capacity, he described how the agency developed a "stable of weapons" in cyberspace.[5] He couldn't give any specific information because, he said, "This is so hideously overclassified, it's hard for us to have an adult discussion about what it is we are or are not doing."

Hayden, who served with the NSA until 2005, then served as the CIA's director from 2006 to 2009, is well versed on any little-known rules governing cyber-espionage attacks coming from and being fielded by the United States.[6] But the rule book is thin. Although Hayden doesn't believe the Russian attacks on the US electoral system are an act of war, but rather more like a covert operation, there are no formal definitions for either in the cyber realm.

Pentagon leaders and members of Congress are still grappling with coming up with an explanation of how cyberspace actions could constitute war.[7]

When I met Hayden in the third-floor interview room at the CBS offices in Washington, DC, less than a week before the elections, where everyone in the newsroom was working around the clock, I found him to be a refreshing interviewee.

Hayden wears glasses and has the kind of distinguished charm of good men of his generation. His expression was always patient and affable, as if he was the kind of guy who had seen it all and so knew the value of a good joke. He was as easy to talk to about his history with the Steelers as he was about the upcoming election. He had an unusual political perspective and an uncanny way of boiling things down so that they were understandable. Since he worked as a private consultant, he was able to speak more freely about his views. He certainly didn't censor himself when it came to speaking about the upcoming elections.[8]

Pegues: Let's start with the connections. Can we talk about Trump's alleged ties to Russia? Is there something there that sort of gives you pause? You've got Mr. Trump who just seems to bend himself into whatever shape he needs to bend himself in order to avoid criticizing the Russian Federation, their foreign policy, or their president. So where does that kind of rationale come from?

Hayden: Well, it could come from a legitimate worldview. I mean there could be parallax that connects all these dots, but I haven't seen all that yet. Frankly, Mr. Trump doesn't have a lot of background in foreign affairs. What he says seems to be stray electrons or, let me be kind, points of light. But I can't find a worldview in which all of those points of light seem to come together.

Pegues: What kind of world does the president face?

Hayden: Here's what I think the real issue is. You have lots of things going on. You have the North Koreans, the South China Sea, there's ISIS, Putin, and then Ukraine. I could go on, but fundamentally I think we're seeing the melting down of the post–World War II American liberal, Bretton Woods, World Bank, IMF [International Monetary Fund] world order. The world order that we largely constructed about seventy-five years ago is no longer adequate to the world in which we find ourselves. So, not only do we see the melting down of that and a growing disorder, now we have to face a fundamental question as a nation. It's hidden in the [2016 presidential] campaign, but you can see reflections of it, and it's fundamentally this: how much of a responsibility are we now going to embrace to build a new global structure? By the way, we did a pretty good job on the last one. I mean, the world has seen remarkable progress in that seventy-five years of American hegemony. Now the choice is, how much do we embrace a responsibility for what goes forward?

Pegues: What does that new world order look like, now that you've brought it up?

Hayden: It looks like a work in progress. How much of that do we want to be influenced by American liberal—small "l"—values? There are an awful lot of other competing value systems out there now. One that's gotten a lot of traction globally—and, frankly, I think we see it reflected in our own election—is authoritarian populism. We see it in Venezuela; we see it in Turkey; we see it in Russia; we see it in a lot of places.

Now what do the ideals of American liberalism have to do with creating a world order in which authoritarian populism seems to be gaining strength?

Pegues: Are you seeing that authoritarian populism here?

Hayden: I have said publicly that the American face of this global movement toward authoritarian populism is the Trump campaign—it's nativism, it's trans-authoritarian, [and] it's certainly a bit isolationist. We see that reflected in other countries as well. This is not a call for American supremacy, certainly not a call for American hegemony.

One definition of an exceptional nation—and we have been described as that in past decades—is a nation that does things for the good of the order, rather than a narrowly defined sense of national self-interest.

One aspect of the [2016] campaign, particularly the Trump campaign, is to pretty much confine all international decisions to a very narrow definition of American self-interest. That may be good, it may be bad, but it's different. It's not the role we played for the last three quarters of a century.

Pegues: And the role that Russia has played, it seems to be some sort of resurgence in the sense that Putin seems to be inserting himself into our political landscape. This idea of the Russians trying to influence the election, is it real?

Hayden: I think it's real. But let me go back to your premise about Russia and what it is or what it is not. I actually go out of my way to say that Russia is not a resurgent power.

Frankly, all the things that Russia needs to be somebody [important] in a global competition, it's running out of. It's running out of entrepreneurship. A growing portion of the Russian GDP is coming out of state-owned enterprises. That's not a winning formula. It's running out of democracy. You've seen that. It's running out of available oil and gas.

And, most fundamentally, it's running out of Russians— that is, a declining population. The life expectancy there is below that of the old Soviet Union. I've said that in other forays he's [Putin's] doing all this troublesome activity, and he doesn't have a pair of sevens in his hand. He's playing a weak hand.

One of the bold moves, as our intelligence community has reported with a high level of confidence, is that Putin is trying to affect the American political process.

Pegues: You've studied Putin?

Hayden: I have studied him. I'm very fond of Bob Gates who, before he became secretary of defense, was in the office I used to occupy at Langley [CIA]. Secretary Gates came back from his first meeting with Putin, kind of paraphrasing President Bush [who said the same thing after meeting Putin], 'I looked into Putin's eyes . . . [and] I saw the KGB.' And you know what? That's really important. We know that the KGB has an endlessly conspiratorial view of the world. They view the world through that lens. Vladimir Putin was convinced that I spent almost all of my nearly three years at Langley thinking up ways to make his life more difficult.

Pegues: Did you?

Hayden: As the director of the CIA—of course! He just expects, given that historical kind of Marxist-shaped view of the world, that that's how other countries treat him.

Pegues: As an intelligence guy you have to sort of get in his head, right? What's his next move? You have intelligence agencies across this country thinking that way now, right? You have to stay one step ahead.

Hayden: Right. You want to use a metaphor? He's got the ball. He's playing offense, and he's going to the line of scrimmage. He's checking out the defense, and whatever ground that defense gives him. That's where that play's going; that's how he's working right now, which is a little bit different than saying this is a strategically resurgent power that's going to be occupying a more massive space in global geopolitics.

It's not. He's not a great strategic thinker. He looks to be of a brilliant tactical one, though.

The interview with Hayden shook me. I thought about it regularly, when I was pouring my girls' cereal, when I was sitting in my office after the morning newscast. It wasn't so much what Hayden said that disturbed me, but the certainty with which he said it.

Hayden was a refreshingly straight talker whose insight about Putin and Trump would hold up as the Russia investigation unfolded. He had earned the right to speak his mind, a position most intelligence officials don't feel licensed to do, even after they are retired. The things he told me were enlightening because they confirmed what I already knew in a succinct way. His authority gave them weight. For example, he implied that Trump may have been compromised by the Russians, that the intelligence community believed Putin is trying to undermine our democracy, and that we weren't pushing back.

It was this last factor that left a bad taste in my mouth. The reason we weren't pushing back at the time was largely because President Obama was being cautious and didn't want to be seen as pandering to one party. Michael Daniel, the former cybersecurity coordinator at the White House during the Obama administration, said the federal authorities didn't tell the states they were hacked sooner partly for the same reason. When they did tell them, they were accused of pandering. Our democracy had fostered a certain defensive divisiveness that was endangering us. What would our unwillingness to push back cost us?

Chapter 18
ELECTION DAY

Intelligence officials, reporters working the Homeland Security beat, and even some network news executives tasked with protecting computer systems from cyberattacks were all watching the election in a different way than most of the rest of the country. We weren't as focused on who was winning each state, as much as whether there would be any cyber disruptions.

I didn't know at the time about the government's formal disaster plan in case a cyberattack occurred. I later confirmed for CBS News that a formal fifteen-page plan had been drafted to deal with multiple kinds of Election Day chaos from cyberattacks, such as voting booth shutdowns or electrical power grid sabotage, to terrorist attacks (al-Qaeda and ISIS reportedly threatened an attack on the day of the election). Plans included moderate measures, for example allowing voting booths to remain open longer or using paper backups in the event voting booths were infected with viruses or made unusable. They also called for more "enhanced procedures" in response to more extreme incidents, which included sending federal law enforcement agents with guns to polling sites and bringing in military units. One serious issue could have involved voting machines being hacked and taken entirely off-line.[1]

Nobody told us any of these plans, of course (though the fact that this document exists means the government anticipated a potential attack). At the time, those of us who had some information about what might happen were on the lookout for incidents like distributed denial of service attacks that would cripple news organizations so we couldn't tally and announce the election results accurately.[2]

We believed these attacks, just like all the cyberattacks in the previous five or six months (such as the attacks on the DNC emails), had been launched at the request of Russian government officials. US law enforcement and intelligence officials at the time were concerned that the Russians would try to disrupt Election Day. The Obama administration had bluntly warned Putin against any type of trouble that day. But the Russian president had ignored Obama's threats before.

US officials didn't seem to know what this kind of attack would look like. My intelligence sources were telling me that they believed the Russian hackers were likely still embedded in our systems and were capable. I imagined massive information blackouts, the newscasters unable to articulate their shock, the way they were during 9/11, even those of us who had rehearsed what we might say if chaos ensued.

I appreciated the way that I had become narrowly, albeit obsessively, focused on the cyber realm, both in the moments leading up to the election and during the election itself. It helped me to keep my emotions in check and out of the picture. Of course, I was human, American, and seeing the way in which the country was being divided. My family's history growing up in the Jim Crow South and then gaining the right to vote was never lost on me.

My parents did their part to ensure that I had equal opportunity. What I see as my contribution is injecting as many facts as possible in an atmosphere of misleading statements and false information in social media and elsewhere. Simply put, I want people to know what's really going on.

I learned how dangerous misrepresenting the facts can be when I wrote *Black and Blue,* a book that came out in May 2017. I was bothered by the fact that many politicians and others would come on TV and misstate the facts, and instead of making a situation better they were making it worse.

While writing that book I explored our country's racial divide by interviewing both police officers and family members whose loved ones had been victims of police brutality. The experience taught me, on a visceral level, how engrained and systematic prejudice is. The 2016 presidential campaign was enflaming the country's long history of racial tension. That aspect of the election, frankly, saddened me. It was, however, beside the point.

Unlike most Americans, I saw the election campaign battle and all it was stirring up in the country as a smokescreen for what was really going on. This disturbed me more. An external enemy had wiggled in, exploiting our weaknesses and undermining our free election system, the same system so many groups of people have vehemently fought for the right to be included in. My focus on that reality may have been emotional, but it was clear and razor sharp.

I was on standby and spent much of my time in the perch of my office watching CBS's live coverage on my television, then traveling downstairs to check in with my producers.

Adam Meyers, the vice president of intelligence from Crowd-Strike, was also there, and like me, he was on standby to spot any anomalies that might pop up. If he noticed something, we'd put him on the air to explain what was going on.

Simultaneously, I wasn't sure anything would happen in the cyber realm. Based on what the pundits were saying, I expected Clinton would win. The polling said she was going to win. Most of the people I knew in law enforcement believed she would win, even though many of them were quietly backing Trump.

A Clinton win in 2016 didn't necessarily mean that the Russian operatives who had messed with our faith in democracy through internet hacking, if not having physically interfered in the election itself, would go away. However, we suspected the fallout would be less. Because of her adversarial relationship with Putin, we suspected that Clinton would acknowledge the cyber threat and deal with it. We didn't know enough of Putin's end game or strategy to ascertain what would happen if she won, but we suspected it would have signaled for him that things didn't go entirely according to plan.

From my perspective, Clinton's winning would have likely made my immediate future less intense. My wife and children would certainly have appreciated that.

For a while things were going just as we had expected them to go. Projections from the Associated Press and other political pundits followed the script. Clinton won Vermont, a state that has voted Democrat in every election since 1988, and Trump took Indiana and

Kentucky, a state that had voted Republican in every election since 1996.[3]

I traipsed downstairs when Trump took Ohio at 10:49 p.m. It was a swing state with eighteen electoral votes. It was a big deal, but I wasn't terribly surprised. Obama had won Ohio both times, but Trump had campaigned in rural areas of the Buckeye State, targeting blue-collar, out-of-work white voters, promising to bring in new jobs and pointing fingers at immigration trends that he claimed threatened their future earning potential. Conversely, Latinos only amount to about 3 percent of Ohio's population. Clinton did not inspire the same black and young voters who had backed Obama.[4]

Nobody in the newsroom seemed incredibly surprised either. I had a quick chat with my producer and Meyers, who informed me that thus far things were copacetic, and no viral threats had been detected, and I went back upstairs to my thinking chamber.

It was admittedly late for me already. I often worked the morning shift, which meant I woke up at about 4:30 a.m., sometimes exercised in my basement, showered, dressed, jumped into the waiting black car (dispatched by the morning show), and left the house while my wife and kids were still sleeping. I would go over my script and notes during the thirty-minute drive into Washington, DC. The grand-slam reporting schedule of those final weeks had messed with my sleeping schedule, and that night I went through the adrenaline/crash cycle. It happened every election year, but this year had been brutal. There was all the coverage of a series of events that shocked many and for which we had no context—that was likely causing all reporters east of the Mississippi to experience some mild burnout.

There also had been much uncertainty about our democracy's future and the doomsday scenarios that were running through half my colleagues', family's, and friends' narratives. Finally, and overshadowing all of this, was the Russian-government-led interference I felt compelled to investigate myself. Yet selling the story to anyone, from my producers to my family and friends, was sometimes like swimming against an ocean tide. Everyone believed the bigger threat was the plain battle between the two candidates.

I was excited about the election, but also looking forward to the moment when I would lumber across the street to the Saint Gregory

Hotel, where I would take a shower and crawl into bed. I was sticking around CBS in case something occurred in the cyber realm and they needed me on camera, but I was expected in the bureau again at about six o'clock the next morning. The office was a quieter, more cocoon-like environment for me to watch the elections.

At 10:53 p.m., when Trump won Florida, and with it twenty-nine electoral votes, I woke up.[5] All the pundits had predicted Clinton would win Florida. For a second, I thought about Florida's checkered election reputation, the battle between George W. Bush and Al Gore, the hanging-chad fiasco. I remembered other disconcerting images from that year of African American voters being turned away, the lines of backed-up cars on streets in poor areas that had been suddenly blocked off, preventing people from getting to the polls. I remembered the more modern-day version of that narrative—Election Day sabotage originating from politicians outside our country. I stood up so hard I nearly knocked the wind out of myself on the edge of the desk, then ran down the steps to the newsroom.

As I headed down, I heard people on television and in the desks off camera trying to figure out Clinton's odds. She still had a shot, but the margin was a lot slimmer.

"I guess more people supported Trump than we thought," somebody said.

Some folks I knew in law enforcement had told me that they believed Trump had more support than people gave him credit for. It occurred to me that was true. It could have been as simple as that. People didn't publicly announce they were going to vote for him, because many people were ostracized if they did so. Still, they voted for him. I think the media underestimated those folks.

I checked in with my producers and with Meyers. I stayed downstairs a while, as if being among other people would provide further verification for what was happening, and to ensure I didn't fall asleep at my desk. I held out while Trump won North Carolina, Utah, and Iowa. At that point, Clinton's only chance was to cinch Pennsylvania, Michigan, and Wisconsin.

Linda's words came back to me for some reason. This was turning into the sort of improbable win that would raise alarms for my trusted intelligence source. She would be repeating what she'd heard in classified briefings. In the run-up to Election Day, she would often whisper, "It's happening." That night, I looked around at all the people in the newsroom. Their expressions ranged from shock to confusion. These were newspeople. We were trained to stay neutral, so it wasn't as if they were taking sides. But what roiled me and so many of my colleagues was that the polls could be so wrong. All the prognosticators who had successfully predicted plenty of elections were wrong. The 2016 presidential election was such an improbable result.

It was a bit different for me. My personal concern wasn't that Trump was winning but that the Russians might have succeeded.

Oh, man, I thought. It wasn't, "How did this happen?" It was, "What the Russians did may have worked!"

I blamed the feelings of nausea I was experiencing on sleep deprivation and copious amounts of coffee. It was midnight. I checked in with my producers one final time, excused myself, and went back to the hotel room.

After showering, I managed to keep the hotel television on until Trump won Pennsylvania, a battleground state, at 1:30 a.m. He was at 264 electoral votes, which essentially cinched it, though the votes were still being counted in Michigan, Arizona, and Wisconsin.

My Justice and Homeland Security beat was about to change dramatically.

Could the Russian operation have worked? It was a sobering thought. I turned off the television and lay in bed. I closed my eyes but couldn't sleep. My brain was wired. The newsroom was going to blow up, but not for the reasons people thought. Trump was going to be president of the United States. I knew things were going to get serious then. The story was just beginning.

Chapter 19

WHAT HAS JUST HAPPENED?

I was in my happy place on a golf course thirty minutes away from Washington, DC. The golf course gave me the same sensation some people experience looking at the ocean. There was something about peering out over the fairways, over the rolling hills, and seeing the sharp emerald trees cutting into the brightening morning sky. I needed the outdoor time, feeling the fresh air on my face, rather than the recycled air in the studio. This was where my personal life began.

The morning was freakishly warm for December. It was almost eight thirty, and I didn't have to be at work until about eleven. I had taken my time practicing my strokes, walking from hole to hole. The task helped me process.

The network was gearing up for a tough stretch. We were incredibly busy, dealing with mass shootings, terrorist incidents, and then the Russia story. We were entering an even more uncertain phase. The Trump administration was spinning from controversy to controversy. It was an unprecedented time, both because of the intensity of the news cycle and the pressure we were under to get the story right. That morning was a nice break from the often twelve-to-fourteen-hour workdays.

This phase we were entering also changed journalism. I am not talking about having to contend with the negativity: President Trump's consistent tweets and statements accusing the media of being purveyors of fake news. There was much more at stake, so a higher level of journalism emerged. The *New York Times* might break one story, and the *Washington Post* will break the next, and then a network may come out with yet another item of news. We're getting bits and pieces of the story without always figuring out how to fit them together or even if they do fit together. There are the pieces of this Russia influence puzzle coming together from different sources speaking to different news organizations as the FBI probed whether the Trump campaign coordinated with the Russians during the 2016 election. My daily existence sometimes made me feel as though I were living in someone else's Hollywood screenplay. It's still hard to imagine being in this place and time where in 2018 a president is being accused of obstruction of justice and where an investigation is triggered in 2017 by the president suddenly firing FBI director James Comey, who was leading the Russia investigation at the time. And the country is in a place where Trump campaign representatives stand accused of seeking "dirt" from the Russians on Hillary Clinton and then potentially accepted assistance from the Kremlin in derailing the Clinton machine. President Trump has called all of the allegations a "hoax."[1]

I practiced my putting stroke a few times, and then my cell phone rang. I jumped. I took my phone out of my pocket and saw Linda's name on the screen. I pushed the green button and walked over to a tree.

"Hello, my friend," I answered, and after some brief small talk, I asked, "What's going on?"

Putin still hadn't responded after President Obama expelled the Russian operatives. Typically, he would have responded by this time. Throughout the transition of power we would hear Obama administration officials and the president himself saying that there is only one president at a time. Intelligence sources were echoing that phrase. I didn't want to try to imagine what was going on at the White House.

Retired lieutenant general Michael Flynn, who had agreed to accept Trump's offer to become his national security advisor, was found to have made false statements to the FBI regarding his contacts with the Russian ambassador Sergey Kislyak over the pending US sanctions for interfering in our election. His contacts would later be the subject of the warning from acting attorney general Sally Yates to President Trump's White House counsel. Yates relayed to the White House official that US intelligence and the FBI believed that Flynn was susceptible to blackmail because of his contact with the

Russians and had likely been compromised by the Russian ambassador. The Russians knew Flynn was lying about his contacts with their ambassador and that he had misled Vice President Mike Pence. Flynn was not fired by the White House until February 14, eighteen days after Yates had warned the administration.[2]

"They're liars," Linda blurted out. At the time, many in the government who were privy to some of the intelligence knew that Flynn had been lying about his contacts with the Russian ambassador.[3]

Linda was angered by the deception. We ended the call, and I went back to focusing on golf for the moment.

We were moving into unprecedented territory. The country had never been down this road before. There were growing questions about the new president's entanglements with Russia. But it wasn't just him. Michael Flynn had been paid by Russian companies, had been reported to be working on corrupt side deals even while he was being considered for national security advisor and then while he was in the White House. And there was that photograph of Flynn and Putin sitting next to each other in Moscow in 2015.[4] There was something odd about how frequently our digging into the new administration kept turning up ties to the Kremlin.

Chapter 20

A SIDENOTE ABOUT COMEY

I t was especially gloomy inside the halls of the famed J. Edgar Hoover Building. There was a dark cloud hanging over the FBI as the sun rose to reveal that the nation had a president-elect who'd beaten the odds. In the early hours of November 9, 2016, Donald J. Trump was declared the winner of one of the most divisive presidential campaigns in US history. Along the way of his victory over Democrat Hillary Clinton, the reputation of the third person in the race had been battered and bruised. FBI director James Comey's image had taken a hit during the election, and it was unclear whether he would ever be able to rehabilitate a public profile that had been decades in the making.

Even the bureau's employees were unsure of what was going to happen next. Reporters were already calling the FBI's National Press Office asking whether Comey would resign. The answer was a resounding no followed by an uncomfortable laugh as the public affairs officials tried to downplay what they knew would be a difficult period for the bureau. The reality was that they really didn't know how to respond since they, too, had doubts about whether their boss would make it.

Comey had taken a huge risk when eleven days before the election he sent a letter to Congress, noting he wanted to amend his testimony in which he stuck by his decision not to bring charges in the FBI's investigation into Clinton's private email server. But he thought Clinton and her aides were "extremely careless" with the way they handled classified or sensitive information.[1] The letter said that the FBI investigation had found additional emails that might be significant and would investigate them. Finally, he stated he couldn't determine how long that investigation would take.[2]

He suspected the emails weren't significant, but felt it was his duty to put what he knew out there. Agents sorting through and categorizing another batch of hundreds of thousands of emails were hard-pressed to come to a conclusion by Election Day. The disclosure was sure to cost Clinton in public opinion polls during the election's waning days.

When Comey sent another letter to Congress the Sunday before the election to announce that there was no evidence of foul play in the emails, it only compounded the damage for him. The FBI director was taking fire from all sides. Democrats, Republicans, and just about anyone paying attention were blasting members of the FBI for being partisan hacks.

At the time, Comey had only been FBI director for about three years. He had reached the pinnacle of law enforcement after a career as a prosecutor that had spanned Republican and Democratic administrations. Prior to his "October surprise," Comey was widely respected not only on Capitol Hill but also among FBI agents and local police. All of that began to change when he announced that Hillary Clinton wouldn't face charges and then chose to wait to disclose new details of the Clinton private email server investigation.

It was sloppy. Some former FBI agents believed that Comey had been talking too much and had now landed the bureau in an awkward position. Rank-and-file employees inside the Hoover Building were feeling the public scorn that Comey's decisions had brought down on the bureau, all while they were tracking the threat from Russia. Ultimately, Comey would take heat for not publicly revealing what Russia had been doing and the concerns about whether the Trump campaign was colluding with Russian operatives. At that time, US officials were beginning to get a clear picture of Russian interference in the election, and they were picking up electronic intercepts that indicated Americans were in contact with Russian operatives.[3] But Comey stayed quiet. The FBI does not comment on active investigations. And the Russia probe was active.

Having studied and covered Comey in my role as Justice and Homeland Security correspondent, I came to view him as someone who had always done what he believed was right, even when his actions were controversial. In March 2004, when he was serving as acting US attorney general (and before President Obama nominated him to be FBI director) while Attorney General John Ashcroft was in the hospital undergoing surgery, he had refused to reauthorize a component of the secret surveillance program known as Stellar Wind. This was an NSA program that was created following the September 11, 2001, attacks and authorized by then president George W. Bush, and involved data mining of private citizens' (a program later leaked by Snowden) telephone records and internet metadata. Comey refused to reauthorize the program on the grounds that he believed that it was illegal.[4]

But even though Ashcroft was hospitalized and Comey was the acting attorney general, the White House wanted to go around Comey to get Ashcroft to sign the documents reauthorizing the program. An outraged Comey let it be known that if it was reauthorized he was ready to quit. "I prepared a letter of resignation, intending to resign the next day, Friday, March the 12th," Comey has said.[5]

That night Ashcroft's distraught wife called the Justice Department to warn that two of the president's top aides were rushing to the hospital to get Ashcroft to sign the documents. Comey later testified that when he found out what was about to happen, he said, "I was very upset. I was angry." He wanted to get to the hospital first. The showdown in the hospital room with White House Counsel Alberto Gonzalez and White House Chief of Staff Andy Card ended with a win for Comey. Ashcroft didn't sign the papers. "I thought I just witnessed an effort to take advantage of a very sick man," Comey said.[6]

Comey had asked for then FBI director Robert Mueller to help him that day. Both men were prepared to resign. President Bush backed down and listened to Comey's concerns, and then gave permission to Comey to institute changes to the program based on Department of Justice recommendations.

Comey and Mueller believed that they were standing up for the Constitution then. How ironic that it might come down to them again. With Mueller now special counsel for the Russia probe and Comey looking on from the sidelines in private life, Comey will play a pivotal role in how the Russia investigation concludes. He was suddenly fired by President Trump on May 9, 2017. By then the Russia investigation was nearly a year old. Comey says during meetings at the White House the president asked him if he would drop the investigation into his former national security advisor Michael Flynn. Flynn had lied about his calls with the Russian ambassador Sergey Kislyak in December 2016 soon after the Obama administration had announced sanctions against the Russians. Flynn had lied to Vice President Mike Pence about the contacts with the ambassador.

Comey kept memos of his interactions with Trump—in part because he viewed the private meetings with the president as inappropriate, especially in the midst of an investigation into the president's own campaign. According to Comey, President Trump said, "I hope you can see your way clear to letting this go, to letting Flynn go. He is a good guy. I hope you can let this go."[7]

After later firing Comey, the president told NBC News anchor Lester Holt in an interview that he was thinking of "this Russia thing" when he fired Comey.[8] I've wondered whether Comey already had enough "dirt" on president to build a case against him. I've also wondered whether Comey took notes of his meetings with the president for that very reason. After all, the FBI was well into its Russia investigation by then.

Comey's firing led to the appointment of his friend Mueller as special counsel. Did Comey know that his firing would trigger the appointment of a special counsel and that the odds were that his friend would be appointed to the job? I think Comey was willing to take that chance. Can you imagine a showdown between President Trump and James Comey in a courtroom? I can. Ultimately, it may all come down to one question: who do you believe? I remember meeting with an FBI source in early 2017. FBI employees are among those who speak a cryptic language when they are talking with reporters. They are (perhaps rightfully so) afraid of revealing too much. At the time, the source told me that at the end of the day the public has to believe what the verdict is at the conclusion of the Russia investigation. What that FBI official told me stands out to this day, especially as the president batters the FBI's reputation and as some Republicans in Congress accuse top FBI officials of having a bias against President Trump.

Will the public believe what the investigators uncover? If so, what happens next? Will the truth be accepted?

These are just a few of the reasons why I believe the informa-tion has been coming out slowly, and is being fed to the public in small doses. For some people it's already too much to absorb. The slow drip of indictments and guilty pleas on their own are unprec-edented. This is where we are in the era of Trump. So much has happened in such a short time that one can't help but feel that the country is spiraling toward some major clash between law enforce-ment and this administration.

We've already seen some "relatively minor" scuffles on the way to a conclusion in this Russia investigation. There is so much at stake. Who will be the heroes at the end? What will the institutions of this democracy look like at the end? That really depends in part on who stands up for the Constitution. During the 2016 election, some would argue that it took too long for the Obama administration to reveal what had taken place, the extent of investigators' knowledge of Rus-sian-led interference with the elections including the DNC emails, how many states had been impacted, and the potential collusion between Trump campaign representatives and Russian representa-tives whose interests ran contrary to ours. By the time the public was made aware of what was happening, it was almost too late.

Comey's old friend Robert Mueller has been methodically building his case. As of early 2018 there had been five guilty pleas in the Russia investigation.[9] Mueller was rolling up witnesses against others up the chain. Former FBI assistant directors whom I spoke with said that this was "classic" Mueller, a hard-nosed investigator who keeps pressing forward no matter what.

A lot of people who've worked with him or covered him over the years might describe Comey that way, and even though he had been villainized for the manner in which he made his public announce-ment about the Clinton email servers or for his lack of candor about Russian cyber espionage during the election, he was far from the only culpable individual. Over the years that I have worked this beat I have noticed the tricky dance that government and intelligence officials have to do when safeguarding and releasing classified infor-mation. I have learned how much we don't know, and probably never will. It is the nature of these organizations to protect information.

When the declassified version of a classified report about Russian interference in the US elections came out, it was a major disclosure, but it still made me wonder what classified information they weren't revealing.

Chapter 21

THERE CAN'T BE TWO PRESIDENTS

Linda and I met again at the hotel restaurant.[1] President-Elect Trump was weeks away from his inauguration. I tried to stay in contact with Linda as much as possible. Intelligence and law enforcement sources were typically more forthcoming when discussing information face-to-face. They were much more reluctant to reveal information over email or in a phone call. These days you just never know when your emails or text messages might turn up in a subpoena. Once again, I wanted to press Linda for more information on what she was hearing and seeing in connection with the Russia investigation. Once we were settled, I asked her what was going on.

"We are on the verge of something here," she said. "A constitutional crisis."

Something about the phrase resonated with me. I wasn't sure exactly what she was saying, but didn't want to push her away. She was more direct than she usually was. She was also being braver, perhaps because there was more at stake.

"People are afraid that the Trump administration will try to suppress the truth from getting out." She inhaled deeply. "So, they're leaking the information. The information about what his campaign did."

"The truth about what specifically? Involvement with Russian diplomats, government officials?"

She nodded. Her face was pinched slightly, as if she was trying to control her temper.

"Who is leaking it? And to whom?"

"I can't say. Everyone."

"Former Obama administration officials, law enforcement, intelligence folks?"

She nodded.

"The reason why it's happening is that people see it as their patriotic duty to get this information out. It's treason," she said.

"What are they leaking?"

"I can't say any more," she said.

Most Americans were still unaware of what was going on and how the Russia investigation was intensifying. Perhaps they were confused about the whole thing. They didn't know what to believe. Or maybe they believed the president's denials and his constant dismissal of the investigation as fake news. "Of course, people who voted for Trump are going to buy into that narrative," I prompted.

I will never forget how unnerved Linda seemed when we spoke. Her unease with what she had been hearing and what she was seeing in the investigation notes kept returning to me. She would often talk about how the Trump campaign was undermining the Obama administration during the transition of power. Linda didn't let on what she meant by that so as not to reveal too much, but it was clear that the intelligence community had human intelligence of electronic intercepts as evidence that there had been contacts between the Russians and the Trump campaign—contacts that appeared to Obama officials to be undermining their response to the Russians' influence campaign. The Obama administration wanted to somehow scold Putin without triggering a cyberwar or some other form of potentially dangerous conflict. But because the Trump campaign's approach to Putin was drastically different, the public messages were in conflict, creating tension between an incoming administration and an outgoing one. In recent memory past Democratic and Republican administrations had not seen this level of discord. Publicly, Obama officials would say that "there's only one President at a time,"[2] almost cryptically something that Linda would say to me— even then—early on in the Russia investigation, sending signals that something just wasn't right. The implication being that the Trump team was working on side deals with the Russians and others.[3]

History was unfolding. I was interested in how Russian interference affected the election. Michael Hayden, the former CIA and NSA director, had mentioned we didn't push back enough, but so far nobody was proposing any alternatives.[4]

To learn more about what caution may have cost the United States, I spoke with Jim Lewis, an expert with the Center for Strategic and International Studies. Over the years at CBS, I have come to trust his insight on a range of cyber-related issues, and early on in the Russia investigation I began leaning on him. He has a way of simplifying complicated issues and making them understandable in a ten-second sound bite.

He spoke about the Russian hackers embedded in our systems.

> This is a country filled with really good mathematicians. They're willing to put a lot of money into this, and they're willing to put years into it. You put that all together and it's very hard to keep them out. In some instances, in the past, there had only been indirect evidence that the Russians were in our network because they're very good at hiding their tracks. We found the noisy ones; if we're lucky, that's all of it. But we don't want to be too sure about all of that.[5]

Once the hackers get into a network, it can take seconds before they've sifted through computer systems. For example, in 2016, CBS News correspondent David Martin reported on how Russian hackers struck at the heart of the US military.[6] The hackers seized the email system used by the Joint Chiefs of Staff. Former Joint Chiefs chairman Martin Dempsey told Martin that the attack proceeded at an alarming speed. Within an hour the hackers had taken control of the unclassified email system. Lewis also discussed the swiftness of the attack.

> Usually, it takes months to prepare for this, and so it's a phased attack. There [are] actions to set it up, to do the reconnaissance, but the moment of execution is really quick. One of the things you hear sometimes is, why didn't the DNC take action? The answer is that by the time they found out, it was too late. The Russians had been in, done what they needed to do, and were out. They're fast, and they are good.[7]

Lewis explained several strategies the United States may use to respond, including overt actions like the sanctions, covert actions like leaking Russian information, or something a little more aggressive. I asked him what kind of activities of ours may be considered more aggressive, such as messing with military computers, which is a riskier prospect.

> **Pegues:** I've talked to people just over the last couple of months who have said, essentially, that the Russians have been hacking the hell out of us, and we're not doing anything to stop it.
>
> **Lewis:** Yes, we've known it was them; we've known what they're up to. One thing we've learned in cybersecurity is that if you don't take action back, it's a green light for the other side.
>
> **Pegues:** What type of action do you think is going to make a difference to Vladimir Putin?
>
> **Lewis:** Well, Vlad is a bit of a tough guy, and so telling him you're going to send him a very angry letter probably won't do it. You need to do things that create political risk for him, and in Russia, political risk comes from relationships and from money—his relationships with other powerful people in Russia, his relationships with the Russian oligarchs, his bank accounts, his money. We have to do something that sends a political message.
>
> **Pegues:** Does that mean sanctions?
>
> **Lewis:** Sanctions are good because the Russians hate them. Second, they send a very public signal that's impossible for anyone to ignore. Third, they do have some effect. Some people always argue about how much effect sanctions have. Having talked to Russians, Chinese, [and] others who have been the targets of sanctions, they really don't like them. That makes sanctions a good option.
>
> **Pegues:** The problem with engaging in a cyber confrontation with Russia and having it escalate is that no one knows where it ends. Right? Especially when you're talking about responding to a cyberattack by using your own offensive cyber, where does that end?
>
> **Lewis:** One of the reasons you've seen people be cautious is

that there's a rough rule in cyberattack: don't do anything that causes physical damage or human casualties. If you stay within that rule, it doesn't justify a violent response. If you go beyond that, you risk war. That's the only rule.

That's not a big rule book for these folks to know. So what happens in this gray area of violence and coercion? No one knows. It's unexplored, unchartered territory, and we're making it up as we go along. That's why there has been some delay. The Russians are not a democracy: they don't have the rule of law. They can be quicker and nimbler than the United States. Putin is willing to take risks that a democracy would never take. You saw that in Ukraine. So Putin has an advantage.

Chapter 22

OBAMA RESPONDS

On December 28, 2016, as he prepared to leave office, Obama ordered sanctions against the Russian government in a response to cyberattacks on Democratic Party officials in an attempt to undermine the free electoral system.[1] These included the expulsion of thirty-five high-level diplomats and declaring them "persona non grata" for "acting in a manner inconsistent with their diplomatic status." US officials believed that several of these individuals were intelligence operatives. They were given seventy-two hours to leave the country.[2]

Lieutenant General Igor Korobov, head of the GRU, Russia's main intelligence directorate, was one of the thirty-five people sanctioned. This group also included Evgeniy Bogachev and Alexey Belan, two men from Russia whom the FBI has linked with cybercrimes for years.[3] The expelled individuals and their families flew on an exclusive Rossiya Airline plane—the carrier that flies Vladimir Putin and other government officials—from Dulles International Airport and arrived in Moscow in time for New Year's.[4]

Concurrently, the State Department shut down two compounds used by Russian intelligence officials in Maryland and New York. The Department of Homeland Security and the FBI released "declassified technical information on Russian civilian and military intelligence service cyber activity, to help network defenders in the United States and abroad identify, detect, and disrupt Russia's global campaign of malicious cyber activities."[5]

President Obama released his most explicit statement about the Russian involvement in the elections: "All Americans should be alarmed by Russia's actions. In October [2016], my Administration publicized our assessment that Russia took actions intended to interfere with the U.S. election process. These data theft and disclosure activities could only have been directed by the highest levels of the Russian government. Moreover, our diplomats have experienced an unacceptable level of harassment in Moscow by Russian security services and police over the last year. Such activities have consequences."[6]

He explained the executive order that he issued. "[The executive order] provides additional authority for responding to certain cyber activity that seeks to interfere with or undermine our election processes and institutions, or those of our allies or partners." And President Obama promised further retaliation: "We will continue to take a variety of actions at a time and place of our choosing, some of which will not be publicized. In addition to holding Russia accountable for what it has done, the United States and friends and allies around the world must work together to oppose Russia's efforts to undermine established international norms of behavior, and interfere with democratic governance."[7]

In a statement at a high-end New Year's Eve party at his Mar-a-Lago resort, Trump issued his own statement, saying that he would have something to reveal. "I also know things that other people don't know, and so they cannot be sure of the situation," he said, referring to the US intelligence agencies' assertion that Russia worked to influence the presidential election in his favor.[8] "I know a lot about hacking," he added, "and hacking is a very hard thing to prove, so it could be somebody else."

That was an early indication that the Trump administration would not be willing to respond with a unified message to the Kremlin's interference. President-Elect Trump was already at odds with the intelligence community, who already knew the Russians had interfered and had backed the Trump campaign.

Without a unified message from the beginning of the Trump administration, Russian influence efforts continued through 2017 and 2018. In fact, they seemed to intensify. Putin was essentially doubling down on his operation to break democracy. Kremlin-backed internet trolls continued to poison social media to shape conversations and debate in the United States. In February 2018, after a gunman shot and killed seventeen students and staff members at Marjory Stoneman Douglas High School in Parkland, Florida, Russian trolls injected themselves in the gun control debate. CNET reported that among the most tweeted two words from Russian bots were "gun control" and "school shooting."[9]

But unlike what was happening during the 2016 election, more people were becoming hip to the tactics being used. But would that be enough of an antidote to neutralize the poison?

Chapter 23

9/11, ANTIFA, AND HAMILTON 68: A CONVERSATION WITH LAURA ROSENBERGER

Laura Rosenberger, director of the Alliance for Securing Democracy and a senior fellow at the German Marshall Fund of the United States, clearly remembers the day she sat in a classroom in Pennsylvania State University's Schreyer Honors College when she heard rumors about a plane hitting the World Trade Center. She was confused, but sat through the class, which had already started.[1]

Forty-five minutes later, Rosenberger walked out of class and to a nearby building where her classmates were crowded around several television sets. She watched the same video feed replaying planes slamming into the towers and people fleeing the streets of Lower Manhattan. Then the footage flipped to show the Pentagon burning. She saw the panicked faces of anchors whose broadcasts were unscripted, and saw the way they struggled to find the words to describe what was happening. Her classmates also lost their language. Many of them were sobbing.

During the hours that passed, Rosenberger's classmates frantically called family members who may have been on the scene of the World Trade Center attack. Several professors held class early so the students could build community. They were in shock. It was hard to wrap their heads around what had happened. They didn't have any real sense of how many people were dead. They didn't know what might follow the attacks. Like many Americans, the trajectory of the world had shifted.

In the clarity of the next morning, Rosenberger, who had always had a deep interest in domestic and foreign policy but had been struggling to pick a career path, decided what she was going to do with the rest of her life.

"I woke up the morning of September 12, and I was like, 'Well, that decision's made.' I need to do everything possible to ensure that that never happens again," she said.[2]

Rosenberger went to graduate school at the American School of International Studies, and later entered the State Department, where she worked for eleven years. She didn't always work specifically on counterterrorism, but instead worked on a broad scale for "our nation's security and for the American people, doing everything we could to make our lives secure and . . . sow greater prosperity and stability and security around the world, which I believe makes us safer."[3]

This included working for Hillary Clinton's 2016 presidential campaign as her foreign policy advisor.

Today, Rosenberger is a studious thirty-seven-year-old woman who is often recognized by her gold-rimmed glasses and thick black hair, and by the pride she takes in being a Yinzer (someone from Pittsburgh) and her love of the Steelers. Her efforts to defend the country have transcended party lines. She runs the Alliance for Securing Democracy with partner Jamie Fly. It is a bipartisan (Rosenberger is a staunch Democrat, while Fly is a staunch Republican), transatlantic organization devoted to interpreting the impact of Russian-led interference on the 2016 election and how to protect the country from future invasions. Like Michael Morell, the former acting director of the CIA, she believes it is akin to what happened on 9/11.

When I asked her how she became involved in the fight against Russian cyber spies, she explained how the attacks on the Democratic National Committee's (DNC) computer system and on democracy overall, while she was advising Clinton, resonated for her because it felt just like 9/11.[4]

No one died in this attack, but I believe that this is existential. I believe that our democracy is the core of our entire being as a country. This is essentially a war without firing a shot. This is an adversary that has attempted to basically implant a cancerous tumor inside of our country and is basically helping it metastasize to kill the body that way.

And that's how I see it, to use a clichéd metaphor. But that's why I'm doing this. This is about our democracy. This is about the centrality of our democracy to our national security. I'm going to do everything possible that I can to preserve it.

I asked her how she gets people to understand the scope of this threat.

Rosenberger: I think it's hard, and that's one of the reasons why it's been difficult in general, I think, to get people really rallying to this challenge. I mean, again, to use the 9/11 comparison, after 9/11, everybody came together. People realized the scale of the problem.

Pegues: Do you think it was because that was easier for us to see?

Rosenberger: Exactly. Yes. I think that's exactly right. This is a much more insidious thing. I mean again, we go back to the cancer inside the body. Sometimes you don't see it till it's too late. It's hard to detect. Even once you know that the tumor's there, you might not feel it. You might feel just fine. . . .

And it's hard to know that it's there. I think that's part of it. I think part of it is that democracy itself is hard to see. I mean, it's an invisible good from which we all benefit on a daily basis. But it's also therefore very easy to take for granted. It's one of those things that we just know so well, and it's been so long since it's ever been challenged that we don't necessarily feel the threat to it in a sort of visceral way.

The discussion then turned to the Alliance for Securing Democracy and the reason why the team is bipartisan.

Rosenberger: I believe it's really strategically important that we respond to this challenge in a unified, bipartisan, transatlantic way. But let's just start with the bipartisan piece. You know, part of Russia's strategy really is sowing and exploiting divisions in societies. . . .

And so much of what we see in Russian information operations and some of their other tactics really has nothing to
do with Russia. I think this is a bit of a misconception; people
think that when we talk about Russian information operations we're talking about propaganda about Russia. And
most of what we're actually talking about has nothing to do
with Russia. . . .

It [involves] operations or attempts to turn Americans or
Europeans against one another. And part of the response to
that has to be refusing to be divided. And that's why what
we're doing at the Alliance for Securing Democracy is bipartisan in its very nature.

Rosenberger explains how in the past she never would have
dreamed she would be working together so closely with Jamie Fly,
who was Marco Rubio's foreign policy advisor and who served in the
George W. Bush administration.

Rosenberger: But both of us have served in national security
in our government and we believe deeply in the bipartisan
nature of national security. We believe that our democracy
is central to our national security interests. And, for me
personally, the whole reason I get to disagree with people
on the other side of the aisle is that we have a functioning
democracy. If we no longer have a functioning democracy,
our ability to disagree with each other disappears. So, I would
rather preserve the framework and the ability for us to have
these debates in the first place.

Pegues: I talked to someone who worked for the Russian-backed
media organization Sputnik. He said, "Putin is using our First
Amendment against us."[5] Do you agree with that?

Rosenberger: He's certainly trying to. One of the most insidious
parts of this tool kit is that, in many ways, it's trying to use and
pervert our free and open society, and in particular turn our
media environment against us. So, if you think about information operations, we have unfettered free speech, which is
one of our greatest strengths in this country. One of the main

tools in the Alliance for Securing Democracy to protect our access to and understanding of media is a web dashboard called Hamilton 68.

Hamilton 68 tracks six hundred monitored Twitter accounts linked to Russian influence operations. These are accounts that include bots and humans and are run by troll factories in Russia and elsewhere, along with sites that clearly state they are affiliated with the Russian government. They also include accounts by the posers, a network of people who aren't necessarily reporting to the Kremlin but jump on the pro-Russian/anti-American bandwagon and join forces. They may come from Russia or anywhere in the world. These are what Putin has referred to as "Patriotic hackers."[6]

Hamilton 68 also tracks people who may be using a wide variety of tools, including information operations, cyberattacks, and financial influence, often through proxy networks. Translation: they hide well and aren't necessarily easy to track. Hamilton 68 helps citizens who tend to get their information from the web (what Laura refers to as the flattening of the media landscape).

Rosenberger: As I'm sure you know, faith in media institutions is really low. People don't necessarily believe as they used to in the role of journalists and editors in vetting sources, in verifying the credibility of information. . . .

A lot of Americans now think that they can judge for themselves. The challenge is that when you have an adversary that is deliberately trying to mislead people, it really becomes a challenge to achieve media literacy and critically evaluate the information that people are receiving. We are trying to think about ways that we can respond to this challenge, to insure that people have as much information as possible about the content they are receiving so that they can evaluate it in the best possible way.

DIVIDED WE FALL: HOW RUSSIAN HACKERS
DOCKED THEIR SHIP IN VIRGINIA

Often, journalists do the hard work for the hackers who are surfing on the media super wave. Our country's crisis becomes their opportunity. Rosenberger explains how this happens.

On August 11, 2017, the Unite the Right Rally occurred in Charlottesville, Virginia, during which Klansmen, neo-Nazis, neo-Confederates, white nationalists, and basically any other garden-variety white supremacist held banners with racist and anti-Semitic words and symbols on them. They carried rifles.[7]

The expressed purpose of the rally was to oppose the removal of a Robert E. Lee statue from Emancipation Park, and came on the heels of the removal of Confederate flags and statues throughout the country. It was billed as a peaceful event until the protestors clashed with counterprotestors. In the middle of the chaos James A. Fields Jr. drove his 2010 Dodge Challenger headlong into a crowd of counterprotestors, killing thirty-two-year-old Heather Heyer and injuring thirty-five other people. Skin and blood were found on the front of the vehicle. A state of emergency was declared in Charlottesville. Fields, who has in the past expressed pro-Nazi racist beliefs, was tried for murder.[8]

Things went from bad to worse when President Trump failed to explicitly denounce white nationalists, and later made a statement about "hatred, bigotry and violence on many sides," and referred to "very fine people on both sides." Many people believed that in doing so Trump had lit a match on the gasoline, and had given white supremacists license to commit acts of violence in the future.[9]

THE ANTIFA APOCALYPSE AND THE RUSSIAN OBJECTIVE:
HOW DO RUMORS GET STARTED?

The uncertainty about the country's future lingered. Rumors flew that members of Antifa (short for anti-fascist), a group of Far Left–leaning radicals donning black costumes and prone toward counter-violence, who were at the Charlottesville rally, would commit various atrocities in opposition to Trump and Fields.[10]

Antifa really refers to a movement and not a group. It originated in Germany and refers to a group of Nazi resisters who later morphed into formal political organizations. There are individuals in the United States who refer to themselves as Antifa and believe in the "eye for an eye" mentality. There are also individuals who consider themselves Antifa who do not believe in violence. There are far more garden-variety survivalists who don't identify with Antifa, and many believe there will come a day when the government will fall and people will take up arms in a revolutionary manner. Antifa and the survivalists are a small subgroup within the overall pool of people whose politics veer more toward the Left.

Those rumors about Antifa died off and surfaced again or died off and morphed until late October when rumors appeared on social media sites such as Twitter, Reddit, Facebook, and a few right-wing news sites like Fox News that it was plotting to launch a civil war on November 4. The imaginary revolution was reported to include house raids, weapons seizures, and violence against random Trump supporters, Republicans, and conservatives.[11]

Although a few demonstrations did occur on November 4, 2017, they were relatively small in scale and little violence occurred.

Rosenberger explains how these false rumors may have been exploited, if not started, by hackers coming from Russia or supporting Putin's goals.

> One recent example that we saw occurred after Charlottesville. It took the networks a couple of days to figure out how to handle that event. But bearing in mind what I said earlier that so much of what the Russian strategy is trying to do is to exploit divisions in American society.
>
> They are going to be pretty keen to take advantage of something like Charlottesville. They took a couple [of] days to kind of figure it out due to the scale of the event. Obviously, the terrorist attack that killed Heather Heyer was not expected.[12]

Rosenberger explained how RT (formerly Russia Today), the Moscow-based, Russian-government-sponsored news channel, started a tweet that led to a story calling for a petition to classify Antifa as a terrorist organization. It followed on the heels of the protest.

And very quickly thereafter, we saw these covert networks, the six hundred monitored accounts, begin to promote that content. That RT story got picked up and became one of the big trending stories that they were promoting. We then saw that RT stopped actually promoting it themselves, but for days thereafter we could still see it on the covert networks—and we still see it occasionally—around different protests. They keep returning to the theme of Antifa as a terrorist organization. . . .

We saw other stories on other websites and other domains that showed up in the networks on the dashboard start to push a similar story. I think that is an interesting example of where we actually saw some overtly promoted content jump to the covert networks.[13]

Rosenberger went on to explain why they were drawn to that particular aspect of the story.

My sense is that they were basically trying to do a couple of things. I'm just speculating here, but it would fortify the sort of "both sides" response that we saw from Trump by discrediting Antifa as a terrorist organization. Number two is the idea of exploiting divisions and fanning the flames of extremism. Something that the Russians see as in their interest. By trying to make Antifa out to be extreme, they were throwing support to the neo-Nazi groups without actually having to overtly support them. . . .

That would put Russia in an uncomfortable place if they were overtly supporting the neo-Nazis. So, instead of supporting them, they are going to attack the other side. We saw that happening there.[14]

In my own research I have seen how sometimes the right-wing or alt-right publications pick up some of these stories, and even Fox News picks up some of them. I asked Rosenberger if these trolls and bots are connected to the Russian government and if they are trying to reach Far Right news outlets.

I think they certainly found an ecosystem in the alt-right media that is favorable to their messaging and that of some other groups. We haven't really written on it ourselves, but a number of other analysts have done some really good pieces looking at the nexus between those two media environments. You mention talking to a Sputnik reporter. I don't know who it is, but if it's who I think it is, this reporter, or former reporter, has also spoken a good bit about that relationship. I think it is certainly a media environment that's favorable. That being said, the Kremlin believes in equal opportunity: this is not ideological for them. They are just trying to sow chaos, weaken us, and exploit divisions. They have made attempts on the Left as well. There are a number of reasons why they have been less successful. And again, I haven't seen any sort of really rigorous analysis of this, but some of the anecdotal points that I have heard commonly made is that, in general, on the Right, and on the alt-right in particular, you have a much more consolidated media environment with Breitbart and a couple of others. . . .

But really Breitbart is where most people go for their sort of news. On the Left you have a much more fragmented media environment. People don't all go to the same place. That makes it harder in an information operation environment to really get a message driven in a concerted way because you just have too many different places to go for news. That's one example given. The other thing I would say in general is that if we take a step back to look at the transatlantic landscape on this, [we'll see] that similar things are happening in Europe. Russia has got some significant ties with the Far Right. I think some of that is just simply Russian opportunism. So much of what they do is taking advantage of existing vulnerabilities and trends. . . .

Given that we have a rise in right-wing populism happening across Europe and the United States that is not necessarily caused by Russia, they certainly sought to jump on it and take advantage of it.[15]

IT'S NOT ALL ABOUT US: AMERICAN DEMOCRACY'S PLACE IN THE RUSSIAN WORLD ORDER

Rosenberger believes that a large percentage of the American population has no idea what really happened during the 2016 presidential election. However, even those who do know have trouble wrapping their heads around it. As when the Twin Towers fell, we have no context for it. Americans haven't really been tracking Russia's interference in democracies throughout Europe for the past decade or so.

Well, I think if we look at the polling, we see continued division among Americans. One of the things that is really concerning to me is that we continue to have a partisan divide about Russia in general and our understanding of Russia's operations that were conducted in the 2016 election. . . .

In many cases, people may have seen coverage of Russia's activities in Ukraine. They see warfare primarily: the illegal annexation of Crimea or the Russian intervention in Eastern Ukraine. But Russians using information operations, cyberattacks, maligned financial influence, support for extremist parties, and economic coercion? That's, well, foreign to Americans. It doesn't feel real, like it fell from the sky. I think part of what we are interested in is being able to explain to people that this is in fact part of a strategy that Russia has been executing for over a decade and, in many ways, is a resurrection of the old Soviet-era playbook but using new tools and technologies.

Chapter 24

RACE-BASED PROPAGANDA: UNDERMINING DEMOCRACY BY TAPPING OUR ACHILLES' HEEL

T he cyber-espionage attacks on the US electoral system are rooted in classic KGB and Soviet government techniques called "active measures" dating back nearly a century.[1]

Service A was a special KGB misinformation unit created in the 1950s. Its agents were a bunch of mad scientists and puppeteers, who concocted nonviolent and macabre schemes to destabilize other countries.[2] One of the chief ways they attempted to destabilize the United States was by exploiting what they viewed as our Achilles' heel, a hair-trigger vulnerability resulting from racial discrimination and our brewing civil unrest.[3]

Our country's oppression of African Americans, particularly under Jim Crow laws in the South, made our democracy look like a sham and earned disfavor in global public policy. Russian officials viewed our bad image as a strategical advantage. In the 1960s, when civil rights campaigns started gaining traction, they were concerned. The KGB didn't like Dr. Martin Luther King Jr. for several reasons. His calls for nonviolent protests in America didn't suit their recipe for stirring up civil unrest. They believed more militant leaders, such as the Black Panthers, were more apt to ignite violence. The way Dr. King associated the movement with the American dream and freedom for all Americans also didn't suit their needs.

During this same period, the Soviet Union's Service A launched a campaign that included forging documents that portrayed King and other prominent civil rights activists as sellouts, calling them "Uncle Toms," who were in cahoots with the US government. They created fake articles and sent them to the African press, to be reprinted in US papers.[4]

The KGB unleashed propaganda that President Lyndon Johnson had secretly planned methods to keep black people in a subordinate status and had bribed King to tame the civil rights movement. Then later, after King was assassinated in April 1968, Service A changed its slant, depicting him as a martyr and implying the US government was behind his assassination.[5]

Service A kept up a steady onslaught of racially charged misinformation during the 1970s and 1980s. For example, in 1971, Yuri Andropov, head of the KGB, okayed the creation of pamphlets laden with racist language to be distributed to militant African American groups and to be blamed on the Jewish Defense League. The pamphlets purportedly urged Jews to avenge attacks on Jewish shops and Jewish people—which never occurred. They also created racially inflammatory pamphlets and fliers and attributed them to the Ku Klux Klan.[6]

Service A's strategy regarding America's long-standing discriminatory practices against African Americans and the intense volatility around racial issues was apt. In the 1960s, race was the most surefire issue to undermine the stability of our political system. In many ways, it still is.[7]

Simultaneously, Russia has not lost this strategic advantage or the desire to tap into it. A Russian hacker group called Secured Borders launched a series of Facebook and Twitter posts intended to stir up hatred. For example, one post attributed to Far Right radicals blared, "They won't take over our country if we don't let them in."[8]

They tried to provoke an anti-immigrant rally in Twin Falls, Idaho, on August 27, 2016, by using Facebook's event and initiation tool. Secured Borders called the city a "center of refugee resettlement responsible for a huge upsurge of violence toward American Citizens." The rally never occurred.[9]

Facebook shut down the Secured Borders group, but investigators noted that there were many more fake sites just like it, including those they have yet to identify. An early internal investigation by Facebook found over three thousand ads costing $100,000 attributed to Russian internet trolls, containing messages about divisive issues, including race.[10] Facebook admits that some of the ads were paid for in rubles. But even that for them wasn't an indicator of suspicious activity "because the overwhelming majority of advertisers who pay in Russian currency, like the overwhelming majority of people who access Facebook from Russia, aren't doing anything wrong."

I occasionally hear from friends, family, and neighbors who are overwhelmed by the news about Russia's interference in the US election and claims about its association with the Trump campaign. Some insist that they've heard enough. Others say that ordinary Americans are just pawns in a game being played by the wealthy and we'll never really know what's going on, so there's no point in listening. More claim that paying any attention to it is playing into the hands of political puppeteers.

Then there are many who believe the most important issue is obviously being played out on our own soil, that being the ever-growing rift between the Left and the Right or the rich and the poor. I know many African Americans, Latin Americans, Asian Americans, and recent immigrants who believe that racism has always spurred violence and exploitation in this country. They believe *that* is the only real issue. I can certainly understand that sentiment. In some sense, I was raised in it.

Chapter 25

THE DOCUMENTS

*A*ssessing Russian Activities and Intentions in Recent US Elections was a declassified report released in January 2017. The report was a compilation of assessments from the CIA, FBI, and NSA. US officials said that what was revealed to the public was a declassified version of another "highly classified assessment" that only a small group of people had been briefed on.[1]

President Obama faced pressure to either "put up or shut up" on the Russia matter.[2] In the overly partisan postelection atmosphere, there were both Republicans and Democrats who denied Russian interference. Law enforcement and US intelligence sources told me then that the Obama administration was trying to get as much information out as possible before the transfer of power. My intelligence sources were telling me that there were concerns in the Obama administration that the incoming Trump administration would attempt to bury some of the evidence.[3]

In the report, US intelligence agencies determined that "Russian efforts to influence the 2016 US Presidential election represent the most recent expression of Moscow's longstanding desire to undermine the US-led liberal democratic order."[4]

On January 6, the CBS News Washington Bureau and my team of producers were busy combing through the declassified document. Producers Andy Triay, Katie Ross Dominick, Julia Kimani Burnham, and I highlighted what we thought were the new revelations. We had already reported some of the information.

The declassified version was about to cause tremors across America. I imagined the classified version would have caused an 8.0 magnitude earthquake had it been released.

The report was stunning, an incredible read. It walked through the analytic process of the information-gathering apparatus of the intelligence community in an attempt to dispel the notion that US officials had just somehow pulled the data from out of thin air. The report was put together using a range of sources and methods. In intelligence circles, that usually means that the FBI, CIA, or NSA was involved at some level, and that they used human intelligence—spies or informants—to collect the data. Or somehow NSA hackers were able to breach computer databases to find the information.

One of the most stunning features of the report noted that Russian president Vladimir Putin ordered an "influence campaign" aimed at the 2016 US presidential election.[5] When the report was issued, CBS News and other news outlets had described what US investigators believed was Putin's goal, but an official report from the intelligence agencies hits closer to home for a skeptical public. The report noted that "Russia's goals were to undermine public faith in the US democratic process, denigrate Secretary Clinton, and harm her electability and potential presidency."[6] By all accounts, Putin despised Hillary Clinton. He was motivated to destroy her as a candidate and as a president, if she were elected.

It was a grudge match. US officials believe that Putin hated Clinton because he believed she had tried to "influence" events in Russia against him. In 2011, the Russian leader accused the United States and Clinton specifically of stirring up protests in Russia. "She set the tone for some opposition activists, gave them a signal, they heard this signal and started active work," Putin told supporters at the time.[7]

Fast-forward to the 2016 election, and at the time most expected Clinton to win. Without weighing too much into politics, most political observers, most Washington insiders, a great many in law enforcement and the intelligence community, and many in the Obama administration thought she was going to win. How could she not win, especially going up against an unproven, undisciplined, unorthodox, un-just-about-everything candidate like Donald Trump?

But Trump had the right mix of what the voters were looking for at the time. He was the Washington antidote. His very nature rubbed the Washington insiders the wrong way, and in 2016 that was a winning formula. I remember talking to one of my old teammates from Miami University of Ohio. I played football there, and most of my teammates hailed from the Buckeye State. They were hard-working, salt of the earth guys. In a phone call early on in 2015, one of them told me he was pulling for Trump. Trump wasn't leading the GOP pack at the time, and I was puzzled by what my old teammate was saying. He insisted that he wanted someone to "blow up Washington!" I was stunned by how much he despised Washington and what it stood for to him and how he was tired of the gridlock. Donald J. Trump was going to be his voice in Washington. And he was going to tear things up.

That message resonated. But the Russian interference certainly helped. What the Russian operation did was amplify the Trump campaign's message. It also injected division into the campaign, tossing the Clinton camp into more turmoil. US officials were seeing signs relatively early on in 2016 that Putin was "out to get" Clinton, but they were slow to act. Again, in our overly partisan campaign atmosphere, they were pussyfooting around Putin's beef with Clinton, because they didn't want to be accused of interfering on her behalf.

US officials assessed in the declassified report that Putin and the Russian government developed a clear preference for President-Elect Trump. We have high confidence in these judgments.[8]

- They assessed that the Russian government tried to improve Trump's chances of winning the election "by discrediting Secretary Clinton and publicly contrasting her unfavorably to him."

    The most public example of that was Russia's disclosure of stolen Democratic Party data and emails. US officials determined that the Russian government used online personas like Guccifer 2.0 (later determined to be a Russian intelligence officer),[9] DCLeaks.com, and WikiLeaks to release the data and emails. Most of it targeted Clinton in one way or another. Then once the stolen data and emails were out in public, social media users and Russian trolls retweeted and spread the information. It created a tsunami of negative headlines for Clinton that, ultimately, she could not recover from and deepened the damage done by her own self-inflicted wounds.

- US officials also determined that "Moscow's approach evolved over the course of the campaign based on Russia's understanding of the electoral prospects of the two main candidates. When it appeared to Moscow that Secretary Clinton was likely to win the election, the Russian influence campaign began to focus more on undermining her future presidency." For that, according to the declassified report they used the same type of tactics, blending "covert intelligence operations—such as cyber activity—with overt efforts by Russian Government agencies, state-funded media, third-party intermediaries, and paid social media users or 'trolls.'"

Here are some of the examples mentioned in the US report:[10]

- In August, Kremlin-linked political analysts suggested avenging negative Western reports on Putin by airing segments devoted to Secretary Clinton's alleged health problems.
- On 6 August, RT published an English-language video called "Julian Assange Special: Do WikiLeaks Have the E-mail That'll Put Clinton in Prison?" and an exclusive interview with Assange entitled "Clinton and ISIS Funded by the Same Money." RT's most popular video on Secretary Clinton, "How 100% of the Clintons' 'Charity' Went to . . . Themselves," had more than 9 million views on social media platforms. RT's most popular English[-]language video about the President-elect, called "Trump Will Not Be Permitted To Win," featured Assange and had 2.2 million views.

Russia, like its Soviet predecessor, has a history of conducting covert influence campaigns focused on US presidential elections that have used intelligence officers, agents, and press placements to disparage candidates perceived as hostile to the Kremlin. This was, of course, much different because technology had made it more potent. Cyberspace took Russian actions to another level. Some of the ads that kept popping up on social media took direct aim at Clinton. One ad touted a petition to remove Clinton from the presidential ballot. It said, "Disavow support for the Clinton political dynasty." That ad was being pushed by a fake group called Donald Trump America. The Russians were behind that. Another ad from a Russian-controlled organization announced a rally in May 2016 to "Stop Islamization of Texas." The Russians were behind that one as well. And there were tens of thousands of more toxic Russian-backed ads in the atmosphere. It is estimated that the posts by Russian-backed Facebook groups alone reached up to 126 million Americans. "I don't think you get it," California Democratic senator Dianne Feinstein said when asked about the impact of the Russian operation on social media. "What we're talking about is a cataclysmic change. What we're talking about is the beginning of cyberwarfare. What we're talking about is a major foreign power with sophistication and ability to involve themselves in a presidential election and sow conflict and discontent all over this country."[11]

But perhaps the most important target of the Russian influence campaign was the state and local electoral boards. US officials in the declassified report concluded that "Russian intelligence obtained and maintained access" to the electoral boards. "DHS assessed that the types of systems Russian actors targeted or compromised were not involved in vote tallying."[12] But could that be said with certainty? What were the Russians really up to when they were scanning and probing voter databases? Multiple sources told me that federal and congressional investigators were trying to determine if by scanning and probing the voter databases the Russians were trying to gather intelligence that could later be used to target ads on social media. One state election official told me it was a possibility that made sense given all of the information available in a voter database.

Chapter 26

PUTIN'S END GAME IN THE UNITED STATES

J im Lewis is an expert with the Center for Strategic and International Studies (CSIS). Prior to working at CSIS he held government positions, which included intelligence assignments. Over the years at CBS I have come to trust his insight on a range of cyber-related issues, and early on in the Russia investigation I began relying more on him. During the course of 2016, 2017, and 2018, we had several conversations about strategy. He explained why Putin had authorized this massive cyber operation.

> You know, at first it was for defense; they felt like Russia didn't come out so well from the Cold War and they needed to regain some land. Under Yeltsin, they had economic disaster, and they blame the Americans for that. Putin is convinced that America has a secret plan to destroy Russia. I know this from people who have spoken directly to him about it. He's convinced, and so he wanted to push back, and in pushing back he discovered he has got a great opportunity to do things here [in the West] that the Russians have wanted to do for decades, like destroy NATO, destroy the transatlantic alliance, and push back on human rights. It started out as a defense, and now it's an opportunity. Remember, he is a former KGB agent. He knows the rule book. . . . He's acting in a way that goes all the way back to the Tsarist intelligence services and to the initial Soviet intelligence services. This is something they're really good at, this kind of disinformation. It's an opportunity for him to do what they've always wanted to do to NATO and the United States.[1]

Lewis explained some of the ways Putin's cyber warriors have wreaked havoc on NATO countries (aka the North Atlantic Alliance), a military alliance between governments of several European and North American states that grew out of the 1940 North Atlantic Treaty.

"They did hack the German congress; they have tried to hack [the British] parliament; they're all over Europe—and these are the incidents we know about," he said. "They're doing other things, too. They're using refugees as a political tool; they're bribing people; they've got RT [previously known as Russia Today], the Russian-government-funded television network. They've got their [internet] trolls. It's a huge campaign to destabilize the United States and our allies."[2]

Lewis also discussed how the Russian hackers were able to penetrate our systems.

> The Russians are among the best in the world. They're at least as good as we are, and in the past, we know they've broken into our networks. It's very hard to find them. . . . When they want to be hidden, they stay hidden.
>
> One of the signs that this was a political action was the Russians were really noisy about it: they didn't mind that we know it was them. It's almost like it's disrespecting the United States. They're the best in the world, and if they want to do this kind of thing, [they can]. They have been doing it since the '80s. Now they've gone public: now they're going for political effect.[3]

Lewis further describes how Russia's particular skill set lends itself to this kind of thing. He said if they aren't still in our computer systems, they have a way to get back in if they want to.

I later asked Lewis what the Russian hackers may be doing specifically to interfere with our elections. Would they break into our voting booths?

> They may have been looking to see if there was some central vulnerability that they could exploit that would really tilt the election or damage the vote count. I think that was the goal: to damage the vote count. But it turns out that it may have been too hard. But they could still complicate things. They could create chaos at some polling places. You could create some bad image that they could

run on Russian television and in papers around the world. . . . This is a PR campaign to damage America's image. . . .

It's a war of ideas. It's not like the old Cold War. It's a war where the Russians are saying, "We were told that Western democracy is perfect and that's the model we all aspire to. But look at this situation. It's such a mess." Clearly that's not true. It's building the case for an authoritarian regime, for rulers who already know what the vote is going to be long before the election. It's to create an alternative model to Western democracy. And it's part of a larger campaign. They're doing things like this in Europe with extremist groups and right-wing groups. Russians have a different doctrine than we do. So, people here worry about cyber Pearl Harbors, or cyber 9/11s. But the Russians never talk about that. They talk about using information to shape opinion, to create political conflict, to destabilize. The Russians are still mad at us for winning the Cold War, so they're yanking our chain.

Lewis may have known then what would eventually become public. US officials would later acknowledge that Russian bots had used Facebook and Twitter to spread misinformation during the 2016 election. The Russian bots exploited controversial topics in the United States and then hyped them up. The *Guardian* reported, "What has now been made clear is that Russian trolls and automated bots not only promoted explicitly pro–Donald Trump messaging, but also used social media to sow social divisions in America by stoking disagreement and division around a plethora of controversial topics such as immigration and Islamophobia. And, even more pertinently, it is clear that these interventions are continuing as Russian agents stoke division around such recent topics as white supremacist marches and NFL players taking a knee to protest police violence."[4]

I asked Lewis if the United States was good at information warfare.

"What we're good at is telling the truth because the truth is on our side, right?" he said. "And that's what we need to do. It's not like advertising; you're not going to make a commercial for a soda pop and then use it to sell propaganda. We're just not good at it. We were never good at it during the Cold War. We're better off if we're just straight with people because the facts are on our side."

Chapter 27

CLUES FOR REPORTERS: THAT NAGGING FEELING

W hile I was working on the Russia investigation, new potential leads to look into would come to me at the oddest
moments, when I was cooking breakfast for my daughters or driving
my car. It was during an oddly meditative, sleep-deprived moment
while I was walking up the stairs to my office when a clue came to me.

A former US official who had seen some of the underlying intelligence told me that there were "massive alarms" going off about the
scope of Russian attempts to breach voter databases in the final weeks
of the election.[1] US investigators had also believed that systems in key
battleground states, including Wisconsin and Florida, particularly,
were in danger. At the time they thought that some voter registration data may have been "exfiltrated" but that investigators weren't
certain. Furthermore, US officials were reluctant to talk about the
breaches out of concern that doing so would reveal methodology,
essentially doing the Russian hackers' work for them.

I walked up to my office and closed the door. I went to my desk,
opened my personal computer, and found the folder with the detailed
notes on the election. Wisconsin was not yet on the list of states that
the Department of Homeland Security (DHS) had officially revealed
as having voter databases that were scanned and probed by Russian
hackers.

On election night I had gone to bed before Wisconsin's votes
came in, but I knew it was a battleground state. That morning I woke
up with the knowledge that Trump had won, and went to my laptop
to watch his victory speech and Clinton's concession. It was an odd

morning for me, as it was for most people. I walked the hotel carpet as if I had just woken up on an alien planet, one with a different air density that I wasn't sure how to take in.

Again, for me it wasn't the fact that Trump was elected. Rather, his election made it clear to me that vulnerabilities had been exposed by the Russian government's influence campaign. Based on the information I had and the information that was coming in from other reporters and the intelligence community, it was almost as if we had been invaded.

I scrolled through my notes on Wisconsin. It had come down to the wire in that state with President Trump winning by just 22,748 votes.[2] It was a fairly thin margin of victory in a state that cast a total of about three million votes. Wisconsin ended up being one of the states that decided who would be the next president. In 2012 President Obama won the state by almost seven percentage points.[3] In a state that hadn't voted Republican since Reagan, it was an unlikely win.[4]

About ten months after the 2016 election, the DHS contacted twenty-one states, telling them that their internet-connected networks were the target of Russian hackers "seeking vulnerabilities and access to U.S. election infrastructure."[5] Wisconsin was on that list along with Ohio, Alabama, Colorado, Connecticut, Florida, Minnesota, Texas, Virginia, Pennsylvania, Delaware, Iowa, Maryland, and Washington State. Arizona and Illinois were confirmed targets about a year earlier. The DHS insisted that there was no evidence Russian hackers were able to change any votes. That notion was backed up by Judd Choate of the US National Association of State Election Directors, who said that "there remains no evidence that the Russians altered one vote or changed one registration."[6] In the months after the election I spoke with an Obama-era DHS official who told me candidly that when they were questioned about whether Russian interference had impacted the vote total they responded with carefully worded statements. The honest answer to that question is that they didn't know. But publicly they kept saying they had "no evidence the actual voting process was interfered with on Election Day."[7]

The effort by the Obama administration to really come to grips with the extent of the Russian intrusion was frustratingly slow. The Trump administration then compounded the problem and seemed incapable of unifying a plan to counter Russian intrusions throughout 2016, 2017, and into 2018.[8] This was largely because President Trump wouldn't acknowledge the issue. He was still calling the story a hoax, purportedly part of some mastermind scheme devised by sore losers after Clinton lost.[9]

Simultaneously, the president and his campaign were under scrutiny by the special counsel that was appointed in May 2017 to investigate whether the Trump campaign conspired with the Russians.[10] Trump often angrily dismissed the accusations and couldn't seem to separate his own interests from those of the country.

It was easy to conflate the two issues. Most Americans couldn't separate the controversy swirling around the White House from the clear and present danger facing our democracy.

In a hearing on Capitol Hill, an official with the DHS confirmed publicly what officials had been saying privately, which was that twenty-one states were targeted by Russian cyberattacks during the 2016 campaign.[11]

I remember the first time when word started leaking out that officials were worried Russian hackers were targeting voter databases and that the DHS was trying to notify states and help election officials determine whether they had been targeted. At the time it seemed to me as if Homeland Security officials were caught off guard and the response was slow and inadequate considering that the country was just weeks away from the election. The Russians' surprise attack had largely gone unnoticed.

Dr. Sam Liles, acting director of the Cyber Division of the DHS, testified in a hearing that Homeland Security officials had no indication that any adversaries, including the Russian government, had been planning activities that would change the outcome of the election. He said the activity by Russian hackers suggested "simple scanning," an act he compared to someone "walking down the street to see if you are home."[12] But future testimony revealed that the Russians had actually broken into some of those "homes" and "manipulated data" where they could.[13] In the same hearing, Senate Intelligence Committee vice chair Mark Warner of Virginia called the Russian cyberattacks on election systems a watershed moment in political history. "This was one of the most significant events any of us on this dais will be asked to address in our careers," he said in his opening remarks to the audience and his fellow senators. "Only with a robust and comprehensive response will we be able to protect our democratic process from even more drastic intrusions in the future."[14]

The consensus was that the Russians would be back in 2018 and then in 2020 as well. The reality was they hadn't left. Most people in the intelligence community figured Russian malware was still lurking in computer systems.

As we learn more about the scope of Russian interference and the delayed and tepid response by the United States, confidence in the election system will likely erode. In 2016, according to a Gallup poll, which was compiled just two weeks before the November 8 election, only 35 percent or about one-third of Americans were "very confident" that their vote would be counted accurately.[15] That poll should trouble anyone who believes in democracy and the values of the Founding Fathers.

Before we know it, the 2018 midterm elections will be upon us. The 2020 presidential election will soon follow. Since 2016, election systems in all fifty states have had to conduct serious examinations of their operations. It has been a time-consuming and costly mission. And at the end of the day it's unclear whether it will be enough to stop the ongoing intrusions by Russian hacking units. Still, what election systems have had to do is unprecedented. As journalists we thought what we were seeing after the "hanging-chad" election in 2000 (involving Florida's voting problems) was earth-shattering. This is a much bigger undertaking because it involves all fifty states. Getting it right this time is more important than ever.

Chapter 28

VOTING BOOTH DINOSAURS

A man walks into a voting booth in Georgia. This joke begins and ends with the booth itself, which is an antiquated dinosaur called the Diebold AccuVote TS—one variety of touch screen voting machine also known as a direct recording electronic (DRE) voting machine. Georgia still uses that particular AccuVote TS, even though that beast has seen better days.[1] Thousands of other AccuVote TS machines outside the great state of Georgia have been scrapped.[2] The state representatives likely have a certain affinity for their voting machines, even though they have been around since the early 1990s.

On the flip side, perhaps the newer machines are too expensive for them to buy. Of course, these machines are used fervently, but they are only used every few years. Perhaps Georgia believes the machines have more staying power.

The volunteer poll workers have given our hypothetical man a plastic smart card. The man inserts the card into the computer, which is attached with old sealant to the thin, notebook-sized touch screen.

This man is older and not necessarily the most technologically savvy person. He still records his business records in ink in ledgers. However, he knows how to work this voting machine, which performs almost like the ATM at his bank. He patiently scrolls through the list of questions with the multiple-choice answers like he did in grade school. He finally gets to the real issue at hand and selects his candidate for president.

Things may go off without a hitch. The man's picks for office are recorded accurately, electronically in its internal flash memory.

Alternatively, things may not work out exactly according to plan.

The man could press the name of his candidate and instead the other candidate's name lights up. This is what happened that same day to his fellow American voters in North Carolina, where Trump lit up for people who pressed Clinton's name, and in Texas, where Clinton lit up for people who pressed Trump's name. His vote flipped.[3]

The problem could be due to human error. The man's finger may be greasy from a snack he might have been eating that morning, and he may have accidentally tapped the wrong button. It is also quite conceivable that the machine was off. The glue may have softened, causing the misalignment of the screen. The software that connects to the touch screen may have lost its calibration. The hardware could also be failing, losing its long-haul efficiency. It is just as likely that the computer, like a person with Alzheimer's, is losing its efficiency throughout the course of the day, specifically because it has performed so many tasks before sunset. On Election Day, then, the moment the Diebold AccuVote TS was created for, the machine malfunctions.

Alternatively, something more ominous could be happening. The machine could have malfunctioned because the system was rigged or compromised, because somebody deliberately practiced vote flipping.

The most vulnerable aspect of all DRE machines, which are currently being used in four other states (New Jersey, South Carolina, Delaware, and Louisiana), is their lack of strong security systems.[4]

While Russian cyberspace operatives were hacking into our voting system in July 2016, Princeton University professor and White House consultant Edward Felten, one of the VIPs seated in the Old Executive Office Building, did think about all DREs, and specifically about Georgia's endearing dinosaur. In 2005, Felten led a team of Princeton graduate students who dissected the Diebold AccuVote TS, piece by piece. A security analysis found extreme problems in the software that would be used in a real election.[5] Felten explained multiple technical means through which an ill-intentioned person could install malicious software. It was relatively easy to reprogram the software in the system to incorrectly count votes. "The machines are fundamentally computers inside, that will do what they are programmed to do," he explained. Since the machines aren't connected to the internet, a person who wanted to reconnoiter a machine would have to physically have access to that machine. However, a software upgrade could be performed in less than sixty seconds.[6]

Hackers could also create viruses in the electronic memory cards that the voting officials use to program the machine through illegal methods, perhaps bribing an electoral official or just stealing a memory card. If you could get your hands on one of these memory cards (in a particular state or county), you could put malicious software on it. The voting machine virus could then spread virally from memory cards to machines, and from machines to memory cards. You wouldn't have to compromise voting booths in multiple states to wreak havoc.

"We also confirmed earlier reports that the machines stored the votes internally—in the order that they were cast, which meant that someone who could get access to the memory cards or the machines could figure out that, say, the seventeenth person who voted that day voted for particular candidates. In most states there are records of the order in which individual voters vote *and* it's possible for observers in the polling place to make those records," Felten said.[7]

Later studies confirmed those results. Other studies showed that different kinds of paperless voting machines had similar vulnerabilities. In "America's Voting Machines at Risk," an extensive 2015 study done for the Brennan Center for Justice, Lawrence Norden and Christopher Famighetti estimated that forty-three states would be using machines bought over a decade ago and that fourteen states would be using machines that are at least fifteen years old.[8]

OPTICAL SCANNING MACHINES

Many states have moved away from those kinds of machines since then, instead adopting optical scanning machines.[9] These machines scan the paper ballots cast by voters, but the paper record is kept as a backup. Optical scans can be more secure than paperless DRE scans, according to Felten. They are, however, far from perfect.

DETROIT, MICHIGAN

In Detroit in 2016, when more than eighty of the optical scanners that registered and counted votes, which were marked on paper, malfunctioned—in many cases the scanners jammed—there were ballot inconsistencies in 59 percent of the precincts.[10] More than 2.1 million votes were recounted before the recount was halted. A Detroit official noted that this kind of chaos happens every election year with their machines.

The recount was spearheaded by Jill Stein, a Green Party candidate running for president, but then the recount was stopped after a judge said Stein's request was invalid.[11] Her petition filed in Pennsylvania noted that the mixed bag of optical scan and electronic machines in the state could be vulnerable to hacking, and requested a complete forensic analysis of the machines. Her petition was rejected on several grounds, including there being no evidence that Pennsylvania's voting system was compromised.[12]

DURHAM, NORTH CAROLINA

The monster was raging in the machine here as well, wreaking havoc on Election Day. A technical glitch in the "electronic poll books" caused volunteer poll workers to scramble to look up and confirm voters' names.[13] In some areas, they had a paper copy backup system in place, but in others there weren't any records. Delays of several hours caused people to leave without voting. Some voters' names had somehow disappeared from the system altogether. Other people were informed that they'd already voted when they hadn't. The Voter Protection Hotline rang off the hook. Various counties petitioned for emergency measures. Voting was extended an extra hour, until 8:30 p.m., for residents in two counties, and also extended an extra hour for residents of six additional counties.

Although officials contended that the glitch was a fluky technological mishap, researchers found that the problem may have originated at VR Systems, Inc., the vendor that supplied digital software to manage voting registrations. US law enforcement later determined that its Florida headquarters were hacked by people believed to be Russian-government-based operatives. During the last week of October, the hackers used a VR Systems' address to send 122 emails to state and local officials across the country whose attachments contained malware, which was reportedly a ruse to mine for enough information to cause disaster, according to an NSA report.[14]

Trump ended up winning North Carolina. It was a swing state that was expected to favor Hillary Clinton. Durham County, in particular, was largely Democratic. The county has more than 38 percent African American voters, three-quarters of whom had voted for the reelection of Barack Obama.[15] Twenty other counties in North Carolina used VR Systems, Inc.[16]

THE MONSTER IN THE MACHINE: THE HANGING-CHAD INCIDENT

This is certainly not the first time our election system has been called into question. And it is not the first time election chaos has been blamed on the monster in the machine.[17] The outcome of the most contentious presidential election in United States, the race between George W. Bush and Al Gore in 2000, hinged on thousands of votes cast on the now defunct Votamic-style punch-card ballots (Votamics were last used in the 2014 general election in Idaho).[18] Voters use a stylus to punch holes in a card for each candidate chosen. The punch goes through the backing to remove a chunk of chad. The hole that is left counts as the vote. In the Florida election, 1.9 million ballots were considered "spoiled votes," which means essentially that the punched holes were indecipherable.[19] These were called "hanging chads," in which some corners of the punched marks still attached to the page and "fat chads," or "pregnant chads," where all the corners were attached but a faint indentation seemed to have been made.[20] The punch cards were counted by optical machines.

According to a report by the US Civil Rights Commission, more than half of these spoiled ballots were used by African Americans, who were largely expected to vote Democrat in that election.[21] Many of the more antiquated machines were in predominantly African

American voting precincts, such as those in Gadsden County, which had in equal measures the highest number of black voters and the highest rejected vote rates. An African American voter was ten times as likely as a Caucasian voter to have a rejected vote. African American voters were less likely than voters in more affluent, predominantly Caucasian counties to receive a replacement ballot if they used the punch cards incorrectly.[22]

Approximately 6,600 votes lost in Palm Beach County were attributed to the butterfly ballot in use there, which opened like the wings of a butterfly and had candidates' names on two sides and punch holes in the middle.[23] (How was this ballot supposed to work, ideally?) Many voters, especially elderly people, claimed they were confused by the way names were listed on the ballot and could well have voted for the wrong candidate.

The pregnant chads, hanging chads, and butterfly ballot mishaps were discovered during an extensive, painstaking recount.[24] The Florida recount occurred following a media super blunder, in which national networks mistakenly called Gore the winner in the state before everyone had a chance to vote. Later, the media reversed their call and gave it to Bush, only to then change their minds again and deem the election "too close to call." The election margin was tight, with Bush leading by just 537 of the 5.8 million votes cast. After thirty-six days of deliberation, Gore ultimately conceded the race to Bush.[25]

There were a multitude of lawsuits against the state, alleging discriminatory practices and overt racism during the election. For example, there was a massive removal of predominately African American voters from the rolls due to a list of nearly sixty thousand suspected felons that was sent to election supervisors prior to the election, which was riddled with mistakes.[26] Following a legal battle between the NAACP and an organization called Database Technologies, the latter reran names on the "purge list" and found that approximately twelve thousand voters who were not felons weren't allowed to vote because they were on the original list sent to the elections office.[27]

Many claimed that the discrepancies were caused by a scheme Florida's former governor, Jeb Bush (George's brother), created to eliminate from the voting rolls those who were projected to vote

Democrat and for Al Gore. This included mostly African American and Hispanic voters who were Democrats.

Three days of hearings were conducted by the US Commission on Civil Rights, during which Floridians gave testimony about some of their problems in voting, including being turned away because they were on the purge list, being blocked from remote polling locations, and because they had difficulties with antiquated voting equipment. The commission concluded that there were significant violations of the Voting Rights Act of 1965—which prevents the Fifteenth Amendment's tenets against voting discrimination, including discrimination on the basis of race.[28]

> The report does not find that the highest officials of the state conspired to disenfranchise voters. Moreover, even if it was foreseeable that certain actions by officials led to voter disenfranchisement, this alone does not mean that intentional discrimination occurred. Instead, the report concludes that officials ignored the mounting evidence of rising voter registration rates in communities. The state's highest officials responsible for ensuring efficiency, uniformity, and fairness in the election failed to fulfill their responsibilities and were subsequently unwilling to take responsibility.[29]

The hearings also determined African American voters were targeted on purge lists; for example, in Miami-Dade, Florida's largest county, black people represented only 20 percent of the population, but represented more than 65 percent of the names on the purge list.[30]

Florida did institute legislation to address problems with the 2000 presidential election.

> The Commission publicly applauded this development as soon as it occurred, and even before the details of the legislative package were finalized. The Commission reiterates that Florida and its leaders deserve credit for the new election law.
>
> However, the same leadership that effectively ensured passage of the recent legislation was missing in the years and months leading up to the November 2000 election. If the same level of leadership had been present, the Commission's investigation reveals that most of the problems during the past election would have been

prevented, and the dire consequences documented in this report could have been avoided.[31]

The maelstrom eventually led to the establishment of the Help America Vote Act (HAVA) of 2002 by Congress, introducing revolutionary changes to voting systems and voting access—and introducing minimum standards for states' election administration. It requires states to implement several procedures that were previously unrequired, like upgrading equipment, creating protections for statewide voter registration databases, and instituting measures to deal with administrative complaints. It also established the Election Assistance Commission to help states comply with HAVA and to give them funding to do so.[32]

While it can be difficult to determine whether glitches in the machine or nefarious humans are the ghosts behind state elections that do not seem to go off according to plan, it seems that in these times it is as important to first shore up the machines as it is to uncover accountability. It seems a no-brainer that states complying with HAVA and that have been part of our country's history would set the bar high for their equipment. To find out why this isn't happening across the board, as well as to learn some of the long-term dangers of keeping our systems outmoded and unchecked in the future, I spoke with Edward Felten.[33]

I asked him first about the AccuVote TS, and why Georgia officials hadn't acknowledged how risky those machines are.[34]

Felten: I think there [are] several factors. One is that they are hearing from some people, including the vendors selling the machines, that there are some people who claim that those risks are overstated. I think that's number one.

Number two is that to change [systems] would cost money. It would be inconvenient. There would be some risk of the change not going smoothly. So, people would prefer not to change. I know in New Jersey the dollar cost of changing the voting machines has been one of the factors that held back a switch to more secure technologies. And the other thing that happens is, in some of these cases, there are public officials who have staked some of their reputations on the idea that these machines are secure enough to use. It can become difficult for them to back down from that position.

Pegues: Is the secretary of state in Georgia one of those guys?

Felten: I don't want to speculate about that particular case. But this is a phenomenon that we've seen in other states, and sometimes in other places. Sometimes changes to the technology become easier when people rotate out of certain positions. Change is sometimes slow in government processes. I think that there's been ample time for Georgia and other states to make changes, and that they should have long ago. We'll see if they're actually going to move forward now. I do think that the threat is higher now than it was back in 2005 [when Felten and his Princeton team first learned of the voting machine vulnerabilities]. I think that's one of the reasons why we may see a renewed push for better technologies now.

Felten believes that the lack of better technologies put us in a vulnerable place for attack by outside entities such as Russian hackers.

Pegues: One of your former colleagues, Alex Halderman, said that he has no doubt that Russian intelligence operatives have the capability to change votes.

Felten: I agree that it's within the technical capability of the Russian intelligence service or other foreign intelligence services to do that, at least on some of the systems that are used. On the DREs, if a couple of graduate students in my lab were able to do what they did, an intelligence service that has more people, more resources, and many less scruples would be able to do a lot more.

However, Felten doesn't believe voting booths were tampered with in the 2016 elections.

Pegues: All right, so when you hear US intelligence officials testifying on Capitol Hill saying that essentially as far as we can tell, no votes were tampered with, I have sources who are telling me that they struggled over what to say about that, how to word their responses when they were asked about that. I'm wondering, do you have confidence in that assessment?

Felten: I do, yes.

Pegues: Why?

Felten: For a couple of reasons. And I need to speak a little bit carefully here, because I was a government official during this time. I need to be careful that I'm not revealing something I shouldn't. But what I would say, generally, is that to understand what a foreign intelligence service might be doing, you might understand . . . by seeing the effects of what they're doing.

You might understand it because you have other intelligence sources that help you understand what they're planning, what orders have been given, and so on. In other words, there are other sources of information about what Russian intelligence services are trying to do and [actually] doing beyond just looking at voting machines.

I think when you take into account the sources of information that the US intelligence community had, the assessment that there was not a Russian attack on the Election Day voting process itself is justified.

Pegues: So, based on what happened with 2016 and the information that is still really coming out about election systems and databases being penetrated, what is your prognosis for the system, or your assessment of the system that we have in place and whether it can stand up to Russian intrusions?

Felten: There are two ways to look at that question. One, what is the likelihood that they could cause trouble or that they could cause parts of the system to fail? I think it's very difficult to prevent a very highly resourced and capable organization like a nation-state-level adversary from causing technical trouble within a system.

The next question to ask is, can we create a system that is resilient enough to deal with that possibility should it happen so that we know what happened, that we have the ability to figure out what the voters actually did, and make sure that people can have confidence in the results of the election, even if there is technical mischief? And in order to do that it requires having safeguards in place and cross-checking different kinds of results against each other, and so on.

So that means having a paper record of each vote that the voters [made], taking care with the chain of custody on those paper records, and then doing postelection audits to make sure that those paper records are consistent with the electronic record. All of these things are part of building a system that is resilient so that if someone does monkey with voting machines, we'll be able to detect it and correct it.

Pegues: Does the state of Georgia have that kind of system in place, as far as you know?

Felten: Georgia does not have a voter-verified paper record. Their voting systems are not secure enough that if some very capable actor were to target a Georgia-based election, it might be impossible to figure out. It might be impossible to know what the voters were really trying to do on that Election Day.

Pegues: What about New Jersey?

Felten: New Jersey has similar problems. Its systems are somewhat older, and in some ways more difficult to tamper with. But still, New Jersey doesn't have the safeguards that it ought to have.

Pegues: If you were still in the White House, and you were looking ahead to the 2018 and 2020 elections, what would you be doing now? What would you be trying to convince secretaries of state or election officials in states across this country to do?

Felten: First of all, to move away from DRE voting machines and to do two things with respect to the Election Day process. One is to use a voting system that has a voter-verified paper record of the vote, a voter-verified paper ballot. Then, second, risk-limiting audits after the elections. [Paper audits are] a way of comparing those paper ballots against the electronic record to make sure that they're consistent.

Pegues: How many states do that currently?

Felten: It's complicated. That's a complicated question, more complicated than it should be, maybe because there are different types of randomized audits that can be done postelection. And some of them are better from a standpoint of being statistically sound.

The majority of states either don't do these postelection audits, or do ones that should be improved. That I can say. I don't want to try from memory to remember which states do this in the best way. I think it would be great to see some kind of national norm that states could agree to about what a sufficient risk-limiting audit looks like. And there are statisticians and other experts who have worked out the technical details of this. But getting states to adopt those procedures would be very helpful.

Pegues: What do you think the Russians were trying to do? I've heard that it was to cause confusion, maybe suppress the vote in some places, maybe alter data.

Felten: Without guessing about what the Russians were trying to do, I can talk about the possible things that an adversary might try to do. I would break those into two categories. The first would be to try to actually modify the result of an election, which means somehow tampering with the casting or tallying of votes in a way that is not detected.

The second thing you would worry about is attempts to disrupt the election or to undermine its legitimacy. That could include things like causing systems to not work on Election Day so that voters show up at the polls and they're not able to vote. That could include things like scrambling the voter registration databases, so when voters show up on Election Day they are told they're not on the rolls.

It could involve things like tampering with machines in ways that are detected in order to cast doubt on the outcome. All these sorts of things might either disrupt or undermine confidence in the election, and that's another scenario that one would need to worry about.

Pegues: That happened in North Carolina.

Felten: You're referring to the electronic poll books in Durham?

Pegues: Yes. US law enforcement believes Russian hackers targeted VR Election Systems, which provided voting systems to North Carolina and also most of Florida. In North Carolina, you had people showing up at the polls amid confusion about whether they could vote.

Felten: In every big national election there are some technical problems, which frustrate people in some places. The question about North Carolina in this instance is [whether] this is an example of that, or is it something that's sort of deeper and more problematic?

And I don't know whether that's the case or not, based on the public evidence I've seen. But it is a question to be asking. Also, we should be clear that the worst case, one that we would lose sleep over, would be much worse than that. It might be voting systems failing to work across a whole state. Really large-scale dislocation or disruption.

Pegues: Are the Russians, in your view, capable of something like that at this point?

Felten: As a technical matter, yes. Our nation-state adversaries are capable of those sorts of things now. Again, we need to be buttoning down the details of our systems to make sure they're as resilient as possible so that people can have confidence that we are able to detect and unwind any kind of attack that happens.

Heading into the 2018 midterm elections, confidence was lacking in the election systems across the country. Even lawmakers in Georgia were introducing legislation to change the sixteen-year-old touch screen voting machines across the state with a paper-based system. The state's twenty-seven thousand machines did not have a paper backup and had proven vulnerable to hackers.[35] Lawmakers estimated that it would cost about $25–$35 million to buy the new equipment and that it wouldn't be in place in time for the 2018 midterm elections. Other states were considering similar upgrades, but the clock was already ticking down to the next major election and the pressure was on state and federal officials to secure systems across the country.

In 2018, about seven months before the November elections, Department of Homeland Security (DHS) officials convened a meeting of state and local election members from across the country. On the weekend's agenda was a onetime-only classified briefing for the state and local officials who hadn't yet gotten security clearances. The DHS was trying to bridge the gap between what they knew about the Russian intrusions in 2016 and what state election officials knew. But it was almost as if the two sides lived in very different worlds from each other. An election official in the meeting told me several people in the room were alarmed when a federal official used an antiquated phrase to describe the voting process. The source told me the DHS official said that "the next time people go pull the levers to cast their votes. . . ." What the federal official didn't seem to know was that the statement had pulled back the curtain on the depth of what the DHS and US intelligence and law enforcement agencies did not know about how elections really work. The election official who relayed the account of the meeting to me was frustrated by the comment and insisted, "We don't pull levers anymore!" Fifteen months after the Russian government worked to disrupt the US presidential election, federal officials tasked with stopping the next influence campaign still had a lot to learn.

Chapter 29

A HOLE IN THE DIKE

O n July 12, 2016, Illinois learned that its voter registration database had been hacked by someone using a SQL (pronounced "sequel") injection—a technique through which hackers inject malware. In the Illinois case, the hackers squirmed into the system and absconded with information for over seventy thousand residents, which included driver's license numbers, names, dates of birth, and other vital information.[1]

There's a reason they are called hackers—they find holes in your system to hack into. In Illinois, the database had a glitch in the online system where residents could apply to register to vote. That is what Kevin Turner, the internet technology (IT) director for the Illinois State Board of Elections, and Kyle Thomas, director of voting and registration systems, called "the hole in the dike."[2] I wanted to interview Turner and Thomas because they were among the unlucky few state election officials whose systems had been breached. Their vulnerability became a cautionary tale for states across the country leading up to the 2016 election.

Pegues: The hackers found a weakness in the system and exploited it?

Turner: Correct. There are many ways that intruders can get into a system. In the case of Arizona, it was a breach through email, which is apples and oranges compared to what happened to us.

In our case, the intruders found the hole in the dike. We discovered that hole as soon as we discovered this degradation of database performance. We found the hole very quickly and obviously immediately plugged the hole. That was on July 12. On July 13, we thought it best to shut the system down, to analyze, "What exactly is going on? What did they get?"

This hack differed from what happened in Arizona because the Illinois State Board of Elections wasn't notified by the government.

Pegues: It was something that you call an anomaly in the system, right? It raises red flags. At that point do you go to DEFCON 5? Did you know at the time—did you have warnings from the Department of Homeland Security (DHS)—that the Russians were breaching some of these systems?

Turner: Absolutely not.

Pegues: So, you didn't know what it was?

Turner: Correct.

Thomas: No, we had no idea. There was no outreach by anybody. We still have not been officially told by anyone, other than reading news reports or watching hearings, that the Russians had any involvement with our breach.

Turner: So, therefore, we have never stated that. We, the [Illinois] State Board of Elections, have never stated that it was the Russians. I mean, that's because nobody has ever officially told us. This is an ongoing investigation with the FBI.

Pegues: Still, to this day?

Both Turner and Thomas answered yes.

RECONNAISSANCE

After finding the intrusion, Illinois election officials began the process of reconnaissance. This included letting folks know their information had been stolen. They took their database off-line for two weeks. Illinois had kept logs about the database. The logs allowed them to ascertain details about when the injection entered the system.[3]

Turner: What we discovered on the back end was that the intruders had begun looking at our system on June 23 [2016]. We had no idea they were in the system. You know, it was like a very slow drip of water. There was nothing, no red flag raised to alert us to any issues whatsoever.

It was on July 12 that they went from zero to one hundred as far as impact to our database. They were in at a two, and then on July 12 it went up to one hundred.

Pegues: Is there a reason why they may have gone to one hundred on that date?

Turner: There is nothing regarding that date that we can associate [the intrusion] with. I think they had done all their sniffing around, and apparently at that point they thought, "We're just going to go for whatever we can get." So, they sent in literally millions of database queries.

Pegues: What did they get?

Turner: Names, addresses, in some cases phone numbers, and birth dates. In some cases, the last four digits of social security numbers. In some cases, driver's license numbers.

In each election jurisdiction in the state there are a number of different vendors that the local election authorities use for their local election systems—VR, voter registration systems. The local number is unique to that jurisdiction. However, it is not unique across the state. So, in other words, John Jones in southern Illinois in jurisdiction A may have the same local election number—the same voter ID—as Jim Smith in northern Illinois, as far as the local ID number goes.

In our statewide voter registration database, everyone has a unique number in addition to that local number. We keep track of the local number, but we also have a unique ID so that in our database, no voter in the state has the same state voter ID as anyone else. They're unique. The number that these actors used was the local voter ID. That's why the information they got back, we can't be 100 percent certain to the nth degree as to exactly whose information they got.

Thomas: The bottom line of that is, as best we could tell, we came up with roughly about seventy-six thousand voters who were breached. Again, we don't know with 100 percent certainty in each of those cases exactly how much information they got.

In Illinois, we have what's called a PIPA, the Personal Information Protection Act, which required us to within— I believe it was—five days [to] notify our legislature of the breach. And there are rules set forth in that act as to how to identify or, rather, how to contact potential victims of the breach. There's a threshold in there, and if it was above five hundred thousand suspected individuals who are breached, then the entity that was breached can simply publish a press release.

Turner: A press release indicating that they had been breached. Because we fell well below that threshold, it was on us to, as best we could, contact individually each of the voters whose information was breached.

We spent several weeks doing this. We composed a letter to the suspected victims, and they were given information to contact the state attorney general's office if they suspected they were victims of identity theft. To this date, we have no evidence of anyone's identity being stolen as a result of our breach.

The hackers weren't able to manipulate or delete information. Neither election official has any idea what the hackers hoped to find in the database.

NOT A SOPHISTICATED ATTACK

I asked them if these attacks were carried out by sophisticated hackers.[4]

Turner: We've been told by the FBI and DHS that, first of all, the tool the hackers used is a common tool that intruders use to attempt to get into databases.

These kinds of tools are available on the internet. If you

have a criminal mind-set and are out to do this kind of thing, it's not difficult to obtain these tools. It's just a question of finding vulnerabilities and finding holes in dikes, so to speak. And they found a hole in ours.

Pegues: If you're saying that anyone could have done this, what does that say about election system security?

Thomas: This was a vulnerability that our system had that no longer exists. And it's not something that's common. It was a programming error that allowed this one field to be unprotected. Our systems are now scanned every week. DHS offers a scanning service where they use basically the same types of tools that hackers would use to scan public websites to find vulnerabilities. DHS is now performing that [scan] for us on a weekly basis. And since that time, they've never found any vulnerabilities within our system.

Prior to the 2016 election the DHS was not offering that service to state election officials. The Russian intrusions changed everything. It exposed weaknesses in voter databases across the country. But Illinois election officials emphasized that the voting machines themselves were not connected to the internet.

Turner: I will state though there seems to be a misunderstanding that voting machines and vote tabulation systems are connected to the internet, and are tied into voter registration systems. That is absolutely not true. In Illinois, they are two totally separate things. The voter registration database—the centralized database—at our level, and all of the databases at the local level, which feed into our database for registrations, [are different things].

Pegues: As the clock ticks toward the next election, given what happened in 2016 in terms of these voter databases—some being breached, some being scanned—are you feeling the pressure to get this right? Are you feeling the pressure for 2018?

Turner: We're doing the best we can to keep security in place. This breach was an education on our part. This was a programming error that, in one field of a public-facing website, allowed intruders to get in. We sealed that hole.

We have found no other evidence of any vulnerabilities. The DHS has, to this date, found no other evidence of any vulnerabilities. Now, I'd be a fool to sit here and say that I'm 100 percent confident that our system is totally safe. No one can state that. If they do, I guarantee you, as the FBI told us, it's not a question of if; it's a question of when.

Chapter 30

CYBER TOOLS

As we now know, Fancy Bear (aka APT28) and Cozy Bear (aka APT29) are nicknames for Russian-government-led cyber-espionage hacking units that are likely to undermine America's free election system. Their objectives look like clues from a yellowing, dog-eared Cold War spy novel.

With monikers like "bots," "troll factories," and "SQL injections," the lexicon that we have to describe our modern-day cyber tools reads like some kind of bizarre hybrid between a stark dystopian novel and languages we previously attributed largely to thirty-five-year-old gamers who live in their parents' basements.

It is tough for many people to care about computer-generated intrusions because, frankly, most of us just don't understand them. We don't understand the culture that spawned the techniques that were adapted to the twenty-first-century cyber terrain, and we don't understand the terrain itself. For people who have been spoon-fed the notion that we are the most powerful country in the world, we are surprisingly unequipped to protect and defend ourselves in cyberspace. How do we know this? Well, first of all, it happened. Russian hackers broke into the emails of political, military, and government officials and scanned and probed state voter databases.[1] Second, we don't necessarily have the resources at present to fight them. Many of our voting systems are antiquated. States struggling to recover from attacks require millions of dollars to fix these systems.[2]

In November 2017, two Democrats appealed to the House Appropriations Committee to free up about $400 million for election security upgrades in states across the country.[3] It was an acknowledgment that the states cannot carry this burden alone. Which frankly wasn't much of a shock considering what state election officials were up against. There is a disconnect between state and federal government. There has been too much inaction on this issue approaching the 2018 midterm elections. And it's not as if most members of Congress don't realize what's at stake.

Democratic congressmen Bennie Thompson of Mississippi and Robert Brady of Pennsylvania wrote in a letter to House Appropriations requesting the $400 million: "We know that Russia launched an unprecedented assault on our elections in 2016, targeting 21 states' voting systems, and we believe this money is necessary to protect our elections from future attack." They called Russia's intrusions on state election systems "an attack on our country," and warned, "We cannot leave states to defend against the sophisticated cyber tactics of state actors like Russia on their own."[4]

By then states had been "flying solo" for months. They were navigating the cybersecurity terrain against topflight Russian hackers largely without the knowledge US intelligence and law enforcement could provide if there was a coordinated response. The response was disjointed from the beginning in part because of a lack of leadership from the top. The very top. The White House. It really came down to priorities. Cybersecurity experts have testified that the $400 million will go a long way to protect voting systems. The Pentagon has been spending more than that on military musical bands.[5]

CYBERSECURITY

The job market is wide open for future cyber juggernauts, wunderkind hackers, and spies. The United States lacks the roughly three hundred thousand cybersecurity experts it needs, according to White House cybersecurity czar Rob Joyce.[6]

Until the United States beefs up its cyber forces, we must work with what we have. One of the first steps is to perhaps acknowledge our culture shock, namely, all the things we do not know. It's almost impossible to know how widespread the Russian cyberattacks really were, and how deeply embedded in US systems the Russian hackers are. These are questions we may never really know the answer to until it's too late. We'll really know—I suspect—when the power starts shutting down in some city grid, which would be similar to what happened in Ukraine.[7]

THE TROLLS

Jim Lewis, a cyber expert with the Center for Strategic and International Studies, describes how trolls aren't in fact the fictional tiny, green, blob-like creatures living under bridges in fantastical countries. Today, they are more like disgruntled government white-collar slobs who work in "troll factories where they are required to muscle into cyberspace."[8] Lewis explains that trolls are an integral technique for the Russian government to break the transatlantic alliance and destroy the world image of Western-style democracy.

> Trolls, internet trolls, are apparently not very well paid, so if they're listening, I apologize. But they sit there, and you can see it [the internet trolls] in some online newspaper.
>
> You can just tell when it's a Russian government employee posting a comment, pretending to be an American or a German or a Brit, saying, "The West is bad; Putin is good." That's basically their theme. They have thousands of people whose job it is to post comments like that [in comment sections of news reports, chat rooms, blogs, etc.]. But they have other techniques as well. And the best technique that they have used so far is to hack into databases, take sensitive information, and then leak it.[9]

He explains that trolls are a major component of information warfare. It is a "new tool they use to get political effect." Alternative names for information warfare are hybrid warfare or political warfare. "They don't need the Red Army anymore. They have the internet," he said.[10]

MALWARE

Malicious software or malware is all the bad stuff. It's a generic term used to describe all the dirty little things that could weasel their way into your computer, including programs like Trojan horses, scareware, spyware, worms, and more run-of-the-mill computer viruses that technicians charge you a small fortune to purge.

As technology becomes more sophisticated and enters our online shopping carts, we become more vulnerable. Many of us are educated and/or paranoid enough about all the ways in which our computers can set us up as marks that we're tempted to put duct tape over our webcams. Some may even pay a yearly fee for software that disguises their IP address so their location can't be tracked through their computer or phone.

The majority of folks out there are either not so savvy or not so concerned. Most are probably wary enough to install antivirus software and leave it at that.

Adam Meyers of the security firm CrowdStrike explained how malware can use seemingly ordinary methods to infect not just computers but devices connected to them, such as digital cameras, cell phones, televisions, and scanners.[11]

Imagine you buy a new wireless high-end printer. It is considered the best of its kind because it is as thin as a potato chip and 0.5 ounces lighter than the previous model and happens to be bedazzled with purple gemstones. You take it out of the box. Experience has taught you that the setup process is less complicated if you don't read the three-page instruction pamphlet with its half-inch text. So, you plug the device in and run through your own version of the setup process, and, boom, it's connected to the internet and you are ready for business. You elect not to create an elaborate, unique username and password because you are sick of passwords. Besides, creating one requires that you type all of your personal information into the printing company's website. You are leery about giving away your personal information that could be used for goodness knows what nefarious purpose, ranging from trying to get you to buy more equipment to selling your name to the highest bidder. Finally, you aren't really great at remembering new passwords and are just as likely to lock yourself out of being able to use the machine as to prevent someone else from getting in. You leave it on the default settings. You are sure signing up would come back to bite you in the bum.

Then one day you realize you should have. A "botnet" has found it and has started to inject its own code into it. Your machine is now a delivery device for malware.

BOTNET

Mirai (aka the Future)

On October 26, 2016, a massive take-no-prisoners cyberattack took down Dyn, a company that takes care of the entire web's domain name system, which lasted for the better part of the afternoon and took down major websites including Netflix, Reddit, and CNN. This kind of attack is known as a distributed denial of service (DDoS) attack. It uses a beast called a botnet to overwhelm a server with traffic until it buckles. Another name for it is an exhaustion attack.[12]

In this case the botnet being used was a special kind of apocalyptic beast called Mirai, which means "the future" in Japanese. Mirai is distinguished from other botnets because it is not just made up of computer parts. Rather, it is made up of "the internet of things," a mishmash of salvaged junk parts from devices like digital cameras and DVD players. This quality makes Mirai a supercharged botnet, which could commit sustained large-scale attacks on multiple "endpoints" with a speed equivalent to a peregrine falcon dive-bombing a pigeon—that's 1.2 terabytes per second in internet talk, an exceptionally high speed.[13]

Another extraordinary element of Mirai is that anyone can get the source code for free. The person who created it claimed to have already made enough money in the lucrative DDoS business and wanted to get out, so the creator put Mirai on open source, which means that essentially anyone who wanted it could use it both as a revenue-generating tool and as a nifty little manual for carrying out a cyberattack.[14]

Meyers also provides the nitty description of a DDoS attack. "It means that when you're attacking a target you distribute the load of the attack across many different hosts [devices]. So, what they do is infect lots of different hosts across the internet and then use those infected hosts to then target the actual end victim."[15] That certainly makes it easier to understand.

Mirai was thought to be a dry run. Its unusual attributes were its strength and the manner in which it was released. Meyers believes the botnet was released "to make a statement about the capability, showing that the capability exists."[16]

Cyber forensic investigators examining the Mirai bot's code found that much of it was written in Russian. By the way, the code also included the sentence, "I love chicken nuggets."[17] Some of these highly skilled hackers seem to have a fairly juvenile sense of humor.

Meyers explained how a botnet like Mirai could be used to impact an election: "If you plan to be broadcasting during the election, this could be used to disrupt signals; it could be used to disrupt your website. During the actual election, depending on what the targets might be, you could use this to disrupt voting stations or the infrastructure involved in tallying votes."[18]

On election night 2016, CBS News and other news organizations were prepping for the potential of that type of attack. Imagine an election night—you're watching your favorite channel, and all of a sudden the numbers start scrambling. The anchor can't figure out what's happening. The IT staff can't figure it out either. Viewers are left puzzled, and doubt starts creeping in about the results, even if the station has these results in some form of a hard copy. Do you trust those numbers? See how damaging any type of cyberattack on an election night could be?

OTHER NIFTY BOTS

Social Bots

When Clint Watts, a Robert A. Fox fellow in the Foreign Policy Research Institute, provided expert testimony before the Senate

Intelligence Committee on Russian information operations, he detailed ways in which Russian operatives may use social media in espionage efforts. The former FBI agent also noted that social bots can be created, replicating "the appearance and speech of the target audience making unwitting observers more likely to engage with and believe the falsehoods they spread. Social bots play on this psychology broadcasting at such high volumes [of hits or views] it makes falsehoods appear more credible." Social bots can be manufactured at "social media sweatshops."[19]

Watts explains how Kremlin-hired hackers can create social bots and inject storylines into not just the web browsing of an unsuspecting public but also the social intercourse of people who should know better, namely influencers such as reporters, political figures, and CEOs of major companies. The dummy narratives arrive in their newsfeeds or emails. In this manner, the public and private sectors can be duped into believing lies told by imaginary people they meet on their screens. In spreading these fake stories, these people can ruin their own reputations. The news these deceitful dummy personas carry can easily replace or usurp what is real news, or influence new policies and legislation.

SATURATION

Social media content is more trusted when it comes from close relations like friends and family. By exploiting these relationships, social bots can create Facebook groups, personas, and pages to saturate social and political discussions with "divisive content designed to enrage competing poles of the US electorate," Watts said.[20] One fake Facebook ad posted by Russian "trolls" came from a group called Stop All Invaders. It showed photos of a woman wearing Islamic religious head covering, and urged followers to stop the spread of sharia law. Yet another ad said, "Down with Hillary!" and it promoted a rally outside Clinton campaign headquarters in Brooklyn.[21]

LAUNDERING

The technique of laundering information that we learned about in chapter 24 when the Russian government tried to discredit Dr. Martin Luther King is less cumbersome to pull off in the information age. Laura Rosenberger, director of the Alliance for Securing Democracy, explains how it works: "Something that will come from Russia—a piece of disinformation or misinformation—will be laundered through covert networks, [such as] the social media or online media environment, so that people can't really tell where it's come from. And then it ends up getting picked up sometimes in credible news sources. And, people don't have any idea where that information has come from."[22] Case in point, in August 2016 there was an active shooter scare at New York's JFK International Airport. At CBS News we were following the story because we saw people on Twitter posting messages about it. But we couldn't figure out if that threat was real. It turns out Russian fake-news writers on social media added to the panic.[23]

Rosenberger detailed a famous case in Germany. A thirteen-year-old Russian/German girl named "Lisa" was reported missing from her home. When she returned home with a bruised face, it was reported that she had been raped by three men who were Muslims.[24] Before the story could be corroborated, Kremlin-controlled print, television, and social media ran with it. This resulted in massive protests against refugees, holding German chancellor Angela Merkel's refugee policy accountable. Among the protestors were members of German right-wing radical groups.[25]

The girl later admitted she lied. But German officials believe the Russian media exploited the situation and controversy, surrounding policies allowing nearly a million asylum seekers into Germany, in order to further discredit Merkel—who opposed Russia's interference in Ukraine.

Rosenberger explains the German government's response. "Now as a consequence in Germany in fact—there's a very high level of awareness about this potential challenge. I don't think we've had quite that kind of 'aha' moment in the United States. And that's not to say I think Germany is totally protected against this either. But it's just to say that that kind of laundering certainly happens. And the media often enough allows that to happen more easily."[26]

Examples of laundering that have occurred in the United States since then include the false news that spread about hate crimes in Idaho, or the Antifa intifada that was picked up by RT.

Vice highlighted an uptick in fake Antifa accounts claiming to belong to the anti-fascist movement that were actually operated out of Russia.[27] In Idaho Russian trolls used Facebook events to set up anti-immigrant protests. The Russians were using false identities to do it.[28] What may have started on social media was then picked up by RT. The Russian-government-backed news network would then trumpet the divisions in the United States to its audience.

Some call cyber laundering propaganda. Watts calls it forgery. He notes how digital forgeries can be distributed through sites laden with conspiracy theories, such as Reddit and 4Chan, and are often far superior to the KGB's active measures efforts at clunky forgeries that were spread using antiquated equipment (wire services and the postal service), which could take years to have an impact and didn't offer much return on their investment. He notes how forgeries can be used by anonymous sources in "smear campaigns and falsehoods that tarnish confidence in America and trust in democratic institutions." He further notes that they can be used strategically to "support conspiracies" and "support anti-government narratives or enflame social divisions in America."[29]

PHISHING

We have seen how a seemingly innocuous email was sent to officials— such as the Arizona secretary of state administrator living in a rural location—and used like bait on a hook to phish out their usernames and passcodes and sell them online. As I reported on CBS News in October 2016, the Arizona worker opened an email attachment and just like that the Russian hackers were into the computer network. The Russian intrusion then spread, endangering Arizona's election infrastructure.[30]

The Russian operation took many different approaches in its attack on democracy. It saturated social media, and by infecting social media it indirectly seeped into the mainstream news cycle. Early on some people in important positions saw the warning signs and spoke out. One person in particular realized that she could not take on the Russians alone.

Chapter 31

SHOULD WE TRUST THEM?

OCTOBER 2016

People traveling into Arizona may first look for the beautiful oddities in the land—giant saguaro fruit-bearing cacti with their twenty-five-foot spiky arms, coyotes walking ancient salt trails, and watermelon-colored sunsets bleeding along the flat expanse of the Sonora.

I am not one of those people. When I am not scoping out a city for a golf course to explore, I am generally viewing a city or state through the lens of its news coverage. I try to see every new place I travel to like an archeologist who has returned to our lost civilization after it has collapsed, to dust off artifacts and try and figure out how we lived. Just as I love to figure out what drives people's personalities, I love to figure out what drives us as a society. That year while I recognized we were on the brink of some kind of major shift, that passion to know how we got to this place as a nation became stronger. Simultaneously, like everyone else, I was feeling a bit of dread.

As my producer Andy and I drove into the eerie, grid-like Arizona metropolitan area demarcated with strip malls, I thought about how Maricopa County sheriff Joe Arpaio's tough war on crime and his anti-immigration projects had made headlines.

These included the world's only female chain gang where women linked by ankle weights limped along the side of the road, performing disconcerting tasks like burying unclaimed bodies, and Tent City, an outdoor jail just south of downtown Phoenix, which Arpaio himself once "jokingly" referred to as a concentration camp.[1]

Tent City held undocumented immigrants, the majority of whom had committed minor crimes like shoplifting, using drugs, or working illegally. The men were housed in green Korean War–era tents in temperatures that could spike to over 120 degrees, and wore black-and-white-striped uniforms with pink underwear and pink socks to humiliate them.[2]

Arpaio often expressed pride in Tent City, and publicly made fun of the men in press conferences.[3] Arpaio fielded nearly a dozen lawsuits in connection to mistreatment of prisoners, which, in more than a handful of cases, led to death.[4] It was the subject of numerous human rights violation charges by Amnesty International and other organizations. Still by the time I traveled through Arizona in October 2016, it was in its twenty-third year of operation.

Perhaps I reflected on Arpaio because his immigration policies were a harbinger of things to come. A Department of Justice (DOJ) investigation, which concluded in 2013, found that the Maricopa County Sheriff's Office had engaged in a "pattern of misconduct that violates the Constitution and federal law."[5] Some of the activities flagged by the DOJ included racial profiling of Latinos at traffic stops, use of excessive force, and retaliation against those who spoke up against the practices. Although the DOJ ordered the Maricopa County Sheriff's Office to stop the practices, they continued. Arpaio's last year as sheriff was 2016, but in 2017 he was convicted of criminal contempt of court for refusing to cease those activities, a crime that he was pardoned for a month later by President Trump.[6] He would go on to announce that he was running for Senate.[7]

For years Arpaio had been operating outside the rules of the game, in the eyes of his critics stepping out of the boundaries of the Constitution. This was exactly the kind of thing that was contributing to the rift that was ultimately making us vulnerable to attack.

We pulled into the parking lot of Arizona's State House, where I would be conducting an interview with Secretary of State Michele Reagan about breaches in Arizona's voter databases. We got our gear and approached the building, a tall, silo-like concrete building on a compound with gravel planters in the parking lot, and a few scraggly-looking trees. The sun was bright. The heat was oppressive, and the air was thick with haze that wavered like grease over a griddle.

I was looking forward to the interview. Although I had only spoken with Reagan on the phone, she seemed deeply concerned about the breaches in the database in a way that transcended politics or party.

Reagan, like former Maricopa County sheriff Joe Arpaio, is a conservative Republican who was elected in the same conservative Republican state. She even shares some of the same kinds of controversial views. For example, she cosponsored state senate bill SB 1070, which was an immigration law that could be viewed as allowing racial profiling.[8] She voted to have Arizona define marriage as a union exclusively between a man and a woman.[9] I was pretty sure she understood that what we would be talking about transcended politics. Also, she seemed to be someone with integrity who always played within the rules.

THE MOON LANDING

The secretary of state's main office was on the seventh floor of a nine-story tower sandwiched between two floors of the governor's office, and the whole floor was under construction. The walls had been opened, and whole sections were cordoned off.

Reagan introduced herself and laughed as our crew started laying out our self-contained, pop-up moveable studio, pulling up lights and working around us. "We call it our moon landing," one crew member told her.

As I got to know her, Reagan surprised me with her down-to-earth, self-described "happy-go-lucky" personality. I was relieved to notice that she wasn't tightly wound. She explained how most people who have reached a certain level of government are more scripted.

"My greatest strength is also my biggest liability, and that is that I am a completely regular person," she later said. She explained how this personality disarms individuals. "I've had people actually show up to events I was going to be at with the intention of heckling me, and then they hear me and they say, 'Wow, she's cool.'"[10]

Reagan's down-to-earth nature and political integrity were sustained throughout a year of utter political chaos. She did what she thought was right when she first learned that her office's computers had been hacked in late June 2016, prompting her to seek out the federal government's help.[11]

She also did what she believed was right a year later, in July 2017, when she refused a request by Trump's Commission on Electoral Integrity for the names, social security numbers, dates of birth, and maiden names of persons from Arizona's voter registration rolls.[12] The commission was created by the Trump administration to review supposed claims of voter fraud, after Trump alleged that millions of immigrants voted when they were not legally allowed to do so. These supposed immigrant voters cost Trump the popular vote, according to Trump. Reagan refused to hand over her state's voter info because she believed the request was illegal, would be ineffective, and because doing so could pose a legitimate cybersecurity threat. Reagan, like most secretaries of state, knew very little about cybersecurity prior to Arizona's voting systems being hacked. In just a year, she had become more of an expert.

THE VIRTUOSO

Reagan's story began in June 2016, when she got a call from the FBI alerting her that the username and password of one of her officials was on sale on the dark web.[13] The dark web is the underbelly of the World Wide Web. You can't gain access to it without specialized software. There are covert sites within the dark web that can't be accessed through a search engine. Someone must provide you with the specific site address. There are a myriad of criminal activities that can be accessed through the dark web, ranging from "darknet markets" where you can buy anything from crystal meth to an AK-47 to an assassin to a human-trafficked woman.[14] It isn't a place where a government agency would want its email to end up.

The hacker had obtained the information by phishing, sending a seemingly ordinary email to the official, which appeared to be from a constituent looking for help.[15] The FBI further informed Reagan that they believed the hacker was from Russia, and was a virtuoso of sorts, having achieved a rating on their hacker scale of 8 out of 10. In other words, the hacker was very good. Eventually, the initial phishing expedition opened the door for a more serious breach. According to Reagan, she was told the voter database had been hacked too. She explained what her first reaction was when she learned that the Russians had hacked into the system.

> Shock and dismay, obviously because this is the reality of a foreign entity, outside intruders if you will, coming into our state and wanting to mess with our election system, wanting to play around and make people feel unsafe.[16]

Arizona, like many of the other states whose databases were being hacked, didn't know exactly what to do. Reagan allowed the FBI and Department of Homeland Security (DHS) to step in. She called in Arizona's cyber troops, a cybersecurity team she later discovered they were lucky to have (not all states have them). The team took Arizona's voter registration off-line to be analyzed for what was supposed to be two days. Two days turned into five, and five into seven.

"We decided to keep it off-line for ten days," Reagan said, "to allow multiple jurisdictions to go through and check it for us because we really wanted to make sure 1) was any information stolen; 2) was any information altered, because that would be just as bad if not worse; and 3) probably the very worst scenario would be if some virus was inserted into the system. So, we were looking for quite a few things before we put [the system] back up. The look on your face is exactly what I felt—it was horrible."[17]

In the ensuing months, Reagan's office put into place eighteen precautionary measures that the DHS and the FBI laid out. She learned other nifty terms unique to cyber espionage, such as cyber hygiene (the steps organizations take to protect against cyberattacks), malware, and trolls.

> These were things that people had never heard of before. Before this attack happened to us, I never heard of the dual-factor authentication; I'd never heard of SQL injections. Who would have heard of these things? I mean we're busy on the ground trying to register people to vote, trying to get them involved in ballot propositions

or learning about different candidates; we're not worried about Russian hackers. Now that's something we need to be worried about, and that again is why I'm so focused on educating other people who, fortunately, haven't had this happen to them, that this is something they do need to also worry about.[18]

They found certain quick fixes: for example, avoid a SQL injection, which is the placement of malicious codes into SQL statements when a site asks a user for input (such as insert your name), via web page, and don't use an exclamation point or a colon when you are entering your name into an address bar—all of which introduce vulnerabilities.

Arizona hired three new IT staff members, which is basically all they could afford. Although Reagan declined to give a hard figure on how much improving cybersecurity could cost, she noted that it wasn't as much as in other states. She admitted, though, that even if her office received just an extra million in the following year's $10 million budget, it would help a lot.[19]

"That's real money," she said, "and when you have an IT staff that's running all of that, over eighty thousand web pages for all of these different divisions, adding a couple of IT people is a big deal in a tiny government agency. I will say again, we don't have the resources of a Pentagon, and we shouldn't be expected to have the resources to fight these kinds of global terrorist threats via the internet. This is a new territory for us."[20]

Unlike some other states, Arizona was assured that the hackers hadn't reached its databases. After the investigation concluded, Arizona's voter registration database went back online. Reagan said that she was confident intrusions wouldn't compromise their election integrity.

Simultaneously, Reagan admitted that the state was reeling from the prospect of protecting the data of its nearly four million voters. Even with the federal government's help, probing continued in Arizona throughout the fall. In September 2016, Reagan learned that the state's systems had 192,000 "intrusions" or "unknown attempts" with 11,000 being deemed so suspicious they were immediately blocked. "That's just in one month," she said, "and this just in a tiny state agency, so I guess what I'm saying is, we need to speak out about how big the scope of this is. We need to recognize that this is something we need to be vigilant about, very diligent about."[21] They continued to seek out help from the DHS and Arizona's DHS, and to partner with "anybody who has best practices," while they waited for the following year's budget allocations.

When other secretaries of state contacted her, asking if they should trust the federal government, she understood their concerns. Reagan said that many states believed federal help came with strings attached.

> The right of states to hold their own elections is baked into our Constitution, and that is something that states protect fiercely, and so states aren't going to want to give it up. I can understand why people aren't going to go running to the federal government saying, "Here's my database, please look it over for me." I can understand that. . . .
>
> Now, going forward, I have the choice of just washing my hands of it and sticking my head in the sand and saying this isn't going to happen again, or saying what are the best practices that the federal government recommends, what are the best practices that my state Department of Homeland Security recommends, and implementing them.
>
> Of course, I'm going to choose . . . those best practices and how I, as an elected official, how can I best protect my state voters. I think that's prudent. I think that crosses party lines. I urge other people to consider doing the same, just as I urge the federal government if states come to you for help, don't put strings on it, just let's all partner together to help each other.[22]

Reagan reiterated that she understood that other states may not necessarily trust the federal government, but that this was a unique situation: "I liken it to when you're being invaded by Russia; you don't decide not to call in your National Guard. At some point you have to say, I need the army, and that's the reality we're living in right now."[23]

I spoke to Reagan again in January 2018 following the controversy when she refused to comply with certain clauses in a letter that Kris

W. Kobach, vice chair of the Presidential Advisory Committee on Election Integrity, sent to her on June 28, 2017, and to all secretaries of state asking for information on their election processes, voter fraud, and election-related crimes that occurred in their states and information about their voters. The letter included these words:[24]

> In addition, in order for the Commission to fully analyze vulnerabilities and issues related to voter registration and voting, I am requesting that you provide to the Commission the publicly-available voter roll data for [Arizona], including, if publicly available under the laws of your state, the full first and last names of all registrants, middle names or initials if available, addresses, dates of birth, political party (if recorded in your state), last four digits of social security number if available, voter history (elections voted in) from 2006 onward, active/inactive status, cancelled status, information regarding any felony convictions, information regarding voter registration in another state, information regarding military status, and overseas citizen information.[25]

It was a lot of personal information to just hand over.

President Trump established the commission in May 2017 to investigate whether his claims that three to five million people committed voter fraud in the 2016 election were substantiated. Vice President Mike Pence chaired the commission.[26]

Although several dozen secretaries of state (including Reagan) refused to comply with the ruling altogether, others submitted partial information.[27] The establishment of the commission also led to several lawsuits: for example, Maine's secretary of state Matthew Dunlap joined the commission and then later sued it to find out what it was doing.[28] In January 2018, the commission was terminated.[29]

Many secretaries of state didn't mince words when refusing to send the information. For instance, Mississippi's representative Delbert Hosemann, a Republican, told the commission to "jump in the Gulf of Mexico."[30] Reagan spoke about why she chose not to cooperate with the federal government's request when her agency's computers had been hacked.

While Reagan says she agreed with the commission's overall

goal—finding out if there was fraud in the system—she didn't agree with the way the commission was going about it, namely, asking for identifying voter information wholesale. She distinguishes her reasoning from that of various Democratic secretaries of state who basically asserted, "We're not sending our information because this is an attempt to suppress voters."[31] Reagan describes the Republican state officials' response this way: "Our philosophy, a number of your Republican ones, is, we're not sending the information, but it's rooted in conservative values and has nothing to do with us thinking they're trying to do something nefarious. It's just that what they're asking for isn't going to do any good."

Instead Reagan, like Hosemann and a select group of fifteen Republican secretaries of state, sent a letter to the commission suggesting alternative ways to investigate alleged voter fraud. They never heard back. "I mean, this wasn't rooted in anti-Trump thought," Reagan explained. "This was [us saying], 'Hey, what you're asking for isn't going to work. Here's some things you could do.'"[32]

Reagan based her decision on a few factors. Foremost among them was that her constituents voiced their objections. Her office received nearly a thousand emails from voters, some angry and others heartfelt, imploring her not to send their information. Many threatened to withdraw their voter registrations. Reagan said that she never had any intention of sending all the requested information, since it was illegal.

> I tried explaining the facts to people. "Here's what we can send; here's what we can't send. Here's the process for public records requests that somebody has to do, according to a lawsuit that was just settled in our state between Project Vote and Arizona."
>
> Sometimes facts are boring. So, I started saying exactly what I really believed. Since when do conservative folks want their information sent to the federal government to be put in [a] database? I mean, isn't this something we're supposed to be completely against?
>
> And how would you have felt if Barack Obama had asked for this information? And I started saying to people on the radio, "You would have lit your hair on fire."[33]

We spoke for a while about these strange times we're living in. We discussed Reagan's new website, See the Money, which actually has the capability to use artificial intelligence, and which tracks politicians' budgets, spending, and donations in a transparent manner so that the public can see what they are doing.

I asked Reagan if she believed that this particular point in time had the potential to be a watershed moment in terms of the American elections and maintaining the credibility of the system. Reagan explained how this is a defining moment in history, but that some people are stuck in an old mind-set and don't see the way our systems are changing.

> There are some people that are still looking at this as just Y2K. But Y2K was a one-time event. Y2K was a computer bug [that] programmers believed may have caused computer web systems to collapse on January 1, 2000, and beyond, causing systems ranging from banking to energy to collapse and causing massive chaos. Some believed it would cause an apocalyptic-type reaction in society, a sentiment echoed by *Time* magazine's January 18, 1999, cover story entitled "The End of the World."
>
> This is something we're going to be dealing with [for some time].
>
> We're still going to be dealing with foreign hackers; we're still going to be dealing with cyber terrorism. It's still going to be there. Let's get in front of it.[34]

The Commission for Voter Integrity was a sign of our very strange times. Simultaneously, federal investigators who had looked into the wunderkind hack that had occurred in states, including Arizona, put up barriers. Reagan had cooperated fully with their investigation, but had been kept out of the loop. She didn't know what they were doing with her state's information, nor did she know if they had reached any kind of conclusion about what the hackers were doing with that information.

They had also given her conflicting accounts of what had actually happened. I learned in early October 2017, about sixteen months after the voter database in Arizona had been hacked, that federal

officials were telling Arizona election officials that suspected criminals had actually been behind the breach, not the Russian government. They were also told, according to my sources close to the
investigation, that the suspected criminal hackers had targeted the
Phoenix Public Library.

Arizona election officials were frustrated by what they were
hearing. They didn't believe federal officials were being transparent.
So they considered responding publicly in a blog to what they had
been told privately. The blog said, "The Secretary of State's office met
with DHS officials earlier this week to discuss alleged intelligence
reports that the Russian government attempted to 'scan' (i.e. search
for weaknesses or access points) in the statewide voter registration
system in 2016. (Note: this meeting was intended to discuss alleged
new information and was completely unrelated to why the Secretary
of State's office briefly shut down the statewide voter registration
database in June 2016). Despite initial reports to the contrary, DHS
could not confirm that any attempted Russian government attack
occurred whatsoever to any election-related system in Arizona, much
less the statewide voter registration database. Thus, while we will
continue to forge a strong partnership with DHS on cybersecurity
issues, we consider Arizona not to be one of the 21 states whose electoral systems were allegedly targeted by the Russian government in
2016."[35] In April 2018, a Trump administration official told Reuters
that suspected criminals were behind the Arizona breach.[36] I wanted
to know more, so I pressed Secretary of State Reagan about her reaction to this new information.[37]

> **Pegues:** Going back to the breach, what were the Russians trying
> to do in Arizona?
>
> **Reagan:** Well, we've been . . . asked by a federal agency to not
> use the term "Russian," but, instead, use the term "foreign,"
> because they can't confirm that it was Russia. It went through
> a server in Ukraine, but that doesn't mean that it emanated
> or started from that area. These folks, as you probably know,
> go through multiple servers to hide their true identity. . . . We
> got the word "Russian" from newspaper reports *and* from
> something that the FBI put out later [in 2016]. Later, in

meetings with Homeland Security and with the FBI, again in 2017—and those were separate meetings—both of them said, "We'd appreciate you not saying 'Russian.'" And I said, "Well, I only said it because it was reported, because it came from something you guys put out." And they said, "Yes, there is no hard confirmation that we can give you that it was the Russians." So, we started using the word "foreign."

Pegues: Were you surprised by that?

Reagan: That was the part of the meeting that we were very surprised about. And, you know, we asked if they knew a little more of where it was coming from or what their [the hackers'] intentions were, [and] what were they trying to do. Were they trying to steal information? Were they trying to sell information? Were they trying to scramble or destroy information? Because if you really want to mess up an election, that would be the way to do it.

You know, people go to the polls, and all of a sudden you're not Jeff anymore; your name is John Smith, and you're registered at a different address. That's probably the biggest thing we were worried about. I didn't get any answer on what that was. I pitched an idea that that was what I thought was [happening], or could have been [happening]. I said, "Have you considered this?" They did not confirm or deny that they had considered it.

Pegues: You also asked federal officials if the scanning and probing of the voter database was connected to the Russian manipulation of Facebook and Twitter ads or posts tailored toward people in a specific age bracket, income level, or who worked for a specific company. It makes sense that the Russians might look into this constituency's tastes or world framework, and tailor ads to hook them on a certain candidate or beliefs.

Reagan: Yes. Right around the time [secretaries of state] were having these meetings with the FBI and with Homeland Security, and I asked them about reports that had come out where Facebook and Twitter came forward and said that there were Russian groups buying ads. Well, in the work that we've done at the secretary of state's office, and the work that various campaigns do, it's no secret that targeting messages [is] a lot more effective than just throwing an ad up on Facebook. I mean, it's targeted, that's the name of the game these days.

What's a better place to get a treasure trove of information about the way people lean and where they live? Does this particular city lean this way or that way? You go to the voter records. I did not get a confirmation or a denial on [my speculation]. That was just talking, and everyone just kind of looked at me.

Pegues: Well, that's another reason why you really have to keep this data safe and secure.

Reagan: Exactly. It was interesting that all of this was coming on the heels of a request, also from the federal government, to just send [information] over.

I thought about everything I had learned from Reagan. Before I'd interviewed her, I understood, theoretically, what affected states might be contending with. Reagan's interview was more impactful; it hit home. A state office under construction in the middle of the Arizona desert has its information sent over the dark web. When they were willing to cooperate, they were provided assistance that helped them come up with a reconnaissance strategy.

After speaking with Reagan, a second time, I had a fuller understanding of why all those states that had refused federal intervention prior to the election did so. Politicians skirting the rules could be negligent and could willfully or inadvertently disregard voters' rights. State officials believed they had the right to be protective of their voters' information. Simultaneously, it struck me that by this point in history there wasn't more trust between the states and the federal government. They couldn't seem to work effectively together.

Chapter 32

THINGS HAVE GONE HORRIBLY AWRY

MAY 15, 2017

I wondered where James Clapper fit into the equation as my crew and I made our way into the Renaissance Washington Hotel in Dupont Circle. Clapper had recently announced that he was resigning from his post as director of national intelligence and was stepping down on January 20, 2017. Even on his way out, critics never let him forget his statements to the Senate Intelligence Committee in March 2013. When asked whether US intelligence agencies were covertly collecting data on millions of Americans, he replied, "No, sir, not wittingly," and "There are cases where they could inadvertently, perhaps collect, but not wittingly."[1] Three months later, former NSA contractor Edward Snowden leaked documents that revealed Clapper wasn't telling the truth.

There were two camps on Clapper's testimony. His critics, some of whom were on Capitol Hill, believed he was overtly lying, and thus was indirectly responsible for allowing illegal activities to continue in violation of citizens' Fourth Amendment rights. They haven't forgiven him. Others in the intelligence community believed Clapper was using language to skirt lines and keep from perjuring himself while trying to safeguard information critical to national security. Clapper had served his country for half a century, capping his career in government between 2010 and 2017 as director of national intelligence.

In early 2017, he had been briefing President Trump, and just prior to the inauguration he had briefed President Obama on the Russia investigation. That's why we wanted to speak with him soon after he left office, while his recollections of the Russia investigation were still fresh in his mind. We sat down for this interview in the days after FBI director James Comey was fired.

I made my way up the elevator to the suite where we would be interviewing Clapper. My producer Andy Triay and I had gone over a list of key points he wanted me to hit upon. These included such things as the manner in which Comey was fired, what former national security advisor Michael Flynn's motivations may have been when he misled the vice president about his interactions with Russian ambassador Sergey Kislyak, the extent of Russian involvement in the election, and whether Clapper had seen evidence of collusion between the Trump campaign and/or the Trump White House and Russia. Andy and I were usually pretty much on the same page when it came to what questions to ask, but I always appreciated his input. At that point, the politics of the country was seemingly becoming a macabre soap opera, and trying to keep track of who lied about what and who was in cahoots with whom was becoming tougher. In that kind of environment, I appreciated Andy's input even more.

Clapper and one of his aides arrived. I introduced myself to him, and within a few minutes the interview began. I was anxious to get his take on the Russia investigation given that he had seen the underlying intelligence from the FBI, CIA, and NSA that helped launch the investigation.[2]

> **Pegues:** Let's talk about Michael Flynn. What happened with him? I know that people who work with him say that something changed. You know, he was obviously out on the campaign trail and an ardent supporter of President Trump. Did something change with him?
>
> **Clapper:** First of all, I think you have to recognize Mike's very distinguished service in the army. Thirty years—months and months and months of deployments in the war zone both in Iraq and Afghanistan. . . .

I've known Mike a long time. I was a co-officiant at his promotion ceremony at the Women's Memorial in 2011 when he was promoted to lieutenant general. He worked with me at the Office of [the] Director [of] National Intelligence for about eleven months, I think. He did fine. I supported him strongly to be the director of [the] DIA [Defense Intelligence Agency] position that I held in the early '90s. But for reasons I won't go into here, it just didn't work out. He stayed for another six months or so, so he could finish three years' service as a lieutenant general, which is the minimum standard for qualifying for retirement in that grade. I lost touch with him after that. My impression is he changed.

Pegues: What do you think changed him? Was it that he was fired?

Clapper: I don't know. That could be. I'm speculating. I really don't know whether he just became angry about it. I don't know.

Pegues: Based on what you know about the public information that's out there now, that the [acting attorney general] Sally Yates ran over to the White House to warn White House officials that Flynn was compromised and yet the White House waited eighteen days [to fire Flynn], would you have waited eighteen days?

Clapper: Again, I'm not going to second-guess what they do. The suggestion was that the White House wanted to ensure due process for Mike Flynn. I can't comment on what their internal dialogue or processes were because my knowledge of White House operations stopped on the twentieth of January.

Pegues: But would you have felt comfortable [with] someone in your office who was alleged to have been compromised by the Russians? Would you have felt comfortable . . . sharing secrets with them?

Clapper: Compromise or not, I would be concerned about the nature of any engagement with an employee of mine if I were aware of engagement with Russians. I'd be concerned about that.

By the end of 2016, Flynn had been indicted and then cut a deal to cooperate with the Russia investigation special counsel Robert

Mueller.[3] Flynn was a key figure in unraveling whether there was coordination between the Trump campaign and the Russians. He could also help investigators determine if the president was trying to cover something up by keeping him on in the White House despite warnings from the acting attorney general. That day in May, Clapper really wanted to discuss the Russian intrusions.

> **Clapper:** That to me is the big message here. The Russians have a long history of messing with elections, both theirs and other people's. . . . There's a history in our election system [of Russian interference] going back to the '60s. But this is the most aggressive, direct assertiveness that we've ever seen. If there's ever been a clarion call for vigilance and action to thwart these Russian activities, boy, this is it.
>
> **Pegues:** Do you think this country has been wounded by what happened over the last two years?
>
> **Clapper:** I do. I think this is an assault on our institutions. And certainly the most hallowed of those, or among the most hallowed, is our election process. The intelligence community didn't reach a judgment on the extent, whether or to what extent, [that] what they did influenced the outcome of the election.
>
> We can't say that. But just [look at] the fact that they interfered and the variety of techniques they used. Not just hacking, but social media and fake news and the standard, classical propaganda, however sophisticated, from the RT network. This campaign they put together is quite aggressive and multifaceted.

Just five days before my interview with Clapper, President Trump welcomed two top Russian officials in the Oval Office. Russian foreign minister Sergei Lavrov along with then Russian ambassador to the United States Sergey Kislyak walked into the White House and Oval Office as if they were taking a victory lap. They smiled and joked while shaking hands with President Trump. We know that only because of the photographs that were released by Russia's state news agency. The White House only allowed a Russian photographer in the meeting. Which is highly unusual. But that wasn't the only thing that caught the national media's attention. During the meeting, which happened a day after the firing of FBI director James Comey, Trump told the Russian officials that firing Comey had relieved "great pressure" on him. He also said, "I just fired the head of the F.B.I. He was crazy, a real nut job."[4] To cap things off, Trump also leaked highly classified intelligence about an ISIS bomb plot to the Russian officials.[5] That must have been music to the ears of Kislyak, who is at the center of the Russia investigation because of his contacts with Trump campaign officials during the 2016 election. The *Washington Post* wrote that "sitting presidents do not usually host foreigners linked to major scandals in their own administration."[6]

After the images of the meeting were made public by Russia's state news agency, I asked some sources at the FBI and in intelligence circles how they felt about the meeting in the Oval Office, and I remember one source saying that people in the office just laughed. Four months into the new administration, I think they were stunned by the degree to which the Russians must have been celebrating over how successful their influence campaign was at getting what they wanted—including a meeting in the Oval Office.

But Clapper was not amused.[7]

Pegues: After the photo op in the Oval Office with Kislyak, Lavrov laughing with the president, how do you think the Russians feel now?

Clapper: They have to be feeling pretty good about their situation and where they are with us.

Pegues: I talked to intelligence, former national, and current officials and law enforcement who looked at that photograph and some people laughed at it. Some people were disturbed by it. What was your reaction?

Clapper: I guess you can put me in the latter camp. I was bothered by it.

Chapter 33

THE NEW PLAYING FIELD

We have come a long way from the days when Michael Hayden first pulled out the National Security Agency's (NSA) desktop keyboard and hacked into elite foreign networks at the dawn of the information age. The ribbon had just been cut on the playing field. The rule book was as implied and undefined as the spycraft profession itself.

We are in the throes of a wild—some would say ridiculous—incarnation of that age now. Computers and the internet have become more the norm than television sets in the modern home; people log more screen time when typing out their own versions of current events. Newspapers are going the way of the T-Rex (but not Georgia's Diebold AccuVote TS), and we have a president who communicates with the American public almost exclusively through his Twitter feed.

Speaking of Twitter, false rumors on the site, which requires you to boil your thoughts into 140 (recently raised to 240) characters with hashtags, have been responsible for massive shifts in the stock market. Twitter also caused the president of Egypt to shut down the great pyramid due to false rumors involving a Masonic cult that would gather there.[1]

Terrorists have used Facebook as a method to recruit young, disenfranchised, would-be suicide bombers across the globe. Military drones have replaced humans on the front lines, and everything is becoming so technologically advanced that former director of the CIA John Brennan can sometimes give himself a headache worrying about alien intelligence.[2]

In the midst of our dependency on social media, we are vulnerable to attack. This was proven to us when our election system was compromised—not just in places where we might expect such attacks would occur (for example, in our antiquated voting booths) but through computer networks at the White House and across all of our states. We learned about all the divisions in our society that increased those vulnerabilities: the widening divisions between Democrats and Republicans, rich and poor, divisions based on race and citizenship status, divisions between counties and states, as well as state and federal governments when it came to holding elections.

Now what? That is the question. What resources do we have to defend ourselves against the Russian-government-supported intruders (or any other government's hackers) who are likely still embedded within our systems, particularly since we have been weakened following this attack? There is increased distrust in our voting systems' reliability, and in our democracy overall. How do we come to understand the hackers' odd, finely honed KGB-era strategies on this new playing field?

Can we admit we were foolish for playing into their hands, for allowing them to be spectators watching us fight each other like gladiators in the Colosseum? But isn't that what democracies claim they want? We want the world to watch as we hammer out our differences in the public and political realms. And, yes, we want the world to see democracy in action and choose to emulate it. But what strategies do we have to maintain a free society while at the same time preventing outside manipulation that could undermine the democratic process?

To answer some of these questions, I looked to White House cybersecurity czar and acting deputy Homeland Security advisor to Trump, Rob Joyce.

When I interviewed Joyce in late 2017, he had only been cybersecurity czar for six months after having spent more than twenty-five years at the NSA. During his last four years at the NSA, he led Tailored Access Operations, the agency's elite hacking unit, honing tools and techniques to exploit computer networks and mine for foreign intelligence.

I believed that hacking foreign adversaries likely teaches a person a lot about our own domestic vulnerabilities. I figured that if anyone knew about weaknesses in our cyber defenses, it would be Joyce. During our interview, in which CBS News was given exclusive access to him, Joyce was blunt about the holes in US cybersecurity.

It had to be close to one hundred degrees outside that day. My producer Katie Ross Dominick and I were rushing over to the White House for the interview, sweating in our clothes. Officially, we would be interviewing Joyce about cybersecurity from a dual government and business perspective. That day he was honoring some of the nation's top collegiate cyber defenders from the University of Maryland, Baltimore County. We had plans to push the limitations of the interview from a college hacker puff piece to something more substantial that would actually make it on the air. As journalists (and in my opinion representatives of the American public), we had limited access to high-level government officials like Joyce, and we had to make the most of the opportunity.

We were supposed to gather at the entrance to the Eisenhower Executive Office Building, adjacent to the White House, at the intersection of State and Seventeenth Streets. However, a mix-up landed us on Pennsylvania Avenue at the press entrance to the White House, where we went through a security checkpoint and were escorted down the driveway along the north lawn.

Although I'd been in the White House several times in the past, I never got over feeling awed, not by the building itself but because of the history of where I was standing. Walking down the driveway and then over to the Old Executive Office Building, I noted all the live shot locations where all the major network crews gathered in the rain or the snow. We passed those and went down and up several steps before we reached the building and eventually the vice president's ceremonial office.

Joyce greeted us with a firm handshake and showed us the vice president's desk. It was a grand mahogany, double-pedestal desk with brass handles and a pullout shelf that had first been used by Theodore Roosevelt in 1902. The desk had survived a fire. It has been written on by presidents ranging from Calvin Coolidge to Richard Nixon. Beginning in the 1940s presidents started to sign its inside top drawer. I took a photograph of the drawer and the desk to show my children.

While Joyce's assistant brought us bottled water, I experienced a strange realization. There was so much history in that room. Yet Joyce and I were about to sit down and discuss the most futuristic of threats. A cyberwar was about to begin, or was already under way, depending on your opinion on the matter. An arms race would surely follow. Joyce later confirmed my suspicion that the United States was ill prepared for the first battle that had passed and those that were still to come.

A group of college students were gathered in the room as well. They were aspiring hackers. "One of the things I care about is making sure we have great people and are thinking about education and how we get the quantities of folks in cybersecurity that the nation needs," Joyce said.[3] Like Brennan, he was intent on recruiting future cybersecurity rock stars. Oddly, they would be entering the field at a disadvantage.[4]

I was stunned to hear Joyce tell the students that the United States lacked the three hundred thousand cybersecurity experts it needs. "We've got roughly three-quarters of a million people doing cybersecurity," he told the students. "If the industry could hire everybody they wanted, they would hire another quarter of a million to almost a third of a million more people."[5]

More than a year after the FBI launched its investigation into Russian meddling in the 2016 election, the United States was still playing catchup. The Russian influence campaign had succeeded, and yet America still needed "troops" to compete with this new threat.

US law enforcement and intelligence officials testified on Capitol Hill, making it clear the Russian cyber spies would be back during the 2018 and 2020 election cycles and beyond, and that their methods of intrusion and influence would progress.

> **Pegues:** It seems like more people—more young people—are becoming aware of cybersecurity as a field to get into, as it relates to government work.
>
> **Joyce:** Cybersecurity is a great career. The country has more needs than it has supply, and I think that people recognize that it's a really important service to do, whether you do it in the government or whether you do it for industry.
>
> **Pegues:** How do you change the mind-set of young college students out there who may not have seen this as a career in the past?

Joyce: I think we need to expose them to hands-on things. I'm a firm believer that trade school–type education will be one of the things that gets us to the quantity of STEM [science, technology, engineering, and mathematics] education, cybersecurity education we need. Everybody doesn't have to do book-level academic work to do computer science—there's a lot of hands-on, and that's what gets people excited, when you're actually doing things.

Pegues: How would you characterize the current cyber threats?

Joyce: The threat from cyber is growing. It's going in the wrong direction. It's going in a bad direction.

As for the upcoming 2018 elections, Joyce believes they will be secure.

> You've got to look at the whole belt and suspenders of how we protect the elections, and that's [from] maintaining the integrity of the machines to the accountability of the people to how that information is verified. I think they've [the Department of Homeland Security] got an exceptional plan and they're looking at the issues that have been raised from the past where people have actually looked for vulnerabilities in voting machines and exposed that back to the companies where they can be improved and fixed.

I left the interview with Joyce surprised by how candid he was about the shortcomings of US cybersecurity. But just look at the daily news headlines. There is usually a cyberattack of some sort that caught someone or some company off guard. Also, more adversaries were targeting US computer networks. This new reality demanded a fresh approach, and recruitment wasn't the only arena where government officials were working to come up with new plans for governing cyberspace. Security experts were attempting to find a new set of rules.

Chapter 34

OUR PLAYBOOK

While speaking with some of the people interviewed in this book, I wondered if our government had a playbook. The Russian hackers may have been operating from a playbook that was grounded in decades of history. As we learned from experts like Michael Hayden, we aren't exactly novices at this. We too have committed acts of cyber espionage. How do we draw on that history and create a playbook that guides the United States in how to respond?

I asked Laura Rosenberger of the Alliance for Securing Democracy if the country had a plan.[1]

Rosenberger: It's hard to have a plan when the president doesn't acknowledge that there's a problem. I don't think that we have [a] responsive playbook, because I don't think we really yet fully understand the threat that we're facing. If you think about other kinds of warfare, you have to understand the weapons systems that are being used against you. You have to understand the different domains they're operating in. And you need to be able to build your own defensive and offensive strategies based on a full understanding of all that. The Russians and Putin certainly see this as a new kind of warfare. We need to understand the weapons systems and the domains in which they're operating in a new and different way in order to really be able to respond comprehensively.

We're trying to build the understanding and the playbook to be able to do [that]. I think until that point, we're just not going to be able to really get ourselves organized around it. That being said, in the last few years there's no question that key parts of our national security apparatus have really started to take on this challenge in a serious way.

Pegues: But it seems to me that this is an arms race that America is losing.

Rosenberger: That is certainly one way of thinking about it.

Pegues: And it's still happening, as [your] Hamilton 68 [website dashboard] points out. This is an ongoing Russian operation.

Rosenberger: Right. That's, I think, the other thing that is lost on a lot of people. This isn't just something that happened in 2016, and maybe they'll come back in 2018 and 2020. They never left. This is an ongoing thing. And it's not just about elections. This is about undermining and weakening democracy and democratic institutions and viewing that as a weapon. This is a weaponized assault on our democracy. Elections are the premier crown-jewel institution in democracies.

A man I speak with regularly at CBS News is former acting director of the CIA Michael Morell. He was traveling with President George W. Bush on September 11, 2001, and he briefed the president on the terrorist attack. Morell has a remarkable reservoir of knowledge and experience, which is why presidents, senators, and many others rely on his counsel.

Morell associated the Russian cyberattacks with an act of war: "We need to see this for what it is. It is an attack on our very democracy. It's an attack on who we are as a people. A foreign government messing around in our elections is, I think, an existential threat to our way of life."[2]

He recommended steps we might take to respond to these attacks in such a way that the results of the attack can be seen. That would serve as a deterrent to the Chinese, North Koreans, Iranians, and anyone else thinking about their own version of the Russian influence campaign.

As for Putin, Morell says, "He has to feel some pain, he has to pay a price here or again, there will be no deterrence, and it has to be seen by the rest of the world as being significant to Mr. Putin so that it can be a deterrent."[3]

In the final weeks of the Obama administration, according to the

Washington Post, officials debated dozens of options for punishing Russia, including a "covert measure that authorized planting cyber weapons in Russia's infrastructure, the digital equivalent of bombs that could be detonated if the United States found itself in an escalating exchange with Moscow."[4] It's unclear whether that action was ever taken. During that period I kept asking US intelligence officials what the response may be, and I was always warned about the uncertainty of an offensive cyber response. "You just don't know where that ends," I was told. As for the Kremlin, it has always denied any involvement. After Special Counsel Robert Mueller indicted thirteen Russian nationals in connection with the influence campaign, one of the men spoke out, dismissing the charges. "They have one-sided justice," said Mikhail Burchik. "It turns out that you can hang the blame on anyone."[5]

The United States' response to the Russian cyberattack has been haphazard. The attack was unprecedented, and there are no real rules. Hayden, the former director of the NSA and CIA, noted that he didn't believe the Russian cyber-espionage attacks constituted an act of war. He also noted that there was no formal definition for an act of war in the cyber realm.[6] Jim Lewis says that the only real rule in cyberattacks was that you don't do anything to cause physical damage or human casualties.[7] Beyond that it is still the Wild West of cyberspace.

For the most part. Although the rule book has not really been written, there are some rough guidelines in place. As aggressive Russian cyberattacks wreak havoc on a global scale, we are beginning to develop new strategies. These are still in their rudimentary stages.

The hefty, 1,220-page *Department of Defense Law of War Manual* was developed over a quarter of a century ago and contains only a fifteen-page section pertaining specifically to cyberspace.[8] However, as Duke law school professor Charlie Dunlap writes, "Though some may complain about its relative brevity . . . the cyber chapter nevertheless represents another step in DoD's growing transparency about cyber operations generally. It was not long ago that most aspects of cyber operations beyond defensive measures were classified."[9]

In the nearly two years since the 2016 election, Putin has not paid a significant price for the influence campaign. In fact, partisan bickering in Washington has allowed the Russian leader to continue his poisonous social media operations with unfettered access to the hearts and minds of the American people. His "patriotic" hacking units continue to poke and pierce computer networks in the United States and across the globe.[10]

Whether there was coordination between the Trump campaign and Russian operatives will ultimately be decided by a judge and jury. But the verdict on the Russian intelligence operation to create doubt and uncertainty in the US election is already in. Now, state election officials are unsure about what they are doing to secure the upcoming elections against the Russian cyber menace. As former president George W. Bush said in February 2018, "It's problematic that a foreign nation is involved in our election system. Our democracy is only as good as people trust the results."[11]

Chapter 35

WHY DIDN'T THEY SEE IT?

It's not as though US intelligence officials didn't see Russian interference in the election coming from a mile away. In fact, for years US threat assessments were telegraphing Russia's intentions. Unlike the United States, where there are limits on a president's powers through legislative and judicial checks and balances, in Russia there really is no cap on how far President Vladimir Putin can extend his influence. The consensus in US intelligence circles is that anything big that happens in Russia has Putin's fingerprints on it. He is the one who gives the go-ahead. Putin has been determined to build an unparalleled cyber army.

Since taking over the Justice and Homeland Security beat for CBS News in 2014, I have made a point of staying on top of US intelligence Worldwide Threat Assessments. It is an interesting read, but it also spells out what US government officials are really concerned about as true national security threats to the country. As early as 2011, observers could see the progression and how the intelligence community's thinking began to evolve.

In March 2011, when then director of national intelligence James Clapper delivered his annual Worldwide Threat Assessment on Capitol Hill, terrorism was at the top of his list of concerns.[1] The "Statement for the Record" began by putting terrorism "at the forefront of our national security threats" and stated that "clear progress" was being made but that "new challenges" were "arising."

I can make the argument that the greatest challenge to US national security at the time was growing increasingly menacing by the day. Cyberspace was fast becoming a battleground, and there were already concerns that America was especially vulnerable.

The threat assessments Clapper would deliver to members of Congress began to change. In 2012, terrorism was still at the top of the list of worries, but concerns about cyberattacks were rising.[2] Then in 2013, on March 12, Clapper's global threat assessment changed dramatically. Terrorism had been knocked out of the top spot, and hacking was now the big item when it came to what threatened Americans' safety. On that day Clapper told the Senate Select Committee on Intelligence that what he was about to tell them really showed "how quickly and radically the world—and our threat environment—are changing." Clapper stated that the current security environment was demanding that he and the intelligence community "reevaluate the way they do business." The threats were more "diverse, interconnected, and viral than at any time in history," and "destruction can be invisible, latent, and progressive."[3]

Clapper also said, "We are in a major transformation because our critical infrastructures, economy, personal lives, and even basic understanding of—and interaction with—the world are becoming more intertwined with digital technologies and the internet. In some cases, the world is applying digital technologies faster than our ability to understand the security implications and mitigate potential risks."[4]

Clapper believed, "In response to the trends and events that happen in cyberspace, the choices we and other actors make in coming years will shape cyberspace for decades to come, with potentially profound implications for US economic and national security."[5]

US intelligence saw Russia's growing cyber capabilities but perhaps misjudged the Kremlin's intentions. Or our intelligence community underestimated how far Putin was willing to go to discredit us. The Russian president, who was a trained intelligence officer, still had a KGB mind-set.

Chapter 36

A PATRIOTIC RUSSIAN HACKER

There are still unresolved questions about how widespread the Russian influence or misinformation operation really was during the 2016 presidential election cycle. A lot of what the US government knows is classified and therefore not available to the public or even to many state and local election officials. For example, it's still unclear how successful the hackers were in breaching voter databases across the country and why they were doing it. Was it to alter data? Was it an effort to create confusion and uncertainty over the vote?

The Department of Homeland Security (DHS) is now working to share more information with states, in attempts to reinforce election systems ahead of anticipated Russian cyberattacks heading into 2018's midterms and the 2020 presidential election. But there is more to do as the threat continues to evolve. In early 2018, Democratic leaders in the House of Representatives and the Senate sent a letter to the Republican majority asking for an additional $300 million to "counter the influence of hostile foreign actors operating in the U.S., especially Russian operatives operating on our social media platforms."[1]

The FBI and DHS will need as much help as they can get. Unlike previous conflicts with foreign adversaries where the military takes the lead, in this new age of cyberwar the FBI and DHS are on the front lines of the battle. As are state and local election officials who must find a way to coexist with the DHS, because without knowing the underlying intelligence, this is a battle they might not be able to win. The DHS must be willing to share.

In early 2018, state election officials and eight different intelligence agencies came together in a secure DHS facility to talk about preparations for the upcoming midterm elections. But some participants in the meeting left disappointed. One source, who is an election official in one of the states targeted by the Russians in the last election, told me that when they met with federal officials in the secure facility to receive the highly classified information, they were told that they could not discuss what they learned outside of the facility. They were warned that if they did share the information with anyone, it would be a "violation of the espionage act." But after the briefing they were underwhelmed: "They didn't tell us anything we hadn't already read in the *New York Times*."[2]

Many local and state officials have been offered federal security clearances but still have yet to complete the paperwork because it takes nine to fourteen hours to fill it out. The delays securing elections systems are evident both at the federal and state level. This is not a well-oiled machine. DHS officials say, "Building any kind of trusted relationship takes time, particularly one that involves multiple partners at the federal, state, and local levels."[3] They insist that they are working to improve in sharing cyber-threat information with the states.

While the Russians appear to be operating at peak efficiency with their multipronged attack, the United States seems to be sputtering along, perhaps heading for another Election Day hangover and wondering what Russia just did to cast doubt on the results. In late February 2018, the outgoing top cyber commander was asked what had been done and what was being done to strike back at the Russians. NSA director Mike Rogers said, "We're taking steps, but we're probably not doing enough."[4] Democratic senator from Missouri Claire McCaskill angrily asked, "I want to know why the hell not? What's it going to take?" Rogers replied, "Ma'am, I'm an operational commander, ma'am. You're asking me a question that's so much bigger than me."[5] Rogers wasn't the only one who had not been ordered to counter the Russian attack by the White House. Earlier that same month, FBI director Christopher Wray responded to a similar question with a now familiar answer. He had not been directed by the president to stop Russian cyberattacks either.[6]

Several of my sources who have been tasked with securing elections tell me that, even without leadership on this issue from the

White House, voters should rest assured that since the 2016 election there have been numerous security upgrades to their systems. Some states have introduced multifactor passwords, paper trails, and they have even hidden data behind layers of security.

But look around America today. The Russia investigation has led to guilty pleas and indictments as well as suspicions about a president who calls the investigation a "hoax."[7] The curtain has been pulled back on the pitfalls of social media and how vulnerable it is to manipulation to the point that it's difficult to separate what's real from what's fake. Our divisions have been amplified. Whether it's about race, guns, or politics, we're at each other's throats.

Americans may share the blame for where we are now, but the Russian influence operation made the situation worse. Vladimir Putin and his intelligence operatives have, at the very least, succeeded in "softening" the ground for further destructive attacks. But the next round may not unfold the way we think it will. It may just be a guy on YouTube. Michael Daniel, who was special assistant to President Obama and cybersecurity coordinator on the National Security Council Staff, told me that in 2016 one of the "worst-case scenarios" White House officials kicked around involved a "patriotic Russian" hacking into a voting machine and then claiming what he/she had done in a post on YouTube or Facebook.[8] All the hacker would have to say is, "We have done this one hundred thousand times across the United States." Even if they hadn't, the misinformation alone would be enough to sow doubt and distrust in democracy as we know it.

> Where you see wrong or inequality or injustice,
> speak out, because this is your country. This is your
> democracy. Make it. Protect it. Pass it on.
> —Thurgood Marshall

AUTHOR'S NOTE

Every effort has been made to provide readers with the latest news about the Russia investigation, but more details are uncovered with each passing day. Please visit my website, jeffpegues.com, to discover the latest information that's come my way since this book was released.

ACKNOWLEDGMENTS

My life has changed dramatically in the last two years. I've authored two books, consistently worked twelve to fourteen hours a day and regrettably missed a lot of important moments at home with my incredible family. I am thankful for the peace, love, and joy they bring to my life in all of this chaos. To my wife, Tareaz, your support means everything to me. I will always need it! To my daughters, Jordyn and Peyton, thank you for working hard in school and playing hard in life! You deserve the best. Also, thanks to Mom and Dad; my big brother, Joseph E. Pegues III; Stephanie Powers Pegues; Gabriel; Zara; Ron; Valerie; Philip; Tiffany; Dorothy Poellnitz; Joseph E. Pegues Sr.; Louise Pegues; Lloyd and Miriam Moore; Stephanie Moore; Ashley Moore; Karen; Celestine; Casey; Carlos; and Morgan.

Thank you, Danielle Wolffe, for your help on this project. Without you this would not have made it to print. You and Kevin Anderson and Associates are difference makers for those of us who need a good editor for projects this big!

To my CBS News family, David Rhodes, Ingrid Ciprian-Matthews, Kim Godwin, Al Ortiz, Laurie Orlando, Steve Capus, Scott Pelley, Norah O'Donnell, Gail King, Jeff Glor, Bob Orr, Ryan Kadro, Diana Miller, Chris Isham, Ward Sloan, Mosheh David Oinounou, Caroline Horn, Albert Oetgen, Chloe Arensberg, Andres Triay, Katie Ross Dominick, Julia Kimani Burnham, Allyson Ross Taylor, Kate Rydell, Mary Walsh, Paula Reid, Duncan McKenna, Grace Lamb Atkinson, Pat Milton, Len Tepper, Julianna Goldman, Alturo Rhymes, Diana Miller, Terri Stewart, Tony Furlow, Caitlin Conant, John Dickerson, Mary Hager, and everyone I wasn't able to mention here who has contributed to my reporting over the years at *CBS This Morning, CBS Evening News, Face the Nation*, CBSN, and CBS Radio. Thank you all!

Thank you to my friends James Lewis, Eric O'Neill, Erroll Southers, and Frank Cilluffo. Men of knowledge and influence!

My agents, Sharon Chang, Henry Reisch, and Bradley Singer have helped guide my career. Thank you to my friends at Prometheus Books, including Steven L. Mitchell, Jeffrey Curry, Hanna Etu, Jill Maxick, Bruce Carle, Jake Bonar, Amy Vigrass, Lynette Nisbet, Catherine Roberts-Abel, and Jackie Cooke. I also want to acknowledge all of the people who have been on my team for years or decades: Christopher Carmichael, Chuck Murray, Mark Edwards, Gregg Burger, Justin Carmichael, Beth Carmichael, KC, Richard Burns, Elizabeth Murphy Burns, Todd Bloom, Kristin Bloom, JR Rodriguez, Cindy Rodriguez, Ron Hosko, Raoul Davis, Leticia Gomez, MB, Cat McKenzie, Rick Martin, Ducis Rodgers, Shefali Razdan Duggal, Molly Fay, Arles Hendershott, Vince Tirola, Barbara Tirola, Randy Walker, Terry Hoeppner, Shawn Watson, Pat Narduzzi, Gordon Benning, Amoury Hollins, Ron Scott, Miami University president Greg Crawford, Hugh Morgan, Dr. Robert Vogel, Miami University, Miami University football, Laddie Lawrence, Staples High School, Staples High School football, and Staples High School track.

NOTES

PREFACE

1. *All The President's Men*, directed by Alan Pakula, written by William Goldman (Burbank, CA: Warner Home Video, 1976), 138 minutes.

2. John P. MacKenzie, "Court Orders Nixon to Yield Tapes; President Promises to Comply Fully," *Washington Post*, July 25, 1974, https://www.washingtonpost.com/politics/court-orders-nixon-to-yield-tapes-president-promises-to-comply-fully/2012/06/04/gJQAZSw0IV_story.html (accessed February 26, 2018).

3. David Folkenflik, "'Deep Throat' Revealed as Ex-FBI Official Felt," NPR, May 31, 2005, https://www.npr.org/templates/story/story.php?storyId=4673957 (accessed February 10, 2018).

4. Devlin Barrett, "US Voting System So 'Clunky' It Is Insulated from Hacking, FBI Director Says," *Wall Street Journal*, September 8, 2016, https://www.wsj.com/articles/u-s-voting-system-so-clunky-it-is-insulated-from-hacking-fbi-director-says-1473368396 (accessed February 19, 2018).

CHAPTER 1. THIS IS WARFARE

1. William Saletan, "Hate Makes Us Weak," *Slate*, March 31, 2017, http://www.slate.com/articles/news_and_politics/politica/2017/03/how_russia_capitalizes_on_american_racism_and_xenophobia.html (accessed January 27, 2018).

2. Julia Ioffe, "The History of Russian Involvement in America's Race Wars," *Atlantic*, October 21, 2017, https://www.theatlantic.com/international/archive/2017/10/russia-facebook-race/542796/ (accessed January 27, 2018).

3. Dr. Carlos J. Bringuier, *Crime without Punishment* (Bloomington, IN: AuthorHouse, 2013), p. 380; Casey Michel, "How Russia Keeps Exploiting Anti-Black Racism in the US," ThinkProgress, September 26, 2017,

https://thinkprogress.org/russias-sordid-history-of-exploiting-anti-black
-racism-in-the-u-s-df3b83b4dd86/ (accessed January 28, 2018).

4. "Vladimir Putin Likely Gave Go-Ahead for US Cyberattack, Intelligence Officials Say," CBS News, December 15, 2016, https://www
.cbsnews.com/news/russia-election-hack-vladimir-putin-personally
-involved-us-intelligence-officials-say/ (accessed January 27, 2018).

5. Bob Dreyfuss, "Russian Trolling of US Social Media May Have Been Much Greater Than We Thought," *Nation*, October 23, 2017, https://www
.thenation.com/article/russian-trolling-of-us-social-media-may-have-been
-much-greater-than-we-thought/ (accessed January 27, 2018).

CHAPTER 2. MINING FOR CLUES AT THE DNC

1. Avi Selk, "The Violent Rally Trump Can't Move Past," *Washington Post*, April 3, 2017, https://www.washingtonpost.com/news/the-fix/wp/
2017/04/03/the-violent-rally-trump-cant-move-past/?utm_term=.e0980
a9ec2a6 (accessed April 10, 2018).

2. Tom Hamburger and Karen Tumulty, "WikiLeaks Releases Thousands of Documents about Clinton and Internal Deliberations," *Washington Post*, July 22, 2016, https://www.washingtonpost.com/news/
post-politics/wp/2016/07/22/on-eve-of-democratic-convention-wikileaks
-releases-thousands-of-documents-about-clinton-the-campaign-and-internal
-deliberations/?utm_term=.7802e667887e (accessed January 22, 2018).

3. Martin Matishak, "Guccifer 2.0 Drops the Dime on the DNC Again," *Politico*, September 14, 2016, https://www.politico.com/tipsheets/
morning-cybersecurity/2016/09/guccifer-drops-the-dime-on-the-dnc
-again-mccain-picks-a-cyber-fight-with-the-white-house-csis-holds-doj
-summit-216319 (accessed February 10, 2018).

4. Ellen Nakashima, "Russian Government Hackers Penetrated DNC, Stole Opposition Research on Trump," *Washington Post*, June 14, 2016, https://www.washingtonpost.com/world/national-security/russian-
government-hackers-penetrated-dnc-stole-opposition-research-on
-trump/2016/06/14/cf006cb4-316e-11e6-11e6-8ff7-7b6c1998b7a0_story.html
?utm_term=.7bb8e65a797c (accessed January 27, 2018).

5. Nancy A. Youssef and Shane Harris, "FBI Suspects Russia Hacked DNC; US Officials Say It Was to Elect Donald Trump," *Daily Beast*, July 25, 2016, https://www.thedailybeast.com/fbi-suspects-russia-hacked-dnc-us
-officials-say-it-was-to-elect-donald-trump (accessed January 27, 2018).

6. Dmitri Alperovitch, "Bears in the Midst: Intrusion into the Democratic National Committee," *CrowdStrike Blog,* June 15, 2016, https://www.crowdstrike.com/blog/bears-midst-intrusion-democratic-national-committee/ (accessed January 27, 2018).

7. Matthew Nussbaum, "The Definitive Trump-Russia Timeline of Events," *Politico,* March 3, 2017, https://www.politico.com/trump-russia-ties-scandal-guide/timeline-of-events (accessed January 27, 2018).

CHAPTER 3. MEANWHILE, BACK AT THE WHITE HOUSE . . .

1. Richard Weingroff, "An Imaginary Tour of Pennsylvania Avenue," US Department of Transportation, Federal Highway Administration, last updated June 27, 2017, https://www.fhwa.dot.gov/infrastructure/pa42.cfm (accessed March 6, 2018); "Our Nation's Ugliest Building," *Curbed* (blog), October 1, 2014, https://dc.curbed.com/2014/10/1/10041050/our-nations-ugliest-building (accessed March 6, 2018); M. Scott Mahaskey, "Photos: Inside the Truman Bowling Alley," *Politico,* May 12, 2014, https://www.politico.com/gallery/2014/05/photos-inside-the-truman-bowling-alley-001752?slide=0 (accessed January 28, 2018).

2. Director of National Intelligence, *Background to "Assessing Russian Activities and Intentions in Recent US Elections": The Analytic Process and Cyber Incident Attribution* (Washington, DC: Central Intelligence Agency, Department of Justice, National Security Agency, January 6, 2017).

3. Ellen Nakashima, "US Investigators Have Identified Russian Government Hackers Who Breached DNC," *Washington Post,* November 2, 2017, https://www.washingtonpost.com/world/national-security/prosecutors-have-identified-russian-government-hackers-who-breached-the-dnc/2017/11/02/f38b9b18-bfd3-11e7-8444-a0d4f04b89eb_story.html?utm_term=.5ab1955632a4 (accessed February 21, 2018).

4. Michael Daniel, in an interview with the author, September 25, 2017.

5. Abby Ohlheiser, "Chinese Hackers Spied on the 2008 Elections, Too," June 6, 2013, *Atlantic,* https://www.theatlantic.com/technology/archive/2013/06/chinese-hackers-spied-2008-elections-too/314506/ (Accessed March 21, 2018).

6. "Democrat Hack: Who Is Guccifer 2.0?" BBC News, July 28, 2016, www.bbc.com/news/technology-36913000 (accessed January 28, 2018).

7. Adam Meyers, in an interview with the author, October 17, 2016.

8. Daniel, interview with the author.

9. United States v. Microsoft Corporation, 253 F.3d 34 (D.C. Cir. 2001), https://www.justice.gov/atr/testimony-edward-w-felten-us-v -microsoft-corporation (accessed December 19, 2017).

10. *Princeton Alumni Weekly* 103 (2002); Academic, s.v. "Edward Felten," 2017, http://enacademic.com/dic.nsf/enwiki/248419 (Accessed January 28, 2018).

11. Robert Vamosi, "Sequoia Voting Systems Site Hacked," CNET, March 20, 2008, https://www.cnet.com/news/sequoia-voting-systems -site-hacked/ (accessed January 28, 2018); Ben Wofford, "How to Hack an Election in 7 Minutes," *Politico*, August 5, 2016, https://www.politico .com/magazine/story/2016/08/2016-elections-russia-hack-how-to-hack -an-election-in-seven-minutes-214144 (accessed January 28, 2018); Marc Ferranti, "Ed Felten on E-Voting: What Can Go Wrong," *PCWorld*, November 2, 2008, https://www.pcworld.com/article/153187/felton _vote_security.html (accessed January 28, 2018).

12. Daniel, interview with the author.

CHAPTER 4. THE DOSSIER

1. Christopher Steele, *US Presidential Election: Republican Candidate Donald Trump's Activities in Russia and Compromising Relationship with the Kremlin* (Company Intelligence Report; Washington, DC: Department of Justice, June 20, 2016),https://www.documentcloud.org/documents/ 3259984-Trump-Intelligence-Allegations.html (accessed February 25, 2018).

2. Kaitlyn Schallhorn, "Fusion GPS's Ties to Clinton Campaign, Russia Investigation: What to Know," Fox News, February 7, 2018, http://www .foxnews.com/politics/2018/02/07/fusion-gpss-ties-to-clinton-campaign -russia-investigation-what-to-know.html (accessed February 25, 2018).

3. Abigail Tracy, "The Ex-Spy behind the Trump-Russia Dossier Left a Clue for Mueller," *Vanity Fair*, November 16, 2017, https://www.vanityfair .com/news/2017/11/christopher-steele-robert-mueller-trump-russia -dossier (accessed February 25, 2018).

4. Julia Manchester, "McCain Associate Invokes Fifth Amendment on Trump Dossier Sources: Report," *Hill*, February 22, 2018, http://thehill. com/blogs/blog-briefing-room/news/375205-mccain-associate-invokes -fifth-amendment-on-trump-dossier (accessed February 25, 2018); I've spoken with three or four sources close to the investigation who

corroborated this information, and to protect my sources I have made their names anonymous.

5. "Alexander Litvinenko: Profile of a Russian Spy," BBC, January 21, 2016, http://www.bbc.com/news/uk-19647226 (accessed February 25, 2018).

6. Brett Samuels, "Trump Calls for Investigation into Clinton Ties to Dossier," *Hill*, October 29, 2017, http://thehill.com/homenews/administration/357700-trump-calls-for-investigation-into-clinton-russia-ties (accessed February 25, 2018).

7. According to my sources close to the investigation.

8. James Carroll, "The True Nature of John McCain's Heroism," *New Yorker*, July 21, 2017, https://www.newyorker.com/news/news-desk/the-true-nature-of-john-mccains-heroism (accessed February 25, 2018).

9. Ibid.

10. Denise Clifton, "Putin's Trolls Are Targeting Trump's GOP Critics—Especially John McCain," *Mother Jones*, January 12, 2018, https://www.motherjones.com/politics/2018/01/putins-trolls-keep-targeting-john-mccain-and-other-gop-trump-critics/ (accessed February 25, 2018).

11. Julian Borger, "John McCain Passes Dossier Alleging Secret Trump-Russia Contacts to FBI," *Guardian*, January 11, 2017, https://www.theguardian.com/us-news/2017/jan/10/fbi-chief-given-dossier-by-john-mccain-alleging-secret-trump-russia-contacts (accessed April 10, 2018).

12. "McCain Corrects Woman Calling Obama an 'Arab,'" CNN, 2008, https://www.cnn.com/videos/politics/2015/09/18/mccain-2008-presidential-campaign-audience-question-on-obama-as-arab.cnn (accessed February 25, 2018).

13. Clifton, "Putin's Trolls."

CHAPTER 5. THEY ARE HACKING THE HELL OUT OF US

1. Linda Power is not her real name. We are disguising the source's identity.

2. Zack Stanton, "Yes, Pence and Trump Have Called Putin a Stronger Leader than Obama," *Politico*, October 4, 2016, https://www.politico.com/blogs/2016-presidential-debate-fact-check/2016/10/yes-pence-trump-have-called-putin-a-stronger-leader-than-obama-229155 (accessed March 17, 2018).

3. Ashley Parker and David E. Sanger, "Donald Trump Calls on Russia to Find Hillary Clinton's Missing Emails," *New York Times*, July 27, 2016,

https://www.nytimes.com/2016/07/28/us/politics/donald-trump-russia
-clinton-emails.html (accessed April 10, 2018).

4. James Comey, "Statement by FBI Director James B. Comey on the Investigation of Secretary Clinton's Use of a Personal E-Mail System," FBI.gov, July 5, 2016, https://www.fbi.gov/news/pressrel/press-releases/statement-by -fbi-director-james-b-comey-on-the-investigation-of-secretary-hillary -clinton2019s-use-of-a-personal-e-mail-system (accessed March 17, 2018).

5. Dmitry Alperovitz, "Bears in the Midst: Intrusion into the Democratic National Committee," *CrowdStrike Blog,* June 15, 2016, https:// www.crowdstrike.com/blog/bears-midst-intrusion-democratic-national -committee/ (accessed February 18, 2018).

6. Ibid.

7. "Adam Meyers," CrowdStrike, 2018, https://www.crowdstrike.com/ adam-meyers/ (accessed March 7, 2018).

8. Robert Hackett, "Hack Investigator CrowdStrike Reaches $1 Billion Valuation," *Fortune,* May 17, 2017, http://fortune.com/2017/05/17/hack -crowdstrike-billion/ (accessed February 11, 2018).

9. Adam Meyers, VP of Intelligence for CrowdStrike, in an interview with CBS News, Jeff Pegues, October 17, 2016.

10. Ibid.

11. Ibid.

12. Ibid.

13. Ibid.

14. Matthew Nussbaum, "The Definitive Trump-Russia Timeline of Events," *Politico,* December 1, 2017, https://www.politico.com/trump -russia-ties-scandal-guide/timeline-of-events (accessed February 18, 2018).

15. Meyers, interview with CBS News, Jeff Pegues.

16. Ibid.

CHAPTER 6. DEAD DROPS, INVISIBLE INK, PROPAGANDA, AND DEEP COVER

1. Olivia B. Waxman, "Q&A: The CIA Officer behind the New Spy Drama *The Americans,*" *Time,* January 30, 2013, www.entertainment.time .com/2013/01/30/qa-the-cia-officer-behind-the-new-spy-drama-the -americans (accessed November 20, 2017).

2. *The Americans,* directed by Joseph Weisberg and Joel Fields, originally aired on January 30, 2013, on FX.

3. "Operation Ghost Stories: Inside the Russian Spy Case," FBI,

October 31, 2011, https://www.fbi.gov/news/stories/operation-ghost
-stories-inside-the-russian-spy-case (accessed January 28, 2018); Eric
Tucker, "Long before New Hacks, US Worried by Russian Spying Efforts,"
Associated Press, March 17, 2017, https://apnews.com/5a189a45ebaf4c86
a330eb87d88beadd (accessed January 28, 2018).

4. Eyder Peralta, "'Ghost Stories': FBI Releases Documents, Videos of
Russian Spy Operation," NPR, October 31, 2011, https://www.npr.org/
sections/thetwo-way/2011/10/31/141881160/ghost-stories-fbi-releases
-documents-videos-of-russian-spy-operation (accessed January 28, 2018).

5. "Did Russian Spy Get Close to Infiltrating Hillary Clinton's
Inner Circle? FBI Warns of 'New Breed' of Moscow Agents," *Daily Mail*,
November 1, 2011, http://www.dailymail.co.uk/news/article-2056301/
Did-Russian-spy-close-infiltrating-Hillary-Clintons-inner-circle (accessed
January 28, 2018).

6. "Operation Ghost Stories," transcript, FBI, November 4, 2011,
https://www.fbi.gov/audio-repository/news-podcasts-thisweek-operation
-ghost-stories.mp3/view (accessed January 28, 2018).

7. "Video 8," May 16, 2004, FBI Records: The Vault, Ghost Stories
Investigation, video, 25 seconds, https://vault.fbi.gov/ghost-stories
-russian-foreign-intelligence-service-illegals/videos?selected=716df32d861
5584588892ba71e02da2c (accessed December 10, 2017).

8. "Video 9," June 6, 2009, FBI Records: The Vault, Ghost Stories
Investigation, video, 1:18, https://vault.fbi.gov/ghost-stories-russian
-foreign-intelligence-service-illegals/videos/mp4/video9.mp4/ (accessed
December 10, 2017).

9. "Video 4," June 8, 2006, FBI Records: The Vault, Ghost Stories
Investigation, video, 44 seconds, https://vault.fbi.gov/ghost-stories
-russian-foreign-intelligence-service-illegals/videos?selected=ecdce6925585
e8960b63a2cbf21f8f8a (accessed December 10, 2017).

10. Brett Forrest, "The Big Russian Life of Anna Chapman, Ex-Spy,"
Politico, January 4, 2012, https://www.politico.com/states/new-york/
albany/story/2012/01/the-big-russian-life-of-anna-chapman-ex-spy-067223.

11. "Video 1," June 26, 2010, FBI Records: The Vault, Ghost Stories
Investigation, video, 1:25, https://vault.fbi.gov/ghost-stories-russian-
foreign-intelligence-service-illegals/videos (accessed January 28, 2018);
"Video 2," January 20, 2010, FBI Records: The Vault, Ghost Stories
Investigation, video, 7:39, https://vault.fbi.gov/ghost-stories-russian
-foreign-intelligence-service-illegals/videos?selected=55731dc5d47151df
61a3f93fe90fa324 (accessed December 10, 2017).

12. Kia Makarechi, "Ousted Russian Spy Anna Chapman Is Now a Trump-Loving Instagram Star," *Vanity Fair*, January 3, 2017, https://www.vanityfair.com/news/2017/01/anna-chapman-instagram-trump (accessed March 26, 2018).

13. Waxman, "Q&A: CIA Officer behind the New Spy Drama."

14. Evan Osnos, David Remnick, and Joshua Yaffa, "Trump, Putin, and the New Cold War," *New Yorker*, March 6, 2017, https://www.newyorker.com/magazine/2017/03/06/trump-putin-and-the-new-cold-war (accessed January 28, 2018).

CHAPTER 7. MODERN-DAY SPIES

1. White House Office of the Press Secretary, "Statement by the President on Actions in Response to Russian Malicious Cyber Activity and Harassment," press release, December 29, 2016, https://obamawhitehouse.archives.gov/the-press-office/2016/12/29/statement-president-actions-response-russian-malicious-cyber-activity (accessed February 5, 2018).

2. Department of Justice Office of Public Affairs, "Russian Banker Sentenced in Connection with Conspiracy to Work for Russian Intelligence," press release, March 25, 2016, https://www.justice.gov/opa/pr/russian-banker-sentenced-connection-conspiracy-work-russian-intelligence (accessed February 6, 2018).

3. Ibid.

4. Lisa Harding, "Russian Spy Ring: The Lure of the SVR," *Guardian*, June 30, 2010, https://www.theguardian.com/world/2010/jun/30/russian-spy-ring-svr (accessed February 13, 2018).

5. "Profile: Russia's SVR Intelligence Agency," BBC, June 29, 2010, https://www.bbc.com/news/10447308 (accessed February 13, 2018).

6. Department of Justice, "Russian Banker Sentenced."

7. "Evgeny Buryakov Pleads Guilty in Manhattan Federal Court in Connection with Conspiracy to Work for Russian Intelligence," US Attorney's Office, Southern District of New York, March 11, 2016, https://www.justice.gov/usao-sdny/pr/evgeny-buryakov-pleads-guilty-manhattan-federal-court-connection-conspiracy-work (accessed March 28, 2018).

8. Ibid.

9. Alan Yuhas, "US Charges Russian 'Spies' Suspected of Trying to Recruit New Yorkers," *Guardian*, January 26, 2015, https://www.the

guardian.com/us-news/2015/jan/26/us-charges-alleged-russian-spies-new -york (accessed February 6, 2018).

10. "US Deports Russian Spy Who Posed as Bank Employee," April 5, 2017, CBS News, https://www.cbsnews.com/news/evgeny-buryakov -deported-russian-spy-posed-as-bank-employee-ice/ (accessed February 6, 2018).

11. "Attorney General, Manhattan US Attorney, and FBI Announce Charges against Russian Spy Ring in New York City," FBI, New York Office, January 26, 2015, https://www.fbi.gov/contact-us/field-offices/newyork/ news/press-releases/attorney-general-manhattan-u.s.-attorney-and-fbi -announce-charges-against-russian-spy-ring-in-new-york-city (accessed February 6, 2018).

12. Harriet Alexander, "Russian Spy Pleads Guilty in New York to Posing as a Banker," *Telegraph*, February 11, 2018, http://www.telegraph .co.uk/news/worldnews/northamerica/usa/12191485/Russian-spy-pleads -guilty-in-New-York-to-posing-as-a-banker.html (accessed March 7, 2018).

13. Criminal Complaint against Evgeny Buryakov, Igor Sporyshev, and Victor Podobny, January 26, 2015, United States v. Evgeny Buryakov, a.k.a. "Zhenya," Igor Sporyshev, and Victor Podobny, 15 Cr. 73 (2015), http:// online.wsj.com/public/resources/documents/2015_0126_spyring2.pdf (accessed February 6, 2018).

14. Ibid.

15. Ibid.

16. "Evgeny Buryakov Pleads Guilty."

17. Jethro Mullen, "Russian Spies Used Tickets and Hats to Try to Hide New York Activities, FBI Says," January 27, 2015, CNN, https://www .cnn.com/2015/01/27/us/new-york-alleged-russian-spy/index.html (accessed March 26, 2018)

18. Ibid.

19. "Evgeny Buryakov Pleads Guilty."

20. "Criminal Complaint against Evgeny Buryakov."

21. Lauren Gambino, Sabrina Siddiqui, and Shaun Walker, "Obama Expels 35 Russian Diplomats in Retaliation for US Election Hacking," *Guardian*, December 30, 2016, https://www.theguardian.com/us-news/ 2016/dec/29/barack-obama-sanctions-russia-election-hack (accessed February 6, 2018).

CHAPTER 8. CONVERSATION WITH A GHOST

1. Toby Harnden, "Eric O'Neill: The Truth behind 'Breach,'" *Telegraph*, September 4, 2007, http://www.telegraph.co.uk/culture/music/rockandjazzmusic/3667507/Eric-ONeill-The-truth-behind-Breach.html (accessed January 28, 2018).

2. FBI, "Robert Hanssen," press release, February 20, 2001, https://www.fbi.gov/history/famous-cases/robert-hanssen (accessed February 19, 2018).

3. Mark Binelli, "Inside America's Toughest Federal Prison," *New York Times*, March 26, 2015, https://www.nytimes.com/2015/03/29/magazine/inside-americas-toughest-federal-prison.html (accessed January 28, 2018).

4. Eric O'Neill, in Interview with Jeff Pegues for the *CBS Evening News*, March 2, 2017.

5. John Kelly and Steve Reilly, "Trump Team Issued at Least 20 Denials of Contacts with Russia," March 2, 2017, *USA Today*, https://www.usatoday.com/story/news/politics/2017/03/02/trump-teams-many-many-denials-contacts-russia/98625780/ (accessed March 28, 2018).

6. "2015 Paris Terror Attacks," CNN, October 31, 2017, https://www.cnn.com/2015/12/08/europe/2015-paris-terror-attacks-fast-facts/index.html (accessed February 19, 2018).

7. Krishnadev Calamur, Marina Koren, and Matt Ford, "A Day after the San Bernardino Shooting," *Atlantic*, December 3, 2015, https://www.theatlantic.com/national/archive/2015/12/a-shooter-in-san-bernardino/418497/ (accessed February 19, 2018).

CHAPTER 9. VLADIMIR PUTIN: WHO IS THIS GUY?

1. Walter Hickey, "39 Photos That Prove Birthday Boy Vladimir Putin Is the Most Badass Leader in the World," *Business Insider*, October 7, 2013, http://www.businessinsider.com/39-photos-vladimir-putin-badass-2013-10?IR=T/#e-of-the-russian-presidents-favorite-hobbies-is-hunting-an-he-frequently-goes-on-expeditions-to-aid-researchers-in-tagging-animals- (accessed February 6, 2018).

2. Ibid.

3. Associated Press, "Russia's Vladimir Putin Plays with NHL Veterans, Scoring 8 Goals," May 16, 2015, http://www.chicagotribune.com/sports/hockey/ct-putin-scores-eight-goals-20150516-story.html (accessed March 29, 2018).

4. "That Time Putin Brought His Dog to a Meeting to Scare Angela Merkel," July 7, 2017, *Business Insider*, http://www.businessinsider.com/putin-merkel-meeting-dog-2017-7 (accessed March 28, 2018).

5. Ibid.

6. Brett LoGiurato, "George W. Bush's Story about Vladimir Putin's Dog Explains So Much," *Business Insider*, April 4, 2014, www.business insider.com/george-bush-vladimir-putin-dog-2014-4?IR=Twww.chron.com/life/article/Which-of-George-W-Bush-s-paintings-is-your-5885691.php (accessed February 6, 2018).

7. Neil MacFarquhar, "Putin Wins Russia Election, and Broad Mandate for 4th Term," *New York Times*, March 18, 2018, https://www.nytimes.com/2018/03/18/world/europe/election-russia-putin-president.html (accessed March 28, 2018).

8. "Edward Snowden: Leaks That Exposed US Spy Programme," BBC News, January 17, 2014, http://www.bbc.com/news/world-us-canada-23123964 (accessed February 1, 2018).

9. Dana Ford, "EU Parliament Votes to Protect Edward Snowden," CNN, October 29, 2015, https://edition.cnn.com/2015/10/29/europe/eu-edward-snowden-vote/index.html (accessed February 1, 2018).

10. Harriet Alexander, "Vladimir Putin Creating 'Worst Human Rights Climate since Soviet Times,'" *Telegraph*, April 24, 2013, https://www.telegraph.co.uk/news/worldnews/vladimir-putin/10015065/Vladimir-Putin-creating-worst-human-rights-climate-since-Soviet-times.html (accessed February 10, 2018).

11. Alev Luhn, "Winter Olympics 2014: Russian President Vladimir Putin Takes on the 'Black Widows' in Sochi Security Crackdown," *Independent*, October 31, 2013, www.independent.co.uk/news/world/europe/winter-olympics-2014-russian-president-vladimir-putin-takes-on-the-black-widows-in-sochi-security-8916428.html (accessed February 6, 2018).

12. Kremlin Press Release, "Putin Personal Website, Biography," March 18, 2018, http://eng.putin.kremlin.ru/bio (accessed March 26, 2018).

13. *Encyclopedia Britannica*, s.v. "Vladimir Putin," last updated February 14, 2018, https://www.britannica.com/biography/Vladimir-Putin (accessed March 7, 2018).

14. Ibid.

15. Laura Rosenberger, in an interview with the author, September 19, 2017.

CHAPTER 10. THE PLAYBOOK

1. Steve Ranger, "Cyberwar: A Guide to the Frightening Future of Online Conflict," ZDNET, August 29, 2017, www.zdnet.com/article/cyberwar-a-guide-to-the-frightening-future-of-online-conflict/ (accessed January 28, 2018).

2. Lisa Brownlee, "Why Cyberwar Is So Hard to Define," *Forbes*, July 16, 2015, https://www.forbes.com/sites/lisabrownlee/2015/07/16/why-cyberwar-is-so-hard-to-define/#10670b1431f1 (accessed March 7, 2018); Andy Greenberg, "How an Entire Nation Became Russia's Test Lab for Cyberwar," *Wired*, June 20, 2017, https://www.wired.com/story/russian-hackers-attack-ukraine/ (accessed February 2, 2018).

3. Kevin Poulsen, "Russia-Linked Hackers Breached 100 Nuclear and Power Plants Just This Year," *Daily Beast*, September 6, 2017, https://www.thedailybeast.com/breaches-at-us-nuclear-and-power-plants-linked-to-russian-hackers (accessed February 2, 2018).

4. Damien McGuinness, "How a Cyberattack Transformed Estonia," BBC News, April 27, 2017, http://www.bbc.com/news/39655415 (accessed March 28, 2018).

5. "Russia 'Was behind German Parliament Hack,'" BBC, May 13, 2016, https://www.bbc.com/news/technology-36284447 (accessed January 18, 2018).

6. Andreas Rinke and Andrea Shalal, "Germany Alarmed about Potential Russian Interference in the Election," Reuters, November 16, 2016, https://www.reuters.com/article/us-germany-election-russia/germany-alarmed-about-potential-russian-interference-in-election-spy-chief-idUSKBN13B14O (accessed February 11, 2018).

7. Ibid.

8. Molly K. McKew, "The Garasimov Doctrine," *Politico*, September 10, 2017, https://www.politico.eu/article/new-battles-cyberwarfare-russia/ (accessed February 6, 2018).

9. Ibid.

10. Ibid.

11. Evan Osnos, Joshua Yaffa, and David Remnick, "Trump, Putin, and the New Cold War," *New Yorker*, March 6, 2017, https://www.newyorker.com/magazine/2017/03/06/trump-putin-and-the-new-cold-war (accessed January 10, 2017).

12. Molly K. McKew, "How Twitter Bots and Trump Fans Made #ReleaseTheMemo Go Viral," *Politico*, February 4, 2018, https://www

.politico.com/magazine/story/2018/02/04/trump-twitter-russians-release-the-memo-216935 (accessed February 11, 2018).

13. Adam Myers, in an interview with the author for CBS News, December 12, 2016.

14. Brad Heath, "Read Robert Mueller's Indictment of 13 Russian Nationals for Election Meddling," *USA Today*, February 16, 2018, https://www.usatoday.com/story/news/politics/2018/02/16/read-robert-muellers-indictment-13-russian-nationals-election-meddling/346688002/ (accessed February 19, 2018).

15. Pam Fessler, "Russian Cyberattack Targeted Elections Vendor Tied to Voting Day Disruptions," NPR, August 10, 2017, https://www.npr.org/2017/08/10/542634370/russian-cyberattack-targeted-elections-vendor-tied-to-voting-day-disruptions (accessed March 28, 2018).

16. Adam Meyers, "Russia's Electoral Endgame," *LinkedIn* (blog), October 14, 2016, https://www.linkedin.com/pulse/russias-electoral-endgame-adam-meyers/ (accessed March 7, 2018).

17. Jay Akbar, "That's One Way to Get a Lift in the Polls: Video of Model and Mayoral Candidate Performing a Striptease Is 'Leaked' Just before Election in Ukraine," *Daily Mail*, October 21, 2015, http://www.dailymail.co.uk/news/article-3283020/That-s-one-way-lift-polls-Video-model-mayoral-candidate-performing-striptease-leaked-just-election-Ukraine.html (accessed February 10, 2018).

18. Luke Harding, "What Are the Panama Papers? A Guide to History's Biggest Data Leak," *Guardian*, April 3, 2016, https://www.theguardian.com/news/2016/apr/03/what-you-need-to-know-about-the-panama-papers (accessed February 5, 2018).

19. Elias Groll, Paul McLeary, and Molly O'Toole, "Moscow Brings Its Propaganda War to the United States," *Foreign Policy*, July 25, 2016, http://foreignpolicy.com/2016/07/25/moscow-brings-its-propaganda-war-to-the-united-states/ (accessed February 27, 2018).

20. "Ukraine's Election: Five Years on in Kiev," *Economist*, January 21, 2010, http://www.economist.com/node/15330489 (accessed February 6, 2018).

21. Michael Daniel, in an interview with the author, September 25, 2017.

CHAPTER 11. PUTIN'S GRUDGE AGAINST CLINTON

1. Patrick Healy and Maggie Haberman, "Donald Trump Opens New Line of Attack on Hillary Clinton: Her Marriage," *New York Times*, September 30, 2016, https://www.nytimes.com/2016/10/01/us/politics/donald-trump-interview-bill-hillary-clinton.html (accessed February 24, 2018).

2. Ashley Gold, "US Election: Do 'Lock Her Up' Chants Mark a New Low?" BBC, July 22, 2016, http://www.bbc.com/news/election-us-2016-36860740 (accessed February 24, 2018).

3. "Donald Trump vs. Hillary Clinton Town Hall Debate Cold Open— SNL," YouTube video, 8:27, satirical look at 2016 Presidential Debate, posted by "Saturday Night Live," October 16, 2016, https://www.google.com/search?client=safari&rls=en&biw=872&bih=1064&ei=UWmRWv_GGIfx_Abs0ofQCQ&q=trump+hovering+behind+clinton+youtube&oq=trump+hovering+behind+clinton+yout&gs_l=psy-ab.1.0.33i21k1.8430.964 5.0.11479.5.5.0.0.0.0.100.415.4j1.5.0....0...1c.1.64.psy-ab..0.5.415...0j33i160k 1.0.vx8jbtOLTzE (accessed February 24, 2018).

4. Michelle Alexander, "Why Hillary Clinton Doesn't Deserve the Black Vote," *Nation*, February 10, 2016, https://www.thenation.com/article/hillary-clinton-does-not-deserve-black-peoples-votes/ (accessed March 28, 2018).

5. Dan Spinelli, "Benghazi Victim's Mother Blames Clinton for Son's Death," *Politico*, July 18, 2016, https://www.politico.com/story/2016/07/rnc-2016-benghazi-patricia-smith-hillary-clinton-225757 (accessed February 24, 2018).

6. Director of National Intelligence, *Background to "Assessing Russian Activities and Intentions in Recent US Elections": The Analytic Process and Cyber Incident Attribution* (Washington, DC: Central Intelligence Agency, Department of Justice, National Security Agency, January 6, 2017), https://www.dni.gov/files/documents/ICA_2017_01.pdf (accessed September 24, 2017), p. ii.

7. Ibid.

8. Michael Crowley and Julia Ioffe, "Why Putin Hates Hillary," *Politico*, July 25, 2016, https://www.politico.com/story/2016/07/clinton-putin-226153 (accessed February 24, 2018).

9. William Harrison, "Medvedev's Liberal Russia: Real or Rhetorical?" *Guardian*, July 7, 2008, https://www.theguardian.com/commentisfree/2008/jul/07/russia (accessed February 24, 2018).

10. James Ball, "Russian Election: Does the Data Suggest Putin Won through Fraud?" *Guardian*, March 5, 2012, https://www.theguardian.com/news/datablog/2012/mar/05/russia-putin-voter-fraud-statistics (accessed February 24, 2018).

11. Miriam Elder, "Russia's Anti-Putin Protests Grow," *Guardian*, December 7, 2011, https://www.theguardian.com/world/2011/dec/07/russia-anti-putin-protest-grow (accessed February 24, 2018).

12. Crowley and Ioffe, "Why Putin Hates Hillary."

13. Ibid.

14. Adam Meyers, VP of Intelligence for CrowdStrike, in an interview with CBS News, Jeff Pegues, October 17, 2016.

CHAPTER 12. THE SEPARATION BETWEEN FEDERAL AND STATE GOVERNMENT

1. Michael Daniel, in an interview with the author, September 12, 2017.

2. Ibid.

3. Eric Geller and Darren Samuelsohn, "More Than 20 States Have Faced Major Election Hacking Attempts, DHS Says," *Politico*, October 3, 2016, https://www.politico.com/story/2016/09/states-major-election-hacking-228978 (accessed March 28, 2018).

4. Daniel, interview with the author.

5. Ibid.

6. "FBI Takes Threat of Election Hack 'Seriously,'" Yahoo, September 8, 2016, https://www.yahoo.com/news/fbi-takes-threat-us-election-hack-seriously-224148411.html (accessed February 19, 2018).

CHAPTER 13. FROM CIVIL RIGHTS TO RUSSIAN INTELLIGENCE

1. *CIA Diversity and Inclusion Strategy* (Washington, DC: Central Intelligence Agency, 2016), https://www.cia.gov/library/reports/Diversity_Inclusion_Strategy_2016_to_2019.pdf (accessed January 31, 2018).

2. "John O. Brennan: Director, Central Intelligence Agency," Central Intelligence Agency, last updated January 5, 2016, https://www.cia.gov/about-cia/leadership/john-o-brennan.html (accessed January 31, 2018).

3. CIA director John Brennan, in an interview with the author, September 12, 2016.

4. Brendan I. Koerner, "Inside the Cyberattack That Shocked the US Government," *Wired*, October 23, 2016, https://www.wired.com/2016/10/inside-cyberattack-shocked-us-government/ (accessed January 28, 2018).

CHAPTER 14. LIVING THE DREAM: BIRMINGHAM

1. CIA director John Brennan, in an interview with the author, September 13, 2016.

2. "Omego Ware: The 'Jackie Robinson of Intelligence,'" Central Intelligence Agency, last updated February 22, 2017, https://www.cia.gov/news-information/featured-story-archive/2017-featured-story-archive/omego-ware-the-jackie-robinson-of-intelligence.html (accessed February 27, 2018).

3. "Director Brennan Delivers Keynote at Miles College," Central Intelligence Agency, September 13, 2016, https://www.cia.gov/news-information/speeches-testimony/2016-speeches-testimony/director-brennan-delivers-keynote-at-miles-college.html (accessed March 28, 2018).

4. Rebecca Shabad, "Former CIA Chief Says There Were Contacts between Russia and Trump Aides," CBS News, May 23, 2017, https://www.cbsnews.com/news/former-cia-director-john-brennan-testifies-on-russia-live-updates/ (accessed January 28, 2017).

CHAPTER 15. MOSCOW ON THE HUDSON

1. Jeff Pegues, "Vladimir Putin Likely Gave Go-Ahead for US Cyberattack, Intelligence Officials Say," CBS News, December 15, 2016, http://www.cbsnews.com/news/russia-election-hack-vladimir-putin-personally-involved-us-intelligence-officials-say/ (accessed July 8, 2017).

2. Gregory Holyk and Gary Langer, "Poll: Clinton Unpopularity at New High, on Par with Trump," ABC News, August 31, 2016, http://abcnews.go.com/Politics/poll-clinton-unpopularity-high-par-trump/story?id=41752050 (accessed April 10, 2018).

3. Harry Enten, "Election Update: Clinton's Lead Is Becoming Safer," FiveThirtyEight, October 6, 2017, https://fivethirtyeight.com/features/election-update-clintons-lead-is-becoming-safer/ (accessed July 9, 2017).

4. Pegues, "Vladimir Putin Likely Gave Go-Ahead."

5. Reuters in New York, "Putin the Peacemaker Banner Hung from Manhattan Bridge, Puzzles Police," *Guardian*, October 7, 2016, https://www.theguardian.com/world/2016/oct/07/putin-the-peacemaker-banner -hung-from-manhattan-bridge-puzzles-police (accessed February 19, 2018).

6. Famous Class (@FAMOUSCLASS), Twitter, October 6, 2016, 10:55 a.m., https://twitter.com/FAMOUSCLASS/status/784089589879373833 (accessed March 13, 2018).

7. Kathryn Peters (@katyetc), Twitter, October 6, 2016, 10:50 a.m., https://twitter.com/katyetc/status/784088398097223680 (accessed March 13, 2018).

8. Natalie Musumeci and Gabrielle Fonrouge, "Putin Banner Mysteriously Appears on Manhattan Bridge," *NY Post*, October 6, 2016, https://nypost.com/2016/10/06/putin-banner-mysteriously-appears-on -manhattan-bridge/ (accessed March 13, 2018).

CHAPTER 16. THEY'RE TALKING

1. Kyle Cheney and Sarah Wheaton, "The Most Revealing Clinton Campaign Emails in WikiLeaks Release," *Politico*, October 7, 2018, https://www.politico.com/story/2016/10/john-podesta-wikileaks-hacked -emails-229304 (accessed March 28, 2018).

2. Zaid Jilani, "In Secret Goldman Sachs Speech, Hillary Clinton Admitted No-Fly Zone Would 'Kill A Lot of Syrians,'" *Intercept*, October 10, 2016, https://theintercept.com/2016/10/10/in-secret-goldman-sachs -speech-hillary-clinton-admitted-no-fly-zone-would-kill-a-lot-of-syrians/ (accessed March 28, 2018).

3. Bryan Naylor, "US Election Systems Vulnerable, Lawmakers Told in Dueling Hearings," NPR, June 21, 2017, https://www.npr.org/2017/ 06/21/533666328/u-s-elections-systems-vulnerable-lawmakers-told-in -dueling-hearings (accessed February 19, 2018).

4. Kevin Drum, "Pussygate Might Be the Final Straw for Donald Trump," *Mother Jones*, October 10, 2016, https://www.motherjones.com/ kevin-drum/2016/10/pussygate-might-be-final-straw-donald-trump/ (accessed February 19, 2018).

5. John Cassidy, "James Comey's October Surprise," *New Yorker*, October 28, 2016, https://www.newyorker.com/news/john-cassidy/james -comeys-october-surprise (accessed February 19, 2018).

6. Linda Power is a pseudonym for an intelligence official author used as a source.

7. "Alec Baldwin's Trump Stalks Hillary as SNL Takes on the 'Second and Worst Ever' Presidential Debate," YouTube video, 5:14, Trump/Clinton Debate, posted by "Breaking News," October 16, 2016, https://www.youtube.com/watch?v=wL8_F_RXfdM (accessed March 7, 2018).

8. "Benghazi Mission Attack Fast Facts," CNN, December 2, 2017, https://www.cnn.com/2013/09/10/world/benghazi-consulate-attack-fast-facts/index.html (accessed February 19, 2018).

9. Cassidy, "James Comey's October Surprise."

CHAPTER 17. THE CYBER REF: A CONVERSATION WITH MICHAEL HAYDEN

1. Paul Bedard, "CIA Director Michael Hayden's Post at the Steelers' Heinz Field," *US News & World Report,* July 29, 2008, https://www.usnews.com/news/blogs/washington-whispers/2008/07/29/cia-director-michael-haydens-post-at-the-steelers-heinz-field (accessed February 5, 2018).

2. General Michael Hayden, "Michael Hayden: In Trump versus NFL, Standing Up for Free Speech," *Hill,* September 26, 2017, http://thehill.com/opinion/white-house/352419-michael-hayden-in-trump-versus-nfl-standing-up-for-free-speech (accessed February 5, 2018).

3. Ibid.

4. Michael Hayden, Chertoff Group, https://chertoffgroup.com/about-us/our-team/244-michael-hayden (accessed February 5, 2018).

5. "How Best to Conduct America's War on Terror," YouTube video, 7:48, CBS News Correspondent David Martin interview with Michael Hayden, posted by "CBS Sunday Morning," February 21, 2016, https://www.youtube.com/watch?v=qaosD8s8zuw (accessed February 5, 2018)

6. Michael Hayden, Chertoff Group.

7. Alyza Sebenius, "Writing the Rules of Cyberwar," *Atlantic,* June 28, 2017, https://www.theatlantic.com/international/archive/2017/06/cyberattack-russia-ukraine-hack/531957/ (accessed February 5, 2018); Bryant Jordan, "US Still Has No Definition for Cyber Act of War," Military.com, June 2, 2016, https://www.military.com/daily-news/2016/06/22/us-still-has-no-definition-for-cyber-act-of-war.html (accessed February 19, 2018).

8. Michael Hayden, in an interview with Jeff Pegues, CBS News, November 1, 2016.

CHAPTER 18. ELECTION DAY

1. Massimo Calabresi, "Exclusive: Read the Previously Undisclosed Plan to Counter Russian Hacking on Election Day," *Time*, July 20, 2017, http://time.com/4865798/russia-hacking-election-day-obama-plan/ (accessed February 5, 2018).

2. Michael Kan, "Election Day in the US Faces Spectre of Cyber-attacks," *PC World*, November 7, 2016, https://www.pcworld.com/article/ 3139283/security/us-election-day-faces-specter-of-cyberattacks.html (accessed February 5, 2018).

3. "US Election Night 2016—As It Happened," *Guardian*, July 14, 2017, https://www.theguardian.com/us-news/live/2016/nov/08/ us-election-2016-polls-trump-clinton-live (accessed February 5, 2018).

4. Ibid.

5. Ibid.

CHAPTER 19. WHAT HAS JUST HAPPENED?

1. Alexi McCammond, "Trump Again Calls Russia Probe a Hoax," Axios, December 29, 2017, https://www.axios.com/trump-again-calls -russia-probe-a-hoax-1515110898-757025c8-532d-4d2a-9d50-2d607f65c099 .html (accessed March 29, 2018).

2. Carol E. Lee and Julia Ainsley, "Focus on Flynn, Timeline Suggests Obstruction Is on Mueller's Mind," NBC News, December 11, 2017, https://www.nbcnews.com/news/us-news/18-crucial-days-what-did -president-know-when-did-he-n828261 (accessed February 19, 2018).

3. Greg Miller, Adam Entous, and Ellen Nakashima, "National Security Adviser Flynn Discussed Sanctions with Russian Ambassador, Despite Denials, Officials Say," *Washington Post*, February 9, 2017, https:// www.washingtonpost.com/world/national-security/national-security -adviser-flynn-discussed-sanctions-with-russian-ambassador-despite-denials -officials-say/2017/02/09/f85b29d6-ee11-11e6-b4ff-ac2cf509efe5_story .html?utm_term=.4b7b7d1d7f6d (accessed February 19, 2018).

4. Dana Priest, "Trump Advisor Michael Flynn on His Dinner with Putin and Why Russia Today Is Just like CNN," *Washington Post*, August 15, 2016, https://www.washingtonpost.com/news/checkpoint/wp/2016/08/15/ trump-adviser-michael-t-flynn-on-his-dinner-with-putin-and-why-russia-today -is-just-like-cnn/?utm_term=.a76532ec71f3 (accessed March 29, 2018).

CHAPTER 20. A SIDENOTE ABOUT COMEY

1. James B. Comey, in letter to Congressional Select Intelligence Committee, October 28, 2016, http://online.wsj.com/public/resources/documents/Binder2.pdf (accessed February 13, 2018).

2. John Cassidy, "James Comey's October Surprise," *New Yorker*, October 28, 2016, https://www.newyorker.com/news/john-cassidy/james-comeys-october-surprise (accessed February 13, 2018).

3. Patricia Zengerle and Doina Chiacu, "Ex-CIA Chief: Worries Grew of Trump Campaign Contacts to Russia," Reuters, May 23, 2017, https://www.reuters.com/article/us-usa-trump-russia/ex-cia-chief-worries-grew-of-trump-campaign-contacts-to-russia-idUSKBN18J2DE (accessed March 29, 2018).

4. Garrett Graff, "What Donald Trump Needs to Know about Bob Mueller and Jim Comey," *Politico*, May 18, 2017, https://www.politico.com/magazine/story/2017/05/18/james-comey-trump-special-prosecutor-robert-mueller-fbi-215154 (accessed February 23, 2018).

5. Ibid.

6. Colleen Shalby, "Comey, Mueller, and the Showdown at John Ashcroft's Hospital Bed," *Los Angeles Times*, May 17, 2017, http://www.latimes.com/politics/la-na-pol-mueller-comey-ashcroft-domestic-surveillance-20170517-story.html (accessed February 23, 2018).

7. Stephen Collinson, Jeremy Herb, and Tom LoBianco, "James Comey Testimony: Trump Asked Me to Let Flynn Investigation Go," CNN, June 8, 2017, https://www.cnn.com/2017/06/07/politics/james-comey-testimony-released/index.html (accessed February 23, 2018).

8. James Griffiths, "Trump Says He Considered 'This Russia Thing' before Firing FBI Director Comey," CNN, May 12, 2017, https://www.cnn.com/2017/05/12/politics/trump-comey-russia-thing/index.html (accessed February 23, 2018).

9. Amy Davidson Sorkin, "Robert Mueller's Distinctly American Indictments," *New Yorker*, March 5, 2018, https://www.newyorker.com/magazine/2018/03/05/robert-muellers-distinctly-american-indictments (accessed March 29, 2018).

CHAPTER 21. THERE CAN'T BE TWO PRESIDENTS

1. Linda Power is a pseudonym. She is a source in the intelligence community.

2. Barack Obama, "Press Conference by the President," Office of the Press Secretary, December 16, 2016, https://obamawhitehouse.archives .gov/the-press-office/2016/12/16/press-conference-president (accessed March 31, 2018).

3. Eric Levitz, "Report: Kushner Told Flynn to Sabotage US Policy with Russia's Help," *New York Magazine*, December 1, 2017, http://nymag .com/daily/intelligencer/2017/12/report-kushner-had-flynn-contact -russia-during-transition.html (accessed February 19, 2018).

4. Michael Hayden, in an interview with Jeff Pegues for CBS News, November 1, 2016.

5. Jim Lewis, in an interview with Jeff Pegues for CBS News, December 16, 2016.

6. David Martin, "Russian Hack Almost Brought the US Military to Its Knees," CBS News, December 15, 2018, https://www.cbsnews.com/ news/russian-hack-almost-brought-the-u-s-military-to-its-knees/ (accessed February 10, 2018).

7. Lewis, interview with Jeff Pegues.

CHAPTER 22. OBAMA RESPONDS

1. David Jackson, "Obama Sanctions Russian Officials over Election Hacking," *USA Today*, December 29, 2016, https://www.usatoday.com/ story/news/politics/2016/12/29/barack-obama-russia-sanctions-vladimir -putin/95958472/ (accessed February 5, 2018).

2. Evan Perez and Daniella Diaz, "White House Announces Retaliation against Russia: Sanctions, Ejecting Diplomats," CNN, January 2, 2017, https://www.cnn.com/2016/12/29/politics/russia-sanctions -announced-by-white-house/index.html (accessed February 21, 2018).

3. White House Office of the Press Secretary, "Fact Sheet: Actions in Response to Russian Malicious Cyber Activity and Harassment," press release, December 29, 2016, https://obamawhitehouse.archives.gov/the -press-office/2016/12/29/fact-sheet-actions-response-russian-malicious -cyber-activity-and (accessed February 5, 2018).

4. "Russian Diplomats Expelled by Obama over Hacking Leave US,"

BBC News, January 1, 2017, http://www.bbc.com/news/world-us
-canada-38484735 (accessed February 5, 2018).

5. *Grizzly Steppe: Russian Malicious Cyber Activity* (Joint Analysis Report;
Washington, DC: Department of Homeland Security, Federal Bureau of
Investigation, December 29, 2016), https://www.us-cert.gov/sites/default/
files/publications/JAR_16-20296A_GRIZZLY%20STEPPE-2016-1229.pdf
(accessed February 5, 2018).

6. White House Office of the Press Secretary, "Statement by the
President on Actions in Response to Russian Malicious Cyber Activity and
Harassment," press release, December 29, 2016, https://obamawhite
house.archives.gov/the-press-office/2016/12/29/statement-president
-actions-response-russian-malicious-cyber-activity (accessed February 5, 2018).

7. Ibid.

8. Brooke Seipel, "Trump: I 'Know Things That Other People Don't
Know' about Hacking," *Hill*, December 31, 2016, http://thehill.com/
blogs/blog-briefing-room/news/312335-trump-i-know-things-about
-hacking-that-other-people-don't (accessed February 5, 2018).

9. Alfred Ng, "Russian Twitter Bots Keep Up after Florida Shooting,"
CNET, February 20, 2018, https://www.cnet.com/news/russian-twitter
-bots-still-a-menace-after-florida-shooting/ (accessed March 29, 2018).

CHAPTER 23. 9/11, ANTIFA, AND HAMILTON 68: A CONVERSATION WITH LAURA ROSENBERGER

1. Laura Rosenberger, in an interview with the author, September 19,
2017.

2. Ibid.

3. Ibid.

4. Ibid.

5. Jeff Pegues, "American Journalist Who Worked for Sputnik Opens
up about FBI Questioning," CBS News, September 17, 2018, https://www.
cbsnews.com/news/american-journalist-andrew-feinberg-worked-for
-sputnik-fbi-questioning/ (accessed March 29, 2018).

6. "Putin Says Russia Has Never Been Involved in Hacking 'at the
State Level,'" CBS News, June 1, 2017, https://www.cbsnews.com/news/
putin-says-russia-has-never-been-involved-in-hacking-at-the-state-level/
(accessed January 28, 2018).

7. David Frum, "The Chilling Effects of Openly Displayed Firearms," *Atlantic*, August 16, 2017, https://www.theatlantic.com/politics/archive/2017/08/open-carry-laws-mean-charlottesville-could-have-been-graver/537087/ (accessed March 29, 2018).

8. Paul Duggan, "Charge Upgraded to First-Degree Murder for Driver Accused of Ramming Charlottesville Crowd," *Washington Post*, December 14, 2017, https://www.washingtonpost.com/local/crime/driver-accused-of-plowing-into-charlottesville-crowd-killing-heather-heyer-due-in-court/2017/12/13/6cbb4ce8-e029-11e7-89e8-edec16379010_story.html?utm_term=.c39346733811 (accessed January 28, 2018).

9. Nancy Cook, "Trump Fails to Condemn White Supremacists in Statement on Charlottesville Violence," *Politico*, August 12, 2017, https://www.politico.com/story/2017/08/12/trump-white-supremacists-charlottesville-violence-241575 (accessed January 28, 2018).

10. Matt Pierce, "Who Was Responsible for the Violence in Charlottesville? Here's What Witnesses Say," *Los Angeles Times*, August 15, 2017, http://www.latimes.com/nation/la-na-charlottesville-witnesses-20170815-story.html (accessed March 29, 2018).

11. Nash Jenkins, "No, 'Antifa' Protesters Aren't Planning on Toppling the Government Tomorrow," *Time*, November 3, 2017, http://time.com/5008829/antifa-november-4-rumors/ (accessed March 29, 2018).

12. Rosenberger, in interview with the author.

13. Ibid.

14. Ibid.

15. Ibid.

CHAPTER 24. RACE-BASED PROPAGANDA: UNDERMINING DEMOCRACY BY TAPPING OUR ACHILLES' HEEL

1. Philip Ewing, "Russia's Election Meddling Part of a Long History of 'Active Measures,'" NPR, May 23, 2017, https://www.npr.org/2017/05/23/528500501/lies-forgery-and-skulduggery-the-long-history-of-active-measures (accessed January 28, 2018).

2. US Information Agency, "How Soviet Active Measures Themes Were Spread," in *Soviet Active Measures in the 'Post-Cold War' Era 1988–1991* (report; Washington, DC: US House of Representatives Committee on

Appropriations, June 1992), http://intellit.muskingum.edu/russia
_folder/pcw_era/sect_03.htm (accessed January 28, 2018).

3. Casey Michel, "How Russia Keeps Exploiting Anti-Black Racism in the US," Think Progress, September 26, 2017, https://thinkprogress .org/russias-sordid-history-of-exploiting-anti-black-racism-in-the-u-s -df3b83b4dd86/ (accessed January 28, 2018).

4. David Robert Grimes, "Russian Fake News Is Not New: Soviet Aids Propaganda Cost Countless Lives," *Guardian*, June 14, 2017, https://www .theguardian.com/science/blog/2017/jun/14/russian-fake-news-is-not-new -soviet-aids-propaganda-cost-countless-lives (accessed January 28, 2018).

5. Ibid.

6. Michel, "How Russia Keeps Exploiting Anti-Black Racism."

7. Ibid.

8. "How Russia-Linked Groups Used Facebook to Meddle in 2016 Election," CBS News, September 13, 2017, https://www.cbsnews.com/ news/how-russia-linked-groups-used-facebook-to-meddle-in-2016-election (accessed January 28, 2018).

9. Ben Collins, Kevin Poulsen, and Spencer Ackerman, "Exclusive: Russia Used Facebook Events to Organize Anti-Immigrant Rallies on US Soil," *Daily Beast*, September 11, 2017, https://www.thedailybeast.com/ exclusive-russia-used-facebook-events-to-organize-anti-immigrant-rallies-on -us-soil (accessed January 22, 2017).

10. Mike Isaac and Scott Shane, "Facebook to Deliver 3,000 Russia-Linked Ads to Congress on Monday," *New York Times*, October 1, 2017, https://www.nytimes.com/2017/10/01/technology/facebook-russia-ads .html?mtrref=www.google.it&gwh=00B64979D5850659A0739AE60ABF43 F2&gwt=pay (accessed January 28, 2018).

CHAPTER 25. THE DOCUMENTS

1. Director of National Intelligence, *Background to "Assessing Russian Activities and Intentions in Recent US Elections": The Analytic Process and Cyber Incident Attribution* (Washington, DC: Central Intelligence Agency, Department of Justice, National Security Agency, January 6, 2017), https://www.dni.gov/ files/documents/ICA_2017_01.pdf (accessed September 24, 2017).

2. Katie Bo Williams, "Obama in Tough Spot on Russia," August 7, 2016, *Hill*, http://thehill.com/policy/cybersecurity/290531-obama-in -tough-spot-with-russia (accessed March 29, 2018).

3. Interview with Linda Power. We are disguising the intelligence source's identity.

4. Ibid., p. ii.

5. Ibid.

6. Ibid.

7. Steve Gutterman and Gleb Bryanski, "Putin Says US Stoked Russian Protests," Reuters, December 8, 2011, https://www.reuters.com/article/us-russia/putin-says-u-s-stoked-russian-protests-idUSTRE7B610S20111208 (accessed February 22, 2018).

8. Director of National Intelligence, *Background to "Assessing Russian Activities."*

9. Spencer Ackerman and Kevin Poulsen, "EXCLUSIVE: 'Lone DNC Hacker' Guccifer 2.0 Slipped Up and Revealed He Was a Russian Intelligence Officer," *Daily Beast,* March 22, 2018, https://www.the dailybeast.com/exclusive-lone-dnc-hacker-guccifer-20-slipped-up-and -revealed-he-was-a-russian-intelligence-officer (accessed March 29, 2018).

10. Ibid.

11. Craig Timberg, Elizabeth Dwoskin, Adam Entous, and Karoun Demirjian, "Russian Ads, Now Publicly Released, Show Sophistication of Influence Campaign," *Washington Post,* November 1, 2017, https://www .washingtonpost.com/business/technology/russian-ads-now-publicly -released-show-sophistication-of-influence-campaign/2017/11/01/ d26aead2-bf1b-11e7-8444-a0d4f04b89eb_story.html?utm_term =.98c96da4b8e4 (accessed February 24, 2018).

12. Director of National Intelligence, *Background to "Assessing Russian Activities."*

CHAPTER 26. PUTIN'S END GAME IN THE UNITED STATES

1. Jim Lewis, in an interview with Jeff Pegues for CBS News, December 16, 2016.

2. Ibid.

3. Ibid.

4. Tom McCarthy, "How Russia Used Social Media to Divide Americans," *Guardian,* October 14, 2017, https://www.theguardian.com/us -news/2017/oct/14/russia-us-politics-social-media-facebook (accessed March 7, 2018).

CHAPTER 27. CLUES FOR REPORTERS: THAT NAGGING FEELING

1. Jeff Pegues, "Election Databases in Several States Were at Risk during 2016 Presidential Campaign," CBS News, June 13, 2017, https://www.cbsnews.com/news/election-databases-in-several-states-were-at-risk-during-2016-presidential-campaign/ (accessed April 6, 2018).

2. Michael Finnegan, "Final Wisconsin Recount Tally Strengthens Trump's Victory," *Los Angeles Times*, December 12, 2016, http://www.latimes.com/nation/politics/trailguide/la-na-trailguide-updates-final-wisconsin-recount-tally-1481584948-htmlstory.html (accessed February 7, 2018).

3. Ken Belson, "State Highlights," *New York Times*, 2012, https://www.nytimes.com/elections/2012/results/states/wisconsin.html (accessed February 7, 2018).

4. Tina Nguyen, "Republicans Just Got a 'Wake-Up Call' in Wisconsin," *Vanity Fair*, January 17, 2018, https://www.vanityfair.com/news/2018/01/wisconsin-state-senate-race-democratic-victory (accessed February 7, 2018).

5. Scott Bauer, "DHS Now Says Russia Didn't Target Wisconsin Voter-Registration System," Bloomberg Politics, September 26, 2017, https://www.bloomberg.com/news/articles/2017-09-26/homeland-security-now-says-wisconsin-elections-not-targeted (accessed February 7, 2018).

6. David Shepardson, "California, Wisconsin Deny Election Systems Targeted by Russian Hackers," Reuters, September 28, 2017, https://www.reuters.com/article/us-usa-election/california-wisconsin-deny-election-systems-targeted-by-russian-hackers-idUSKCN1C32SQ (accessed February 24, 2018).

7. Missy Ryan, Ellen Nakashima, and Karen DeYoung, "Obama Administration Announces Measures to Punish Russia for 2016 Election Interference," *Washington Post*, December 29, 2016, https://www.washingtonpost.com/world/national-security/obama-administration-announces-measures-to-punish-russia-for-2016-election-interference/2016/12/29/311db9d6-cdde-11e6-a87f-b917067331bb_story.html?utm_term=.50d6436b0707 (accessed February 27, 2018).

8. Martin Matishak, "Trump Hasn't Directed NSA Chief to Strike Back at Russian Hackers," *Politico*, February 27, 2018, https://www.politico.com/story/2018/02/27/trump-russia-hackers-nsa-response-368241 (accessed February 27, 2018).

9. Saisha Talwar, "Trump Calls Russia Election Hack a 'Big Dem Hoax,'" ABC News, June 22, 2017, http://abcnews.go.com/Politics/trump-calls-russia-election-hack-big-dem-hoax/story?id=48206952 (accessed February 7, 2018).

10. Tom McCarthy, Jon Swaine, and Ben Jacobs, "Former FBI Head Robert Mueller to Oversee Trump-Russia Investigation," *Guardian*, May 17, 2017, https://www.theguardian.com/us-news/2017/may/17/trump-russia-investigation-special-counsel-robert-mueller-fbi (accessed February 7, 2018).

11. Tal Kopan, "DHS Officials: 21 States Potentially Targeted by Russia Hackers Pre-Election," CNN Politics, July 18, 2017, https://www.cnn.com/2017/06/21/politics/russia-hacking-hearing-states-targeted/index.html (accessed February 7, 2018).

12. Emily Tillett and Julia Kimani Burnham, "DHS Official: Election Systems in 21 States Were Targeted in Russia Cyber Attacks," CBS News, June 21, 2017, http://www.cbsnews.com/news/dhs-official-election-systems-in-21-states-were-targeted-in-russia-cyber-attacks/ (accessed August 14, 2017).

13. Michael Riley and Jordan Robertson, "Russian Cyber Hacks on US Electoral System Far Wider than Previously Known," Bloomberg Politics, June 13, 2017, https://www.bloomberg.com/news/articles/2017-06-13/russian-breach-of-39-states-threatens-future-u-s-elections (accessed September 4, 2017).

14. Emily Tillett, "DHS Official: Election Systems in 21 States Were Targeted in Russia Cyber Attacks," CBS News, June 21, 2017, https://www.cbsnews.com/news/dhs-official-election-systems-in-21-states-were-targeted-in-russia-cyber-attacks/ (accessed April 6, 2018).

15. Ibid.

CHAPTER 28. VOTING BOOTH DINOSAURS

1. Lily Hay Newman, "The Simple Fix That'd Help Protect Georgia from Election Hacks," *Wired*, June 15, 2017, https://www.wired.com/story/georgia-runoff-election-hack-audit-vote/ (accessed February 5, 2018).

2. Ben Wofford, "How to Hack an Election in 7 Minutes," *Politico*, August 5, 2018, https://www.politico.com/magazine/story/2016/08/2016-elections-russia-hack-how-to-hack-an-election-in-seven-minutes-214144 (accessed February 5, 2018).

3. Nicole Perlroth, Michael Wines, and Matthew Rosenberg, "Russian Election Hacking Efforts, Wider than Previously Known, Draw Little Scrutiny," *New York Times*, September 1, 2017, https://www.nytimes .com/2017/09/01/us/politics/russia-election-hacking.html (accessed February 5, 2018).

4. Jessica Schulberg, "Good News for Russia: 15 States Use Easily Hackable Voting Machines," *Huffington Post*, July 17, 2017, https://www .huffingtonpost.com/entry/electronic-voting-machines-hack-russia _us_5967e1c2e4b03389bb162c96 (accessed February 5, 2018).

5. Ariel J. Feldman, J. Alex Halderman, and Edward W. Felten, "Security Analysis of the Diebold AccuVote-TS Voting Machine," Center for Information Technology Policy at Princeton University, September 13, 2006.

6. Ibid.

7. Edward Felten, professor of computer science and public affairs at Princeton University, in an interview with the author, September 12, 2017.

8. Lawrence Norden, Christopher Famighetti, "America's Voting Machines at Risk," Brennan Center for Justice, September 15, 2015, https://www.brennancenter.org/publication/americas-voting-machines -risk (accessed February 5, 2018).

9. Abby Goodnough and Christopher Drew, "Florida Moves to End Touch-Screen Voting," *New York Times*, February 1, 2007, http://www .nytimes.com/2007/02/01/us/01cnd-voting.html?pagewanted=print (accessed February 5, 2018).

10. Charlotte Alter, "Detroit Voting Machine Failures Were Widespread on Election Day," *Time*, December 14, 2016, http://time .com/4599886/detroit-voting-machine-failures-were-widespread-on -election-day/ (accessed February 5, 2018).

11. Max Blau, Mayra Cuevas, and Emily Smith, "Michigan Recount Halted," CNN Politics, December 8, 2016, https://www.cnn.com/2016/ 12/08/politics/michigan-election-recount/index.html (accessed February 5, 2018).

12. Roger DuPuis, "Jill Stein's 'Irrational' Pa. Recount Request Denied," *Central Pennsylvania Business Journal*, December 12, 2016, http:// www.cpbj.com/article/20161212/CPBJ01/161219974/jill-steins-irrational -pa-recount-request-denied (accessed February 11, 2016).

13. Perlroth, Wines and Rosenberg, "Russian Election Hacking Efforts."

14. Director of National Intelligence, *Background to "Assessing Russian Activities and Intentions in Recent US Elections": The Analytic Process and*

Cyber Incident Attribution (Washington, DC: Central Intelligence Agency, Department of Justice, National Security Agency, January 6, 2017), https://www.dni.gov/files/documents/ICA_2017_01.pdf (accessed February 22, 2018).

15. Perlroth, Wines, and Rosenberg, "Russian Election Hacking Efforts."

16. Aaron Mak, "Evidence of Russian Election-Data Tampering Mounts as Urgency to Investigate It Does Not," *Slate*, September 1, 2017, http://www.slate.com/blogs/the_slatest/2017/09/01/did_russian _hacking_of_vr_systems_affect_election_in_durham_county_new_york .html (accessed February 22, 2018).

17. Jeff Zeleny, Michael J. Berens, and Geoff Dougherty, "Ballots, Rules, Voter Error Led to 2000 Election Muddle, Review Shows," *Chicago Tribune*, November 12, 2001, http://www.chicagotribune.com/sns-ballots -tribune-story.html (accessed February 5, 2018).

18. Verified Voting, "Votomatic," https://www.verifiedvoting.org/ resources/voting-equipment/ess/votamatic/ (accessed April 6, 2018).

19. Greg Palast, "Vanishing Votes," *Nation*, April 29, 2004, https:// www.thenation.com/article/vanishing-votes/ (accessed February 5, 2018).

20. Samantha Levine, "Hanging Chads: As the Florida Recount Im- plodes, the Supreme Court Decides Bush v. Gore," *US News & World Report*, January 17, 2008, https://www.usnews.com/news/articles/2008/01/17/ the-legacy-of-hanging-chads (accessed February 5, 2018).

21. "Voting Irregularities in Florida during the 2000 Presidential Election: Executive Summary" (Washington, DC: US Civil Rights Commission, June 2001), http://www.usccr.gov/pubs/vote2000/report/ exesum.htm (accessed February 5, 2018).

22. Ibid.

23. John Lantigua, "How the GOP Gamed the System in Florida," *Nation*, April 12, 2001, https://www.thenation.com/article/how-gop -gamed-system-florida/ (accessed April 6, 2018).

24. Wade Payson-Denney, "So, Who Really Won? What the Bush v. Gore Studies Showed," CNN, October 31, 2015, https://www.cnn.com/ 2015/10/31/politics/bush-gore-2000-election-results-studies/index.html (accessed February 5, 2018).

25. Ibid.

26. Lloyd Vries, "Presidential Election Lawsuit Ends," CBS News, September 4, 2002, https://www.cbsnews.com/news/presidential-election -lawsuit-ends/ (accessed February 5, 2018).

27. Ford Fessenden, "Florida List for Purge of Voters Proves Flawed," *New York Times*, July 10, 2004, http://www.nytimes.com/2004/07/10/us/florida -list-for-purge-of-voters-proves-flawed.html (accessed February 5, 2018).

28. "Voting Irregularities in Florida."

29. Ibid.

30. Ibid.

31. Ibid.

32. Ibid.

33. Felten, interview with the author.

34. Ibid.

35. Mark Niesse, "Lawmakers Propose Switching Georgia from Digital to Paper Ballots," *Atlanta Journal-Constitution*, January 22, 2018, https:// www.myajc.com/news/state-regional-govt-politics/lawmakers-propose -switching-georgia-from-digital-paper-ballots/DnMzFdOpB2fA52cZt 8D4xO/ (accessed April 7, 2018).

CHAPTER 29. A HOLE IN THE DIKE

1. Joe Uchill, "Illinois Voting Records Hack Didn't Target Specific Records, Says IT Staff," *Hill*, May 4, 2017, http://thehill.com/policy/ cybersecurity/331981-ill-voting-records-hack-didnt-target-specific-records -says-state-it (accessed February 19, 2018).

2. Kyle Thomas and Kevin Turner, in an interview with the author, August 28, 2017.

3. Ibid.

4. Ibid.

CHAPTER 30. CYBER TOOLS

1. Brett Samuels, "DHS Cyber Chief: Russia 'Successfully Penetrated' Some State Voter Rolls," *Hill*, February 7, 2018, http://thehill.com/ policy/cybersecurity/372816-russia-successfully-penetrated-voter-rolls-in -some-states-report (accessed February 10, 2018).

2. Cory Bennett, Eric Geller, Martin Matishak and Tim Starks, "Cash-Strapped States Brace for Russian Hacking Fight," *Politico*, September 3, 2017, https://www.politico.com/story/2017/09/03/election-hackers -russia-cyberattack-voting-242266 (accessed January 10, 2018).

3. Morgan Chalfant, "Dems Call for States to Get $400 M Election Security Upgrades," *Hill*, November 20, 2017, http://thehill.com/policy/cybersecurity/361263-dems-say-congress-should-send-400m-to-states-for-election-cyber-upgrades (accessed February 11, 2018).

4. Rep. Robert Brady and Rep. Bennie Thompson, in letter to Chairman Rodney Frelinghuysen and the Honorable Nita M. Lowey, Congress of the United States, November 16, 2017, https://democrats-homeland.house.gov/sites/democrats.homeland.house.gov/files/documents/appropstf.pdf (accessed March 13, 2018).

5. Ellen Mitchell, "The Pentagon's Battle of the Bands," *Politico*, May 22, 2018, https://www.politico.com/story/2016/05/pentagons-bands-battle-223435 (accessed February 11, 2018).

6. Rob Joyce, in an interview with Jeff Pegues for CBS News, August 22, 2017.

7. "Was Russian Hacking of Ukraine's Power Grid a Test Run for US Attack?" CBS News, June 23, 2017, https://www.cbsnews.com/news/russian-hacking-of-ukraines-power-grid-test-run-for-us-attack/ (accessed February 6, 2018).

8. Jim Lewis, in an interview with Jeff Pegues for CBS News, December 16, 2016.

9. Ibid.

10. Ibid.

11. Adam Meyers, in an interview with Jeff Pegues for CBS News, December 19, 2017.

12. Nicky Woolf, "DDOS Attack That Disrupted Internet Was Largest of Its Kind in History, Experts Say," *Guardian*, October 26, 2016, https://www.theguardian.com/technology/2016/oct/26/ddos-attack-dyn-mirai-botnet (accessed February 10, 2018).

13. Lily Hay Newman, "The Botnet That Broke the Internet Isn't Going Away," *Wired*, December 9, 2016, https://www.wired.com/2016/12/botnet-broke-internet-isnt-going-away/ (accessed March 8, 2018).

14. "Source Code for IOT Botnet Mirai Released," Krebs on Security Newsletter, October 16, 2016, https://krebsonsecurity.com/2016/10/source-code-for-iot-botnet-mirai-released/ (accessed February 6, 2018).

15. Meyers, interview with Jeff Pegues.

16. Ibid.

17. Jeff Pegues, "Hackers Exploited Connected 'Smart' Devices for Massive Cyberattack," CBS News, October 24, 2016, https://www.cbsnews.com/news/hackers-exploited-connected-smart-devices-for-massive-cyberattack/ (accessed April 6, 2018).

18. Meyers, interview with Jeff Pegues.

19. *Extremist Content and Russian Disinformation Online: Working with Tech to Find Solutions, Before the US Senate Committee on the Judiciary Subcommittee on Crime and Terrorism*, 115th Cong. (2017) (statement of Clint Watts, Robert A. Fox Fellow, Foreign Policy Research Institute), https://www.judiciary.senate.gov/imo/media/doc/10-31-17%20Watts%20Testimony.pdf (accessed January 28, 2018).

20. Ibid.

21. Craig Timberg, Elizabeth Dwoskin, Adam Entous, and Karoun Demirjian, "Russian Ads, Now Publicly Released, Show Sophistication of Influence Campaign," *New York Times*, November 1, 2017, https://www.washingtonpost.com/business/technology/russian-ads-now-publicly-released-show-sophistication-of-influence-campaign/2017/11/01/d26aead2-bf1b-11e7-8444-a0d4f04b89eb_story.html?utm_term=.98c96da4b8e4 (accessed February 24, 2018).

22. Laura Rosenberger, in an interview with the author, September 19, 2017.

23. Jeff Pegues, "'Follow the Trail of Dead Russians': Senate Hears Testimony on 'Cyber Invasion,'" CBS News, March 20, 2017, https://www.cbsnews.com/news/russian-meddling-investigation-misinformation-tactics-senate-intelligence-committee/ (accessed February 24, 2018).

24. Stefan Meister, "The 'Lisa Case': Germany as a Target of Russian Disinformation," *NATO Review*, 2016, https://www.nato.int/docu/review/2016/Also-in-2016/lisa-case-germany-target-russian-disinformation/EN/index.htm (accessed February 24, 2018).

25. Ibid.

26. Rosenberger, interview with the author.

27. Beckett Mufson, "A Fake Antifa Account Was 'Busted' for Tweeting from Russia," *Vice*, September 28, 2017, https://www.vice.com/en_ca/article/59dwed/a-fake-antifa-account-was-busted-for-tweeting-from-russia-vgtrn (accessed February 24, 2018).

28. Ben Collings, Kevin Poulsen, and Spencer Ackerman, "Exclusive: Russia Used Facebook Events to Organize Anti-Immigrant Rallies on US Soil," *Daily Beast*, September 11, 2017, https://www.thedailybeast.com/exclusive-russia-used-facebook-events-to-organize-anti-immigrant-rallies-on-us-soil (accessed February 24, 2018).

29. *Extremist Content* (Watts).

30. Jeff Pegues, "After Hack, Arizona Working to Keep Its Elections Database Secure," CBS News, October 13, 2016, https://www.cbsnews

.com/news/after-hack-arizona-working-to-keep-its-elections-database
-secure/ (accessed February 24, 2018).

CHAPTER 31. SHOULD WE TRUST THEM?

1. Veleria Fernandez, "Arizona's 'Concentration Camp': Why Was
Tent City Kept Open for 24 Years?" *Guardian*, August 21, 2017, https://
www.theguardian.com/cities/2017/aug/21/arizona-phoenix
-concentration-camp-tent-city-jail-joe-arpaio-immigration (accessed
February 4, 2018).

2. Ibid.

3. Ibid.

4. Michael Lacey, "Prisoners Hang Themselves in Sheriff Joe Arpaio's
Jails at a Rate That Dwarfs Other County Lockups," *Phoenix New Times*,
November 24, 2015, http://www.phoenixnewtimes.com/news/prisoners
-hang-themselves-in-sheriff-joe-arpaios-jails-at-a-rate-that-dwarfs-other
-county-lockups-7845679 (accessed February 4, 2018).

5. Department of Justice, "Investigation of the Maricopa County
Sheriff's Office," Civil Rights Division, August 6, 2015, https://www.justice
.gov/crt/investigation-maricopa-county-sheriffs-office (accessed February
4, 2018).

6. Julie Hirschfeld Davis and Maggie Haberman, "Trump Pardons Joe
Arpaio, Who Became Face of Crackdown on Illegal Immigration," *New York
Times*, August 25, 2017, https://www.nytimes.com/2017/08/25/us/politics/
joe-arpaio-trump-pardon-sheriff-arizona.html (accessed February 4, 2018).

7. Gabrielle Levy, *US News & World Report*, "Sheriff Joe Arpaio Says
He's 'Seriously' Considering Run for Jeff Flake's Senate Seat," AOL,
December 8, 2017, https://www.aol.com/article/news/2017/12/08/
sheriff-joe-arpaio-says-hes-seriously-considering-run-for-jeff-flakes-senate
-seat/23302009/ (accessed February 4, 2018).

8. Mary Jo Pitzl, "Sec'y of State Candidate Gets Endorsement from SB
1070 Co-Author," *Arizona Republic*, June 17, 2014, https://www.azcentral
.com/story/politicalinsider/2014/06/17/arizona-secretary-state-kobach
-endorsement/10674329/ (accessed February 4, 2018).

9. Howard Fischer, "Bid for Ban of AZ Gay Marriages Is Derailed,"
Arizona Daily Star, April 4, 2008, http://tucson.com/news/local/bid-for
-ban-of-az-gay-marriages-is-derailed/article_cb1bcb85-7a59-5573-8341
-8114fd6ae870.html (accessed February 4, 2018).

10. Michele Reagan, Arizona secretary of state, in an interview with the author, January 12, 2018.

11. Ellen Nakashima, "Russian Hackers Targeted Arizona Election System," *Washington Post*, August 29, 2016, https://www.washingtonpost .com/world/national-security/fbi-is-investigating-foreign-hacks-of-state -election-systems/2016/08/29/6e758ff4-6e00-11e6-8365-b19e428a975e _story.html?utm_term=.6b798f97750c (accessed February 4, 2018).

12. Arizona Secretary of State, "Secretary Reagan Rejects Request of Voter Data from Presidential Commission," press release, July 4, 2017.

13. Nakashima, "Russian Hackers."

14. Barbie Latza Nadeau, "Inside 'Black Death Group,' the Dark Web Gang That Kidnapped a Model," *Daily Beast*, December 7, 2017, https:// www.thedailybeast.com/the-case-of-the-kidnapped-model-exposes-dark -corners-of-the-deep-web (accessed February 19, 2018).

15. Nakashima, "Russian Hackers."

16. Michele Reagan, Arizona secretary of state, in an interview with Jeff Pegues for CBS News, October 12, 2016.

17. Ibid.

18. Ibid.

19. Ibid.

20. Ibid.

21. Ibid.

22. Ibid.

23. Ibid.

24. Kris W. Kobach, in letter to North Carolina, June 28, 2017, https://www.documentcloud.org/documents/3881856-Correspondence -PEIC-Letter-to-North-Carolina.html(accessed February 4, 2018).

25. Ibid; Jessica Huseman, "Presidential Commission Demands Massive Amounts of State Voter Data," ProPublica, June 29, 2018, https:// www.propublica.org/article/presidential-commission-demands-massive -amounts-of-state-voter-data (accessed February 4, 2018).

26. Ali Vitali, Peter Alexander, and Kelly O'Donnell, "Trump Establishes Vote Fraud Commission," CNBC, May 11, 2018, https://www .cnbc.com/2017/05/11/trump-to-establish-vote-fraud-commission.html (accessed February 4, 2018).

27. Arizona Secretary of State, "Secretary Reagan Rejects Request."

28. Associated Press, "Judge Backs Maine Secretary of State in Lawsuit against Trump Voter Fraud Panel," *Press Herald*, December 22, 2017, https://www.pressherald.com/2017/12/22/judge-backs-maine-secretary

-of-state-in-lawsuit-against-trump-voter-fraud-panel/ (accessed February 4, 2018).

29. Jordan Fabian and Brandon Carter, "Trump Dissolves Voter Fraud Commission," *Hill*, January 3, 2018, http://thehill.com/homenews/ administration/367343-trump-dissolves-voter-fraud-commission (accessed February 4, 2018).

30. Geoff Pender, "Hosemann Tells Trump Commission 'Go Jump in the Gulf' on Voter Records," *Clarion Ledger*, July 1, 2017, https://www .clarionledger.com/story/news/politics/2017/06/30/hosemann-voter -records/444623001/ (accessed February 4, 2018).

31. Reagan, interview with author, January 12, 2018.

32. Arizona Secretary of State, "Secretary Reagan Rejects Request."

33. Reagan, interview with author, January 12, 2018.

34. Ibid.

35. Arizona Secretary of State, "Russian Hack Update," October 12, 2017, https://www.azsos.gov/about-office/media-center/azsosblog/1328 (accessed April 10, 2018).

36. Dustin Volz, "Arizona Election Database Targeted in 2016 by Criminals, Not Russia: Source," Reuters, April 8, 2018, https://www .reuters.com/article/us-usa-cyber-election/arizona-election-database -targeted-in-2016-by-criminals-not-russia-source-idUSKBN1HF11F (accessed April 8, 2018).

37. Reagan, interview with author, January 12, 2018.

CHAPTER 32. THINGS HAVE GONE HORRIBLY AWRY

1. Steve Nelson, "Lock Him Up? Lawmakers Renew Calls for James Clapper Perjury Charges," *U.S. News and World Report*, November 17, 2016, https://www.usnews.com/news/articles/2016-11-17/lawmakers-resume -calls-for-james-clapper-perjury-charges (accessed April 7, 2018).

2. Director of National Intelligence James Clapper, in interview with Jeff Pegues for CBS News, May 14, 2017

3. Abigail Tracey, "'A Really Really Good Deal': Mike Flynn's Guilty Plea Suggests He's Turned on Trump," *Vanity Fair*, December 1, 2017, https://www.vanityfair.com/news/2017/12/mike-flynn-guilty-plea-donald -trump (accessed April 6, 2018).

4. Matt Apuzzo, Maggie Haberman, and Matthew Rosenberg, "Trump Told Russians That Firing 'Nut Job' Comey Eased Pressure from

Investigation," *New York Times*, May 19, 2017, https://www.nytimes.com/2017/05/19/us/politics/trump-russia-comey.html (accessed April 4, 2018).

5. Jeff Stein, "Trump's Russia-ISIS Slip Unprecedented in US Presidential History," *Newsweek*, May 16, 2017, http://www.newsweek.com/trump-russia-isis-israel-putin-lavrov-kislyak-oval-office-netanyahu-610500 (accessed February 24, 2018).

6. Julie Vitkovskaya and Amanda Erickson, "The Strange Oval Office Meeting between Trump, Lavrov, and Kislyak," *Washington Post*, May 10, 2017, https://www.washingtonpost.com/news/worldviews/wp/2017/05/10/the-strange-oval-office-meeting-between-trump-lavrov-and-kislyak/?utm_term=.d0b7fc1a218c (accessed February 24, 2018).

7. Clapper, interview with Jeff Pegues.

CHAPTER 33. THE NEW PLAYING FIELD

1. Jack Shenker, "Egyptian Pyramid Closes Briefly Over 11/11/11 Rumour Mill," *Guardian*, November 11, 2011, https://www.theguardian.com/world/2011/nov/11/egypt-great-pyramid-closes-111111 (accessed February 24, 2018).

2. CIA director John Brennan, in an interview with the author, September 12, 2016.

3. Rob Joyce, in an interview with Jeff Pegues for CBS News, August 22, 2017.

4. Jeff Pegues, "W. H. Cybersecurity Coordinator Warns against Using Kaspersky Lab Software," CBS News, August 22, 2017, https://www.cbsnews.com/news/kasperksy-lab-software-suspected-ties-russian-intelligence-rob-joyce/ (accessed February 24, 2018).

5. Ibid.

CHAPTER 34. OUR PLAYBOOK

1. Laura Rosenberger, in an interview with the author, September 19, 2017.

2. Michael Morell and Suzanne Kelly, "Fmr. CIA Acting Dir. Michael Morell: 'This Is the Political Equivalent of 9/11,'" Cipher Brief, December 11, 2016, https://www.thecipherbrief.com/fmr-cia-acting-dir-michael-morell-political-equivalent-911-1091 (accessed February 26, 2018).

3. Ibid.

4. Greg Miller, Ellen Nakashima, and Adam Entous, "Obama's Secret Struggle to Punish Russia for Putin's Election Assault," *Washington Post*, June 23, 2017, https://www.washingtonpost.com/graphics/2017/world/national-security/obama-putin-election-hacking/?utm_term =.e234621e3524 (accessed February 26, 2018).

5. Associated Press, "Russian Indicted in Election Probe Says US Justice '1-Sided,'" *Business Insider*, February 17, 2018, http://www .businessinsider.com/ap-russian-indicted-in-election-probe-says-us-justice -1-sided-2018-2 (accessed April 8, 2018).

6. Michael Hayden, in an interview with Jeff Pegues for CBS News, October 2016.

7. Jim Lewis, in an interview with Jeff Pegues for CBS News, December 16, 2016.

8. *Department of Defense Law of War Manual* (June 2015; Washington, DC: Office of General Counsel, December 2016), https://www .defense.gov/Portals/1/Documents/pubs/DoD%20Law%20of%20 War%20Manual%20-%20June%202015%20Updated%20Dec%202016 .pdf?ver=2016-12-13-172036-190 (accessed February 27, 2018).

9. Charlie Dunlap, "Cyber Operations and the New Defense Department Law of War Manual: Initial Impressions," *Lawfare*, June 15, 2015, https://www.lawfareblog.com/cyber-operations-and-new-defense -department-law-war-manual-initial-impressions (accessed April 4, 2018).

10. Krishnadev Calamur, "Putin Says 'Patriotic Hackers' May Have Targeted US Election," *Atlantic*, June 1, 2017, https://www.theatlantic.com/ news/archive/2017/06/putin-russia-us-election/528825/ (accessed February 10, 2018).

11. Jamie Ross, "George W. Bush: Russia Definitely Meddled in the 2016 Election," *Daily Beast*, February 8, 2018, https://www.thedailybeast .com/george-w-bush-russia-definitely-meddled-in-the-2016-election (accessed February 10, 2018).

CHAPTER 35. WHY DIDN'T THEY SEE IT?

1. James R. Clapper, *Statement for the Record on the Worldwide Threat Assessment of the US Intelligence Community for the Senate Committee on Armed Services* (transcript; Washington, DC: Senate Committee on Armed Services, March 10, 2011), https://fas.org/irp/congress/2011 _hr/031011clapper.pdf (accessed March 13, 2018).

2. Ibid.

3. James R. Clapper, *Statement for the Record, Worldwide Threat Assessment of the US Intelligence Community* (transcript; Washington, DC: Senate Committee on Armed Services, April 18, 2013), https://www.dni.gov/files/documents/Intelligence%20Reports/UNCLASS_2013%20ATA%20SFR%20FINAL%20for%20SASC%2018%20Apr%202013.pdf (accessed April 4, 2018).

4. Ibid.

5. Ibid.

CHAPTER 36. A PATRIOTIC RUSSIAN HACKER

1. Democratic leaders in the House of Representatives and the Senate, in letter to the Republican majority, Congress of the United States, February 21, 2018; quoted in Ed O'Keefe, "Top Democrats Seeking $300 Million for FBI to Fight Foreign Election Interference," *Washington Post*, February 21, 2018, https://www.washingtonpost.com/news/powerpost/wp/2018/02/21/top-democrats-want-300-million-for-fbi-to-fight-foreign-election-interference/?utm_term=.a6c53b05ee88 (accessed February 24, 2018); "Following Recent Mueller Indictments in Russia Investigation, Schumer & Klobuchar Call on Trump Administration to Issue Public Report on Russia Efforts to Interfere in 2018 Elections, & Call for Major Increase in Federal Funds to Protect Integrity of American Elections," Senate Democrats, February 21, 2018, https://www.democrats.senate.gov/newsroom/press-releases/following-recent-mueller-indictments-in-russia-investigation-schumer-and-klobuchar-call-on-trump-administration-to-issue-public-report-on-russia-efforts-to-interfere-in-2018-elections_call-for-major-increase-in-federal-funds-to-protect-integrity-of-american-elections- (accessed April 7, 2018).

2. Election official, in an interview with the author, February 2018.

3. DHS Official, in an interview with CBS News, October 2017.

4. "NSA Chief Spelled Out Russian Threat: Is Trump Listening?" *Washington Post*, February 28, 2018, https://www.washingtonpost.com/opinions/the-nsa-chief-spelled-out-the-russian-threat-is-trump-listening/2018/02/28/0849aef4-1cb4-11e8-b2d9-08e748f892c0_story.html (accessed April 7, 2018).

5. Matthew Rosenberg, "White House Has Given No Orders to Counter Russian Meddling, NSA Chief Says," *New York Times*, February 27,

2018, https://www.nytimes.com/2018/02/27/us/politics/michael-rogers
-nsa-cyber-command-russia-election-meddling.html (accessed February 27,
2018).

6. Dan Friedman, "Intelligence Chiefs: Trump Has Not Directed Us to
Stop Russian Meddling," *Mother Jones*, February 13, 2018, https://www
.motherjones.com/politics/2018/02/intelligence-chiefs-trump-has-not
-directed-us-to-stop-russian-meddling/ (accessed February 19, 2018).

7. Alexi McCammond, "Trump Again Calls Russia Probe a Hoax,"
Axios, December 29, 2017, https://www.axios.com/trump-again-calls
-russia-probe-a-hoax-1515110898-757025c8-532d-4d2a-9d50-2d607f65c099
.html (accessed March 29, 2018).

8. Michael Daniel, in an interview with the author, September 12,
2017.

INDEX